WHEN HELL FREEZES OVER

OTHER BOOKS BY TOLLER CRANSTON
The Nutcracker
A Ram on the Rampage
Zero Tollerance

OTHER BOOKS BY MARTHA LOWDER KIMBALL
Zero Tollerance (with Toller Cranston)
Robin Cousins

WHEN HELL FREEZES OVER

SHOULD I BRING MY SKATES?

TOLLER CRANSTON

WITH MARTHA LOWDER KIMBALL

Cloth edition published 2000
Trade paperback edition published 2001

National Library of Canada Cataloguing in Publication Data

Cranston, Toller
   When hell freezes over, should I bring my skates?

ISBN 0-7710-2336-7 (bound). – ISBN 0-7710-2337-5 (pbk.)

1. Cranston, Toller. 2. Skaters – Canada – Biography. I. Kimball, Martha Lowder. II. Title.

GV850.C73A3 2000   796.91'2'092   C00-931195-5

We acknowledge the financial support of the Government of Canada through the Book Publishing Industry Development Program for our publishing activities. We further acknowledge the support of the Canada Council for the Arts and the Ontario Arts Council for our publishing program.

Typeset in Berkeley by M&S, Toronto
Printed and bound in Canada

McClelland & Stewart Ltd.
The Canadian Publishers
481 University Avenue
Toronto, Ontario
M5G 2E9
www.mcclelland.com

1 2 3 4 5   05 04 03 02 01

To Brenlee Carrington Trepel,
a dear friend and a
Canadian intellectual phenomenon

T. C.

To Lauren Kimball
and to Elizabeth, Timothy, and Kate Petras,
my newest and dearest inspirations

M. L. K.

Contents

III. Coming to Terms with Life, Death, and Retirement

When Hell Freezes Over

On the garden steps in San Miguel.

Preface

Artists are born. Visual art, the art of words, and the art of physical movement are all natural inclinations. Almost from the first enchanted moment I set foot on the ice of a small pond in Swastika, Ontario, at the age of six, I knew just where my destiny lay. It is a huge advantage in life to have, at such an early age, the certain knowledge of what one wishes to become. Figure skating offered me the athletic and artistic release that I craved even then. The problem was that I possessed no passport to the world of skating, no map to lead me to success. There wasn't really anywhere to go in remote Swastika.

After Grade 1, I moved with my parents, Montague (Monte) and Stuart Cranston, my older sister, Phillippa, and my younger twin brothers, Guy and Goldie, to Galt, Ontario. Later we migrated northeast to Baie d'Urfé, a suburb of Montreal, Quebec. We never held familial discussions, at least as far as I remember, about my future, my talents, or my inclinations. I was cut from the same checkered cloth as my mother. In addition to our uncanny physical resemblance, we evidenced similar instincts, eccentric personalities, and artistic abilities, although we shared no particular artistic rapport. I was an island, even within my own family.

Each child with great aspirations must first come to terms with who and what he is, then learn to make the best of it and acquire coping skills. He must accept some values and reject others, forming the basis of character. From my youngest days, I exhibited an inborn tendency to go against the grain, but it was unconscious. Somebody with a different physical and emotional make-up might have been able to hide that propensity.

As teachers know, children who march to their own drummers are frequently the ones who grow up to achieve noteworthy accomplishments. Those who huddle in the security of their cliques may end up pumping gas. It is the strength to act as an individual that arms a child for the world outside the school doors. That strength and its consequences temper his character, like steel, for the struggle to come.

Many skaters of my era, whether because of our driven personalities, our artistic proclivities, our inborn sexual orientations, or our insistence on pursuing a solitary sport, were different from other children our age. I was an old soul in a child's body, waiting restlessly to fulfill my adult potential, finding little amusement in the toys and games that occupied my peers. From earliest memory, I had a clear sense that I was different in every conceivable way. Later in life, experience confirmed that innate knowledge. I felt that I was playing for time, waiting to grow into my skin, waiting to become what I was destined to be. Meanwhile, I found welcome support among unlikely and diverse adult companions. Few of them skated.

Most members of the skating world failed to understand my unusual, dramatic, and sometimes flamboyant style. They could not relate to me, did not like me, or even felt intimidated by me. Once I rose to the senior level and became the Canadian champion in 1971, however, at least they had to acknowledge me. I was the number-one male skater in Canada for six years in a row.

For one reason or another, I was denied (or I denied myself) the ultimate recognition in my sport, an Olympic gold medal. That failure festered within me and in large measure dictated the course of my next two decades. My lust for acceptance and recognition led me to the trials I described in *Zero Tollerance*: black dramas involving charlatans, drugs, lawsuits, exaggerated personal behaviour, and ruinous (as well as humorous) conspicuous consumption.

At the same time I led a parallel existence on a brighter plane: an existence filled with world travel, wonderful opportunities, and colourful personalities. Since my earliest days as a figure skater, I have met people, seen places, and undergone experiences that I would not have been privileged to enjoy had I not skated. The richest of those experiences, however, in the most fundamental sense, have had little to do with figure skating per se and everything to do with life's larger issues and humankind's search for meaning.

If I didn't connect with my more normal peers, I was powerfully drawn to others who were different like me. Many of them were men, but more often they were strong-willed and accomplished women. Some of those people offered me moral and financial support. Some became my companions. Still others pursued me for their own neurotic ends. Together they formed an idiosyncratic human tapestry that coloured my life.

There was something else on the plus side of my ledger sheet. As a counterpoint to the abyss of the Innsbruck Olympics, I had the joy and fulfillment of the 1974 Munich world championships,[*] where I won a bronze medal entirely on my own terms. The fame that I was able to achieve as a result of events in Munich was the passkey to a life of adventure – good, bad, and bizarre – and an entree into privileged circles.

This book, then – a contrapuntal companion to *Zero Tollerance* – is ultimately about fame. Through what struggles does one win it? What gifts does it bring? What dilemmas does it pose, especially as it inevitably wanes? Fame is as slippery as the ice on which I skated for more than forty years, yet as textured as the canvases on which I daily continue to paint.

---

[*] Worlds (the annual World Figure Skating Championships) is an event consisting of four individual championships: Men's Singles (Men's), Ladies' Singles (Ladies'), Pairs, and Dance. As is customary, we will use the term "world championships" to refer to the collective event and "world championship" to refer to one of the four divisions.

I

The Making of a Skater-Artist

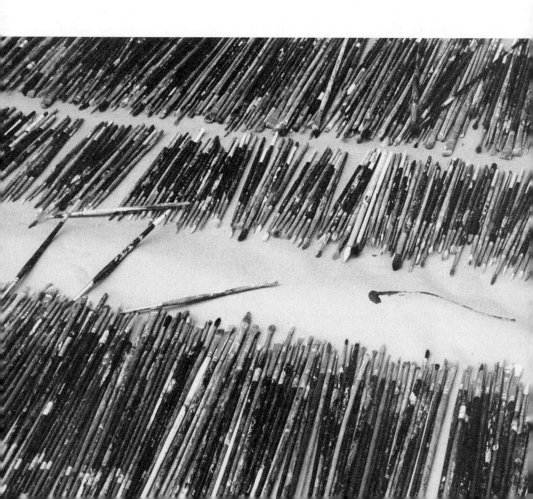

1

Chess

Seven, generally perceived as a lucky number, has consistently been the most negative for me. In Grade 7, when I was twelve years old, a humiliating and utterly unexpected event happened to me at Dorset School in the homeroom class of Mr. Bennett, a British expatriate who looked like a walrus but turned me on to the joys of world history. For the latter I thank him. The study of history has brought me pleasure throughout my life. Mr. Bennett served as both my homeroom advisor and social studies teacher.

We students were required to line up outside the school and wait for the bell before we could march into homeroom. As male readers know, the nascent sexuality of boys that age is often beyond their control. Standing in the queue one day, I developed an enormous erection. The front of my pants bulged, and I was mortified. Every single person in the queue, both male and female, saw my embarrassment and discomfort. I was powerless, yet I could not run away. The school bell was about to ring. I was rooted to the spot.

Children can be unspeakably cruel. From one day to the next, I became *persona non grata*. Suddenly none of my classmates spoke to me. In that vortex of humiliation, there was absolutely no one with whom I could discuss my sudden change in status, and I did not understand why it had occurred.

Until that day, however different I may have felt emotionally, I had been able to behave more or less like everybody else in the pack. I had chatted, played soccer, and walked home with the other children. Then I became social strychnine.

Grade 7 was a crucial, confusing developmental year for us all. Every child had opinions, crushes, peeves, and yearnings, but how many children were strong enough or confident enough to manifest them in original behaviour? Only conformity afforded safety. I suppose that it was understandable that no one broke ranks to defend me.

To protect myself when I got home from school, I began going straight to my bedroom to take comfort in my books. My mother, however, no doubt with the best of intentions, declared that it was unhealthy for a boy my age to stay indoors and read on a nice day. She demanded that I go out and play with my friends – but I didn't have friends any more. I was ostracized.

My mother did more than make suggestions. She locked me out of the house and told me, "Do not come back until dinner-time." I didn't know where to go. Sometimes I knocked on the doors of the class nerds, but even they rejected me. I roamed the streets almost every sunny day in a state of high anxiety from 3:30 until 6:00 P.M.

The Ambush

Walking home from school alone, I regularly took a shortcut through fields of high grass. One day a gang of boys waited for me in the overgrowth, sprang at me from all directions, and beat me up. It was a scene straight from *Lord of the Flies*. The shock of that sudden attack was more severe than the beating itself.

To make matters worse, the commotion roused the red-winged blackbirds that nested in the grass, and they dive-bombed at me from every angle. It was a real-life Alfred Hitchcock nightmare. The assault was two-pronged, ground and air, and I was terrified.

When the incident ended, I couldn't explain to anybody, including my mother, why those boys had beaten me. The reason was too embarrassing to disclose.

Playing for Acceptance

My ostracism didn't end after a week or two. It persisted for all of Grade 7, tarnishing my reputation as I prepared to enter MacDonald High School the following fall. (MacDonald began with Grade 8.)

But something positive occurred as a result of my shunning that set the tone of my life from that point on. Mr. Bennett introduced his students to the game of chess. Whenever we finished our work and had spare time, we were allowed to play chess with each other. Every single student was rated from one to thirty. If someone wanted to improve his chess rating, he had to challenge a higher-ranked student.

For reasons that had little to do with chess, I acquired such proficiency that I became the champion. I was perfectly conscious of what I was doing. I was forcing other children to make contact with me. Even if they didn't like me, and even if they could not relate to me, at least I garnered their respect. Anyone who wanted to become the champion was required to challenge me.

The same thing later happened during my skating career. Chess in Grade 7 was the dry run for a pattern that repeated itself again and again throughout my life.

Full Circle

In the years since my beating and the concurrent red-winged blackbird bombardment, I haven't bumped into any of the perpetrators, human or avian. However, Bill Oliver, another acquaintance from my youth, attended my painting exhibition in Ottawa while I was promoting *Zero Tollerance* in 1997. He came with hat in hand and asked, "Do you remember me?"

I answered, "Yes. You were a tough guy. I was afraid of you. I thought that you were going to beat me up or something."

"Well, I'm sorry about that," Bill said. "Why don't you phone me?"

In maturity, we had come full circle.

2

Odessa Carrion

Black participants were uncommon in the elite and costly sport of figure skating in 1964. Even more than two decades later, national and world champion Debi Thomas, with her thoroughbred body and light-brown skin, was the rare dark horse in a herd of Lippizaner stallions.

Early in the summer of 1964, when I was fifteen, a black woman and her daughter came to the Town of Mount Royal arena from the depths of the Bronx, New York, and shook things up in the staid Montreal skating world. Odessa and Jeanine Carrion set up temporary quarters in a local motel so Jeanine could skate every day.

The only black people someone like me would have encountered in suburban Montreal were the conductors on the CN trains. I didn't know about black people. I had never carried on a real conversation with someone of colour. Since I was raised in a civilized environment, I was inclined to overreact, to be more kind than I would have been to a fellow Caucasian. Struggling with mixed motivations, stabs of racism, and guilt, I befriended the Carrions and defended them to other skaters' mothers.

Odessa Carrion, a formidable woman, had been born in Kentucky on Independence Day in 1916. When I met her, she was on the cusp of forty-seven. She had spoollike hair, a broad smile, and a strange laugh, incongruous with her physical appearance, that ascended to a high register. She displayed a penchant for rather tasteless clothes (in my opinion), but she dazzled me with the rings on her long fingers: sapphires, rubies, and emeralds. Although the stones were small, they were genuine. That impressed a middle-class boy who was susceptible to such things.

Jeanine was somewhat younger than I. She had a beautiful face, fine mulatto-coloured skin, a tiny waist, long black hair that hung in ringlets, and perfectly aligned white teeth. With colossal thighs and a larger derrière than had ever before been seen on the ice of Mount Royal, she displayed the exotic bearing of an African princess.

Jeanine's training clothes attracted a great deal of criticism among members of the local skating club. In the 1960s, young women (even champions) practised in little woollen skating skirts and matching bonnets their mothers had sewn. Jeanine's practice clothes were more like today's competition dresses, vibrant in colour and thick with sequins.

My Personal Therapist

Mrs. Carrion, a distinguished psychotherapist at Lincoln Hospital in the Bronx, fulfilled several critical functions for me. I needed someone who would care for me, talk to me, and give me an economic boost. More than that, I needed somebody who believed in me. Mrs. Carrion fit the bill.

Someone like a young Elvis Stojko[*] would have been monitored daily by his mother in that most matriarchal of worlds. His mother would have driven him to the Toronto Cricket Skating and Curling Club, watched him while he practised, and acted as every-

---

[*] Elvis Stojko, born on March 22, 1972, in Newmarket, Ontario, is a six–time Canadian champion, three–time world gold medallist, and two–time Olympic silver medallist.

thing from gofer to provider to publicist to mother lion. That was normal and typical. I was simply deposited at the rink. My parents rarely participated directly in my skating. (Maybe I didn't want them to.) Mrs. Carrion stepped in and assumed the maternal role.

I was emotionally torn. Deep down inside, I was almost embarrassed to be seen with Mrs. Carrion in public in my all-white world, yet she was the only one, I thought, who cared about me and helped me. (If my parents did, I refused to see it.) As though plucking a perfect high C on a Stradivarius violin, she told me – and she was the first person in my life to do so – exactly who I was and what I was destined to become. She spoke of world championships, Olympic Games, and fame as an artist. This woman who came to me from out of the blue, who knew virtually nothing about figure skating, told me all the things I wanted to hear. Like Doug Leigh, skating coach of Canadian champions Brian Orser and Elvis Stojko, she understood the value of positive energy. I breathed in the magical perfume of her encouragement.

I had one unfortunate tendency in those days. Like an alert army ant, I held my antennae straight up in the air, seeking opportunities and social conquests that might somehow help me to achieve my skating goals. I welcomed anything from a pat on the head – *Gee, you really have a lot of talent, Toller* – to something more tangible: *You good little boy, may I take you out for dinner and perhaps buy you an extra figures patch for the week?*

One way to harpoon my affections, I regret, was through money or gifts. Skating was extremely expensive because of the high costs of ice time, equipment, and travel. Few family resources remained for the sartorial splendour I craved. Mrs. Carrion returned from trips home to New York with bags full of clothes she had bought for me. At the time I thought they were Bloomingdale's haute couture, but I later learned that they came from Alexander's on Third Avenue. My mother, and perhaps rightly so, was horrified by Mrs. Carrion's largesse. She felt threatened by Odessa Carrion and tried to wean me from her.

Mrs. Carrion, for her part, spent the summer turning me against my mother, whom she dismissed as psychotic. *Your mother hates you. Your mother is jealous of you. Your mother is trying to destroy you.* Whether those assertions were true or not, I sensed they were. Even so, I did not like hearing them.

Mrs. Carrion made one particular remark that grabbed me like white-hot tongs around my neck. She said, "If you do not leave your mother and her influence, you will become a homosexual."

I recognized Mrs. Carrion's kind intentions. Nevertheless, with regard to my personality and my brain chemistry, the die had been cast. There wasn't anything she could do to change the person I was, but she saw all the signs and tried very hard to protect me.

Ensconced in the Bronx

Several times I flew alone to La Guardia Airport to visit the Carrions in New York. They drove me into the heart of the Bronx, to a high-rise apartment building that housed only blacks and Puerto Ricans. Mrs. Carrion and her daughter slept in one of the two bedrooms. Jeanine's toothless grandmother, "Ma," whom I never knew to wear anything but a nightgown, kindly slept on the living room couch while I occupied her cubicle. What a strange and foreign environment that was for a boy from the snow-white sport of skating in the equally snow-white suburbia of Baie d'Urfé.

The Carrion apartment contained all sorts of foods that I hadn't tasted at home: fancy buns, hunks of meat, good cookin'. I remember the delicious smells that permeated the building in the insupportable summer heat of the Bronx. I was never entirely at ease in the Carrions' milieu, however, because mine was the only white face for miles around.

At that age, and throughout my life, I felt equally compelled both to skate and draw. Mrs. Carrion allowed me to set up shop and execute drawings in her living room. She thought that every one of those drawings was better than Michelangelo's. It is funny how you can be told things that you know are absurd and completely unrealistic, yet you want to hear them, so you don't disagree. Mrs. Carrion urged me to move to New York to study art at the Pratt Institute or Parsons School of Design.

If Mrs. Carrion could not actually adopt me, then she wanted me to marry her daughter. Yet I felt uncomfortable whenever she tried to match us up, boy and girl.

"Toller, go off with Jeaniny," she frequently urged me.

She gave us money to go to the movies in downtown Manhattan or to attend performances at Radio City Music Hall, a treat that I loved. But what I truly wanted to do was cut loose and walk the streets by myself. Mrs. Carrion would not allow that, which was wise.

The Eighth Labour of Hercules

Figure skating progress, hence admission to various competitive levels, was measured by a rigid test structure in compulsory figures and freestyle performance. Free skating came easily to me, but I worked and laboured and slaved on my figures.

In those days the eighth figure test – the gold test that would qualify me to eventually compete for the first time in the senior, or championship, division and open up access to the real competitions, the national and world championships – was excruciatingly difficult. We had to trace and retrace twelve figures six times each at a high standard of accuracy. I realized that, in order to pass, I needed to commit myself to six patches a day.[*] The norm was two daily patches. Three was a hefty number. Six was extreme.

The big day arrived. I was mentally prepared to become a senior skater. Years earlier, I had been so ill prepared for my tests that I had trembled and sobbed with nervousness. During the eighth and final test, I did not feel nervous at all. My personal psychotherapist saw to that.

---

[*] "Patch," in the vernacular of the day, meant a clean strip of ice on which to practise figures for a set period of time.

My teacher, Eva Vasak, an important coach, a dear friend, and a refined Czechoslovakian woman, for some reason ceded her place that day to Mrs. Carrion. Like Surya Bonaly's mother, Suzanne, whatever Mrs. Carrion knew about me, whatever she knew about psychology, and whatever she knew about the world of competitive ice, the one thing about which she knew nothing was skating technique. Nonetheless, at that particular moment, Mrs. Carrion was exactly the person I needed.

When a child in those days first met with his judges, it was like Louis XVI having a chat with his executioners. I remember being polite and cheerful, doing everything that I could to influence those ogres to like me more and to make the outcome go my way. Most of the gold-test judges had been imported from Toronto, which reinforced my certainty that Canadian skating power resided in Ontario.

I knew that it was quite possible that I would be kicked off the ice after my first or second figure if I did not meet the standard, so the eighth test was a case of sudden death. If, while practising my next figure, I noticed out of the corner of my eye that the judges were forming a huddle, I realized that either they were having a friendly visit or they were discussing my imminent demise.

Mrs. Carrion allowed me to practise each figure as long as I wanted to. As a result, in all the annals of figure skating, I am convinced that no eighth test has ever taken as long. The twelve figures, the twelve hurdles that I had to leap, took a total of three and one-half hours.

My first figure, I heard later, was below standard. The next was barely adequate, so my account was still in the red. However, the longer I practised, and the more Mrs. Carrion counselled me, the better my figures became. The last figure was one that was particularly difficult for many skaters, but it was, and would always remain, a favourite of mine. It was the back left bracket change bracket, and I was partial to using my left foot. When the judges held up their marks, I was thrilled to see a 5.6 (out of a possible 6.0). That generous assessment pushed me over the hump. I passed the test.

After three and one-half hours of figures, I was then told to put on my free-skating boots and perform my long program. It went well.

I hurried home and carbon copied a drawing of myself sitting on a big gold medal, proclaiming that Toller Cranston had passed his gold test. I sent the announcement out by post to virtually every person I knew and possibly to some baffled strangers as well.

The Backstage Goodbye

The last time I saw Mrs. Carrion was for a fleeting moment backstage at Radio City Music Hall in 1983, which was as appropriate a place as could have been chosen. Although I might not have known it then, Ice at Radio City, where I shared the bill equally with Olympic gold medallists Robin Cousins and Peggy Fleming, was among my greatest accomplishments as an entertainer.

So much water had flowed under the bridge since Mrs. Carrion stood at the boards coaching me through my eighth test. Now, at least in her eyes, I was a glittering star with my name in lights, encased in a silver spandex costume. I was a bit uneasy: perhaps because of all the years that had gone by without contact between us; perhaps because I was embarrassed that I had failed to show her proper appreciation once I became far more successful than either she or I had honestly thought I would.

During that brief meeting, there were simply too many things for us to discuss. Our conversation remained superficial. I learned that Jeanine, once destined to be my African queen, had gone to university and had married someone else. Mrs. Carrion and I promised each other that we would get together again, but we never did.*

---

* Odessa Carrion died in April 1987. Educated at Wayne State University and the University of Michigan, Carrion had taught at the City University of New York, had been the director of social work for the Health and Hospitals Corporation, had served as a liaison to the Congressional Black Caucus, and was a member of many boards and associations at the time of her death. She is listed in the fifth edition of Who's Who Among Black Americans.

Everything that Mrs. Carrion predicted for me had come true by then, both the good and the bad. Even on my lofty perch that night at Radio City Music Hall, I felt defenceless. She could still see right through me.

3

Kathleen Morris

The Cranston family was one of thirteen that owned property in Marshall's Bay, a private enclave that stretched some two miles along the coast of a widened section of the Ottawa River known as Shaw Lake. For generations, the cottages in Marshall's Bay were the collective summer seat of the same thirteen extended families. Various factions within those families feuded with one another, but there was a certain comfort in the perennial antagonism. Like the feud between the Montagues and the Capulets, it was historical and occasionally assumed almost noble proportions.

One reached Marshall's Bay through a working farm owned by Ross Elliott. Occasionally, if Mr. Elliott took offence at the cut of someone's jib, he closed his private road and blocked our access to the cottages. Marshall's Bay was the special and strange little spot where I spent all my childhood summers.

The Woman Who Talked to Chipmunks

Kathleen Morris, a chief member of Montreal's Beaver-Hall Hill school of painting, lived just around the point, five minutes from my family's cottage. Like the Cranstons, the Morris family had spent summers there for generations. The unmarried daughter of wealthy parents, Kathleen travelled, along with her housekeeper, all the way from Montreal by taxi. That struck me as an unimaginable luxury.

During my childhood I was never sure how old Kathleen was. Congenital deformities masked the usual means of estimation. She had a twisted spine. Her neck and head attached to her shoulders at a 45° angle. Her masculine feet were shod in sensible shoes, while her sparrowlike body was clad in old-fashioned calico summer frocks that spinster aunts of an earlier age might have worn. Her gnarled, veiny, arthritic hands were mannish, almost like a labourer's. I found that most unusual for an artist with a deft, sensitive touch.

Kathleen, I learned in adulthood, had been born in 1893. She turned fifty-six in 1949, the year in which I was born. She had been an invalid from birth. Less courageous parents in those days might have institutionalized her, but her mother and her father cared for her and nurtured her strength of character. Some perceived her as a fragile, tortured being, but God sometimes sprinkles magic on such people. In her case, the magic was in her extraordinary painting ability.

My mother rhapsodized about Kathleen's charm, integrity, and spirit. As a child, I had difficulty seeing those spiritual attributes when her odd physical characteristics were so obvious. Her appeal to me lay in the affinity that sometimes exists between equally unusual people. Neither of us had been dealt an ideal hand in the poker game of life. I was an adult in a child's body. My interests were eccentric. I felt that I was different, and distant, from my peers. With Kathleen's and my meeting, two strange creatures with crosses to bear, one physical and the other emotional, had miraculously intersected.

Whether or not it was true, I believed that Kathleen Morris sensed in me a kindred spirit. That gave me strength and inspiration. She paid attention to me, artist to artist, although my work was the antithesis of hers. Mine was mystical, dark, exotic, decorative, fantastic, and not of this world, while Kathleen's depicted rural life and the honesty of nature.

A narrow, meandering path through the forest passed by Kathleen's cottage. The house was somewhat ramshackle, but she probably liked it that way. Although she could easily have afforded to make improvements, through the years it remained essentially unchanged. I recall walking along the wooded path, my footfall cushioned by a lush carpet of generations of pine needles. As I passed the Morris cottage, Kathleen often came out to greet me (as she greeted the other children of Marshall's Bay). She made grotesque Martha Graham-like gestures and spoke in the odd manner of someone whose hearing impairment had affected her speech. She often removed her false teeth, which made it even more difficult to understand what she said.

For all of that, she was gracious and gentle. When she laughed, she covered her mouth so that her toothless gums wouldn't frighten the children who visited. She retained a girlishness, a kind of coyness, despite her appearance and age. Her most endearing quality – it left one entirely defenceless – was her ability to joke about her own physical defects.

In the Cranston cottage, chipmunks and squirrels were perceived as vermin. For Kathleen, they were companions. The chipmunks, her particular friends, had individual names. They allowed Kathleen to pet them and feed them by hand. Skunks and raccoons inhabited various niches in her cottage as well. After Kathleen brought a pet canary from Montreal, she and her bird entertained me with duets.

Kathleen painted in enormous straw hats adorned with big floppy bows or wilted flowers. The hats, while keeping the sun out of her eyes, made her appear a bit ridiculous, like a caricature, but for me they indicated her complete lack of pretension and inhibition.

My mother was a painter too, but not of Kathleen's calibre. Together she and Kathleen went off on jaunts to farmers' fields, where they painted haystacks, cows, barns, clouds, and pine trees.

Kathleen was so effusive, so complimentary about my mother's work and so pejorative of her own, that one could almost forget how famous she was.

Years after I became acquainted with Kathleen, I enrolled at the École des Beaux-Arts in Montreal. When Kathleen saw my portfolio of elaborate mixed-media drawings coated with layers of shellac, she asked meekly if I would trade a drawing for one of her paintings. I was flattered, but for some reason I never acted on the offer. That was a very foolish oversight.

The Chickadees

Kathleen painted oil sketches: often quite simply and sloppily, I thought. Then she took those sketches to her swanky Montreal apartment on Côte-des-Neiges and used them as studies for much larger, more serious paintings. Once, as a teenager, I was taken to that apartment. The Kathleen Morris whom I saw there was the same Kathleen Morris I had known since birth at Marshall's Bay, but the rustic environment had been transformed into blue-blooded, well-bred Montreal sumptuousness, with fine oriental rugs, old family silver, and maids in attendance.

Beside a window overlooking the Montreal cityscape was a painting on which Kathleen was working. She was no longer physically able to hike out into the fields, so she used the subject matter at her disposal. She fed chickadees on her snowy window ledge, high up from the ground, then painted the birds in the snow against a grey, wintry Montreal sky. Her sensitivity to the subject and her mastery of colour were supreme. I found the painting of the chickadees to be among her finest.

In 1976, I attended a retrospective of Kathleen Morris's work at the Sherbrooke Street gallery of Walter Klinkhoff, her long-time art dealer. Over the mantelpiece hung a large chickadee painting, as charming and enchanted as any in the world. All the glorious works of art I saw that day had begun as the familiar sketches Kathleen had painted as she sat beside my mother in the fields of Marshall's Bay.

As a gesture of friendship, Kathleen had given my mother a number of paintings. My mother, with unprecedented largesse, presented one of them to each of her four children. The one I received was the best, I think: a sketch of two Clydesdale horses in an Ottawa winter market scene. When I divested myself of most of my worldly possessions in 1991, Sotheby's Canada sold that tiny painting for $25,000. It helped substantially to finance the property on which I now live during part of the year in San Miguel de Allende, Mexico, a paradise of natural beauty that Kathleen Morris would have relished.

Genius is not always easily perceived. Van Gogh and Gaugin, though equally worthy, did not enjoy the success that Picasso did during his lifetime. Similarly, Kathleen Morris failed to reach the heights commanded by Emily Carr, a more famous Canadian landscape painter, yet I see little difference between the best of Carr and the best of Morris. In both, the honesty rings true.

Eric Klinkhoff, Walter's son, told me that Kathleen Morris would probably never become more famous than she was on the day of her retrospective.[*] Collectors were so enamoured of her work that they didn't resell the pieces. As a result, the paintings wouldn't circulate, pique interest, and appreciate in value. Kathleen's star would ascend no higher because collectors loved her work too much. What a fitting tribute to an artist who was as gifted, sensitive, and courageous as ever lived in Canada.

---

[*] Eric Klinkhoff gladly admits that he was proven wrong in that assessment. As the original owners of Morris's works have died, paintings have reappeared on the market. Today, those works generate lively interest and command substantial prices.

4

The God of the Pole Vault

God dealt me, as I mentioned, a strange collection of cards. I was artistic and inclined to be intellectual, yet I was also the best athlete in my school. You cannot be classified as a nerd if you are the athlete of the year, so what you become is a strange hybrid: not exactly on the nerd level, but definitely not Mr. Popularity either.

Throughout high school, but particularly in Grades 8 and 9, the measuring stick for the male students, as it always has been and continues to be in Canada, was who could make the football and soccer teams. Everyone aspired to be one of the big wheels, the studs. That was the supreme masculine ambition.

The tryouts were in the fall. Team events were not to my liking. I didn't enjoy sharing the stage. Nonetheless, I went out for the teams to show that I could make them. I qualified easily, but instead of jumping up and down when I saw my name on the list posted in the hall, I dismissed the honour. I was really more interested in skating. I had no time to play soccer and football.

In trying out, I did what everyone else did. But then I changed direction and did just the opposite. That stymied my classmates and teachers and probably contributed to my inability to fit in. I suppose that it also stymied my father, Monte, the former Queen's University football quarterback.

I did follow through with one sport, however. I eventually became all-Montreal pole-vaulting champion.

Pole vaulting shares a common denominator with figure skating: the act of becoming airborne for brief periods of time.

Being an ace in pole vaulting during my final year at MacDonald High School* was a natural for me.

There was no formal technical instruction. *This is the pole. You use it to get over the bar. Do it in any way you can.*

In my typical unconscious/conscious way, I became madly creative. Instead of concerning myself with height, I was interested in the many variations on the theme of going over the bar in artful positions. I didn't actually ascend in stag position or perform arabesques and pikes, but I freely experimented. We had an aluminum pole. If it looked like the lance of a knight in shining armour, it was no less heavy and awkward. Today pole vaulters use flexible fibreglass poles that contribute spring to the jump. By comparison, our equipment was primitive.

Pole vaulting wasn't high on my list of favourite activities, but my body wasn't particularly well suited to sprinting, which I might have preferred. I didn't have long enough legs to be a champion sprinter, and I wasn't tall enough. Pole vaulting was just the ticket to success. I also competed successfully in the broad and high jumps. In my minuscule pond, I was a big fish.

One of the terribly glamorous aspects of being on the track team – how silly it is to think of it now – was going off by bus to track meets at such illustrious sites as Lachine High School, Hudson High School, and, best of all, McGill University. We athletes got out of school three-quarters of an hour early when everyone else was left behind to study French.

Beyond my conspicuous physical eccentricities (that I honed to the finest edge in my skating career), I was unremarkable in appearance, especially when I wore the same colour and style of shorts and jersey as everyone else. I was also shy.

There was one particular boy who did stand out in the crowd. He attended one of the other high schools. I was filled with deep

---

* Toller attended MacDonald High School from 1961 through 1965. He completed Grade 11, then pursued advanced studies at the École des Beaux–Arts in Montreal from 1965 through 1967.

admiration for him and enjoyed watching him compete. His name, to the best of my recollection, was Julian Soldendick.

Julian was Adonis. Dark-blond hair topped a body that could have sprung off the screen from *Chariots of Fire*. Julian seemed to me to be of British stock, leggy, and well built. He was among the friendliest people I have ever met, and he had a drop-dead smile: natural, unselfconscious, and intensely enviable in the eyes of someone who has never smiled easily. He was tremendously encouraging to everyone at the track meet, the ultimate champion. His generosity of spirit was probably based in part on his confidence that he would ultimately win.

At one particular track meet in Lachine, Julian and I were leading the pole vault neck and neck. Then he missed. I missed too.

I have never really had the killer instinct. That deficiency was the root of some of my problems in figure skating. Only if I had previously embarrassed myself did I possess sufficient desire to go in for the kill. I never harboured the innate motivation to beat the shit out of my competitors. I preferred to fight against myself.

On his last attempt, Julian cleared the bar. Instead of firing me up, that magnificent feat thrilled me. I was being beaten by a god. I suspect that I tried to do well in my final attempt, but I didn't try as hard as I might have. I essentially threw in the towel. Julian was far more a champion than I was, and I felt it was fitting that he win. Second was a comfortable position for me.

I won't claim that passing up the chance to win that pole-vault event was totally without conscious motivation, but it sprang primarily from a deep reservoir of unconscious inclination and character traits. The pattern was to repeat itself often in my life, notably at the 1976 Olympics. The magnificent Briton John Curry, who won the gold medal in men's figure skating at the Games in which I took the bronze, was just the latest incarnation of Julian Soldendick, the golden god of the pole vault.

5

The Monkey Suit

When Linda Hunt won an Academy Award for the 1983 film *The Year of Living Dangerously*, she remarked that receiving such an award was as rare as getting water from the moon. In the early 1960s, the ability to train figure skaters to the world and Olympic level was just that rare. As a result, certain senior coaches in each country taught all the top skaters. A student had to undergo their tutelage in order to gain their secret knowledge. No one with whom I came into contact during my early teens had that special water-from-the-moon knowledge. As a result, the best I could hope for was luck in competition. That was rarely enough.

I did manage to win the Canadian Junior Men's Championship in 1964, at the age of fourteen. Holding the title (and passing my eighth test) catapulted me into the senior ranks. In one sense, that meant I was closer to making the Olympic team. In reality, though, I felt further away, because the chasm that I had to leap, the prerequisite for a senior male skater, was the mandatory five-minute long program. Simply surviving a five-minute program was physically more difficult and demanding than learning individual jumps and other technical elements. The secret was conditioning and stamina. I had neither, nor did I know how to develop them.

I was a suburban boy, and boys like me were supposed to go to our cottages during the summer. I was allowed only one month of summer skating. Lake Placid, in Upstate New York, was one of the meccas. I was duly scheduled to compete in the 1964 Lake Placid

Summer Free Skating Competition in late July. By then I had turned fifteen (my birthday is in April).

One of the things that separated the men from the boys at that time was whether you owned a "monkey suit": a multilayered costume that included a formal shirt, a bow tie or cravat, a jacket like those worn by restaurant maître d's, a jumpsuit that pulled up under the jacket, suspenders, and, in my case, false cuffs adorned with my father's cufflinks. Like getting one's first long pants in an earlier era, being allowed to own one of those monkey suits was hugely significant in a young male skater's life. It was the skating world's equivalent of the bar mitzvah.

A dressmaker, the mother of skater Pinkie Hill, made my first jumpsuit, which was of royal-blue wool jersey. Competition day was like Christmas morning. It was *the* special day, and that was when you put on your special costume. You never, ever tried out your costume beforehand. To skate in it in advance would have been unheard of. That custom had egregious consequences.

Mother and Son

The previous summer, competing in the silver division with just a three-minute program, I had won handily, and my mother had basked in the glory. Perhaps she now hoped to relive those glory days when I had been the toast of the competition. For whatever reason, she decided to drive me to Lake Placid this time as well. It was to be a mother-and-son expedition.

I would skate my new five-minute program to difficult, intense classical music, Dvořák's *New World Symphony*. Two facts should have given my mother pause. I had never yet run through a complete five-minute program in my life. More daunting, I was going to compete against the likes of John Misha Petkevich,[*] who at the time

---

[*] In the summer of 1964, John Petkevich was a rising star. He subsequently captured the American junior men's championship and won one senior bronze medal, three silver medals, and the 1971 U.S. men's title.

was America's golden-haired boy – half god and half Tab Hunter.

I remember certain details as though the event occurred yesterday. My mother and I stayed at the Caribou Lodge, part of the Mirror Lake Inn. I clearly recall that, for some odd reason, the two of us were given an enormous room with five beds.

On the day before the competition, I went to senior men's practice. John Misha Petkevich entered the rink in a trench coat. Immediately everyone in the rink – and I have not seen anything like it since – cleared the ice and appeared to undergo full-blown paralysis. It was as though the Prophet had arrived. We were all his competitors, yet nobody else seemed to exist, thanks to his larger-than-life personality.

Two other extremely talented skaters in the rink that day were Paul McGrath, and Bobby Black from the Skating Club of Boston. They were part of skating history, and both have since died of AIDS.

The men competed late the next evening, and whatever could go wrong for me did. The royal-blue wool jersey jumpsuit was exceedingly stretchy. Within a minute and one-half, its crotch was bobbing around my kneecaps. Not only did that impede free movement, but I was highly embarrassed by the huge, unaccustomed *thing* between my legs.

In addition, I had tied the cravat too tight. Just as I was running out of breath because of the arduousness of the five-minute program, I was also running out of air due to the tourniquetlike grip of the cravat. I almost suffocated on the ice. People noticed and later remarked that I was sweating profusely and my face was as red as a beet.

It was a summer night, and although Lake Placid was comfortably cool in the evening, the more I sweated, the more the wool jersey itched. I remember thinking in the middle of my number, "If only I could just tear off this bloody costume and skate naked!" My thoughts were entirely focused on extricating myself at the first possible moment from my personal torture chamber. My poor skating, my uncomfortable costume, and Dvořák's ponderous music all conspired to strangle me to death.

At about the two-and-one-half-minute point, one of the false cuffs studded with my father's cufflink fell onto the ice and became a further source of humiliation. I had to keep skating past it as my program unfurled. I don't exactly know how I finished the number, but I was definitely in a somnambulistic state, semiconscious and literally ready to faint. I keeled over onto a rinkside bench, gasping and sputtering.

Although I was practically *non compos mentis*, I do remember watching the performance of John Misha Petkevich through glazed eyes and being absolutely hypnotized by his charisma. He jumped like a gazelle.

I changed clothes and left the building in disgrace. My mother, Stuart, did not speak to me again for two weeks. In our room at the Caribou Lodge, with its five beds, she occupied the bed at one extreme and I slept miles away at the other. That was her choice. I had humiliated her. I had made her trip from Montreal to Lake Placid a living nightmare, an embarrassment, and a waste of time.

Not a word passed between us the next morning at breakfast. We bore the two-and-one-half-hour drive home in our forest-green Mustang in utter silence.

It is at just such times when dialogue between parent and child can make things better, offer hope, promote understanding, and encourage future efforts. But the longer we travelled, the more frighteningly deafening the silence became.

When we got home, my mother told my father that she would never again have anything to do with my skating career.

Father and Son

The next major event in my schedule was the Central Ontario Summer Free Skating Competition. In some ways, that was even more daunting than the Lake Placid event. At the time, Central

Ontario was the main centre of skating in the country. The likes of Jay Humphry, David McGillivray, Charles Snelling,[*] and all the other people from the big clubs with the water-from-the-moon knowledge would be at the competition. It was decided that my father would take time off from work to drive me to Toronto and remain with me during the event. Not a word was ever spoken, but I sensed that my mother expected some kind of redemption. There was a great deal of pressure on me, I thought, to save face.

I crawled out of the emotional wreckage of the Lake Placid catastrophe and left behind the itchy royal-blue costume and the indignity of the audience's amused reaction to it. I was hardly in fighting form, although I could actually be quite good for thirty seconds at a time.

The day before the Central Ontario event, my father took me to a practice rink in Mississauga. A strange and disastrous thing happened there that forever changed my physical skating vocabulary. I fell on my wrists. I don't think that I broke them, but I must have severely sprained them. They both became dislocated. I could pop them in and out of joint. I kept the knowledge to myself and didn't seek medical treatment. Years later, I found that I was able to move my hands as no one else did. I had more flexibility than other men, and I made good use of it in my choreography. But at the time, at age fifteen, the condition was just terribly, terribly painful.

My father, who was far more empathetic than my mother but certainly didn't know anything about skating, had to endure an experience similar to what my mother had endured in Lake Placid. I was competing, in essence, against the Canadian world team, and I completely ran out of steam after thirty seconds. I did a few good jumps, then dropped to zero. I crawled through five minutes of Dvořák's *New World Symphony* as Hannibal crossed the Alps. The

---

[*] Charles Snelling was the five–time senior champion and the 1957 world bronze medallist. Jay Humphry would win the Canadian title in 1968 and 1969, David McGillivray in 1970. Ultimately Humphry would rise as high as sixth in the world, McGillivray tenth.

task was cold, bitter, unpleasant, and nearly impossible. All I could think was "Oh, God, I wish it were over."

I didn't quite swoon at the end of my program, but I felt emotionally numb. I had failed again, and this time my father had been privy to my ignominy.

Years later I met Ellen Burka, who had been teaching Canadian bronze medallist Jay Humphry at the time. She reported to me that the buzz at the practices had been "Oh, Toller Cranston is very talented, but don't worry about him. In thirty seconds, he'll be dead." That was perfectly accurate. No matter how hard I might have tried to impress people, the word was already out that I had no conditioning.

My father and I drove home the next day. Instead of discussing my skating, what had gone wrong, and how the problems could be fixed, we talked about everything else. The conversation contained an enormous doughnut hole. We didn't address the real problem. It couldn't be discussed. We circumvented it. It was as though the competition hadn't occurred.

I remember returning to 701 Dowker Drive in Baie d'Urfé and getting out of the car, knowing that my father had to tell my mother what had happened at the competition. Even though he was kind, another tsunami of hostility washed over me. I had done it again. A lot of money was going into my skating, and I didn't deserve the investment. I was unworthy.

Retribution

The story ended on an even sadder note. In the Town of Mount Royal arena, there were several people (as there always were in my life) who saw my real talent and potential. One of those was a New York woman, Mrs. Kerr. Her daughter, Honey Kerr, became a minor star in America. The Kerrs bonded with me, understood me, and knew that I really had the stuff. They offered to take me to Lake Placid for two weeks of training. Although they had little more money than my parents did, they planned to pay all my expenses.

Going to Lake Placid would be a way for me to end the summer on a high note, training with many world-class skaters.

My mother, as punishment for humiliating the family with two dreadful competition performances, forbade me to go to Lake Placid that summer. Moving heaven and earth would not have changed her mind.

To a fifteen-year-old, that was an enormous and almost insurmountable emotional mountain. Someone else might not have recovered. I am not laying blame on my parents. I am simply saying, *This is what happened. This was their reaction.* I share the story because my situation was bleak and desperate, yet I was eventually able to escape that physical and mental morass, learn from the experiences, find a teacher with the water-from-the-moon knowledge that I needed, and become an Olympic medallist – albeit at a great psychological price.

6

The Summer of '68

At the age of nineteen, I finally convinced my parents that I had to leave the Town of Mount Royal arena to train in Lake Placid, a bigger pond in the skating world, though geographically a remote Adirondack hamlet. That summer is deeply etched onto my soul. At the time I was a lost child in every conceivable way. The only thing that seemed clear to me still was my sense of my skating destiny, but that destiny was a lighthouse on a distant rock, and the ocean raged between us. I still had no means, no strategy for getting there. All I could do was stand on the beach and watch it twinkling in the mist.

During the 1967–68 skating season, while studying art at the École des Beaux-Arts in Montreal (which I did for two and one-half years after high school, leaving just short of graduation), I had whipped myself into fighting form in unorthodox ways in order to qualify for the 1968 Olympics in Grenoble, France. I had sneaked through the back door of the Colisée building every day and run up all nineteen flights of fire stairs. Rather than going to a gym and working out with a trainer as skaters do now, I had hoped that by simply exerting myself to the point of exhaustion, I would become more fit. That was what I could afford. Strangely enough, the regimen worked to some extent.

The de facto qualifier, the Canadian national men's championship, had taken place early in the year. I was last to skate on that Sunday afternoon in Kerrisdale, British Columbia, just outside of Vancouver. Having finished fifth in the figures[*] behind Jay Humphry, Steve Hutchinson, David McGillivray, and Paul Bonenfant, I needed to pull up two places to make the Olympic team. I skated a performance that ranked among my most historic. I distinctly remember receiving marks from first place to last, falling short of an Olympic berth by a hair.

Steve Hutchinson, who finished in third place overall and went on to Grenoble, missed two double Axels and a triple toe loop. I hit my double Axels, double loops, double flips, combinations, and everything else, but nonetheless placed fourth overall. My free-skating marks ranged from mediocre to near-perfect. The audience booed the low ones.

I considered retiring after that performance, but Ellen Burka, coach of the reigning Canadian champion, Jay Humphry, fortified

---

[*] In *Zero Tollerance*, Toller recalled placing fourth in the figures in Vancouver. According to the March 1968 issue of *Skating* magazine, he finished fifth in figures, fourth overall.

my spirit with a pep talk behind the grandstand. I took the red-eye flight home and had a nervous breakdown *à la* Virginia Woolf in my Baie d'Urfé bedroom. I had achieved what I wanted to achieve in the sense that I had caused a public sensation, but I had not reaped the coveted reward from the judges. I took to my bed for a week.

That may sound artificially dramatic, but I was a hypersensitive artist who felt things more deeply than anyone I knew. I was as frustrated and confused as a salmon heading upstream to spawn but unable to jump over a waterfall. I knew that spawning was my biological imperative, but the force of the crashing water constantly washed me back downstream.

When summer came, I went to Lake Placid[*] to study with Howard Nicholson, a celebrated coach who was known for teaching school figures, my Achilles' heel. Scott Ethan Allen also took lessons from Mr. Nicholson. I was in awe of Scott and covetous of his family's seemingly unlimited resources. Scott and I were about the same age, but he was the two-time American champion, the 1964 Olympic bronze medallist, and the 1965 world silver medallist while I had not yet broken out of the Canadian national ranks to advance onto the world scene. As it turned out, I eclipsed Scott in the end. In the summer of 1968, however, I could not imagine ever competing with his likes on an even par.

The Colour of Skating

It was in Lake Placid that I had my first painful encounter with outright racism. (On the Canadian side of the border, prejudice was subtler.) Mrs. Carrion thought that it would be wonderful if Jeanine could move into the skaters' dormitory at the Mirror Lake Inn, a local landmark constructed from an old estate in the 1920s by the original Fuller Brush man and his wife, and train beside me. The mother of one of the other skaters, a member of a well-known

---

[*] In *Zero Tollerance*, Toller placed this event in 1969. Subsequent research has shown that it took place a year earlier.

local family whom I can still name, looked at me with cold blue eyes and said, "We can't have niggers staying in a place like this."

I was completely torn between addressing the wealthy, powerful skating mother (*How dare you say that, you bigot?*) and caving in to her imperious, intimidating demeanour. I said nothing, which I regret to this day.

I apologetically reported the incident to Mrs. Carrion. For whatever reasons, Jeanine did not train at Lake Placid that summer.

Moving into the Garage

On the financial level, I was more than a fish out of water. The athletes' dormitory cost what seemed to me an enormous amount of money: $50 a week. Serious skaters today have sponsors and retinues, as all Eastern Bloc athletes and a number of Americans did then. I was on my own. I obtained a job as a waiter at the Mirror Lake Inn, a job for which I was particularly ill suited.

Like every other time in my life, I could not fit into the group. I didn't want to stay in the rowdy dormitory with the other summer waiters and bartenders: beer-swilling, womanizing jocks from American universities. Somebody suggested that the vacant garage high on the hill at the back of the hotel could serve nicely as my summer quarters. I agreed that the garage was just the place for me.

It was a tiny, derelict structure with a worm-eaten wooden floor and a manually operated overhead door. Its interior smell was an unsavoury cross between ancient woodshed and mildewed attic. Cobwebs hung in profusion from sombre brown beams. The room must have previously served as living quarters. It contained a sink and a toilet. Those were the only amenities. The hotel staff brought in a bed for me.

Fortunately my days as a waiter were short-lived. I was asked to assume the official title of groundskeeper of the Mirror Lake Inn.

There was a second groundskeeper, a mentally deficient redheaded man. Even my fellow gardener was not destined to become my friend.

The Incomparable Josie

We all repeatedly gravitate towards the same types of people and make the same mistakes over and over again. The patterns are embedded in the rhythms of our psyches. Ever since childhood, I had befriended older women. (That was before the film *The Graduate* made it fashionable.) While I was in Lake Placid, as so often in my past, I was kind to a particular older woman and she, in response, was kind to me.

Josie was a frail, itsy-bitsy chambermaid with one of the town's hotels. Her hair was badly permed, and her tremendous nose protruded like Olive Oyl's sausage-shaped proboscis. Her social bearing indicated that she had lived in rural Upstate New York all her life, like generations before her, and she was genuinely good-hearted and probably lonely. She had a crush on me. To the likes of Josie, I was an unusual specimen.

Josie took it upon herself to decorate my room with every available amenity at her disposal. Any item that a chambermaid could furnish to the guests in the fancy rooms, I had in my garage: piles of perfumed soaps, crisp white sheets, an unlimited number of bath towels, blankets, fluffy robes, and packets of bubble bath. I had maid service three times a day.

I suspect that Josie periodically invaded the cutting gardens of her place of work. I lived among a plenitude of flora. My environment was rapidly transformed from a dusty, mildewed garage into a hideaway on the scale of *The Thousand and One Nights*. On one hand, it was primitive; on the other hand, it was the apogee of luxury. Meals began to arrive from the kitchen without my intervention. The situation was unusual, to say the least, and it persisted all through the summer.

Lady Chatterley

I was happy with the Josie connection, but I lusted after bigger fish, something the size of a muskellunge. I was looking for a sponsor, someone who could help me achieve my elusive skating destiny. I just was not going anywhere in the skating hierarchy, thanks in part to the copious butter that the Mirror Lake Inn insinuated into every culinary delight, particularly the pies. With twenty pounds of increased weight as ballast, I was spiralling downward, and I knew it.

I became friendly with the mother of one of my fellow skaters. Mrs. S. was perhaps thirty-six years old to my scarcely nineteen. Her husband was out of the country. That left her free to live in a rented house in Lake Placid while her daughter trained at the Olympic Centre. Mrs. S. was lonely, sexually frustrated, and probably not too very interested in her distant husband when push came to shove.

Although I was utterly inexperienced, living the celibate life of a monk, I knew there was sexual energy in the air whenever Mrs. S. was around. Her farewells were just a little too passionate. Her hand on my shoulder gave off certain vibrations that other hands on my shoulder did not emit. She hinted that I should move in with her and her daughter and remain in Lake Placid to train full-time. Our friendship became too intimate. There was the tiniest whiff of something unhealthy about it. But how would a serious-minded, well-bred teenager in the innocent 1960s know about that? After all, I was the groundskeeper, not the gamekeeper.

I allowed Mrs. S. to be kind to me. That meant taking me out for lunch or a steak dinner at the swanky Steak and Stinger restaurant or giving me small sums of money: $10 here, $20 there. As in the biblical case of the forty pieces of silver, when one takes money in return for an unsavoury favour, the money does not offer much pleasure. Granted it is more fun having money than not, but there are ways of earning it that afford greater satisfaction. Still, I had to survive, and I was prepared to do it in any way I could.

On one particular evening at dusk, near the end of the summer, Mrs. S. drove me home from practice along a back road on the upper property of the Mirror Lake Inn. We lingered in the car for a private chat. Again, sexual energy filled the air. I was aware of it, although it did not excite me. I watched from outside my skin, an observer enjoying our cat-and-mouse game (with me definitely playing the role of the cat and Mrs. S., or so I believed, playing the mouse).

When I bid the mouse farewell and pushed up my garage door, she suddenly stepped on the gas and drove into my living room. She steered her car right up to my bed. The door banged down again.

It was at that point that my cat melted into a mouse and Mrs. S.'s mouse mushroomed into a cat. She lunged from hand to thigh to crotch within less than a minute. She undid my fly with amazing dexterity and, without a moment's hesitation, performed oral sex on me. Like any teenage boy, I responded immediately and dramatically. Fortunately Josie had left me plenty of towelettes and guest soaps.

Wait for the Beep

If Mrs. S. longed to make love on the bed, I was not the least bit interested. I told her briskly, "I think you have to leave."

Undaunted, she replied, "People in small towns talk. When I visit again, I'll just honk the horn. Pull the door up, and I'll drive in."

She backed her car out of my bedroom and drove away into the orange summer sunset. She may even have been whistling.

There were many times when I reclined on my bed, reflecting on that strange interlude. I felt disappointed when I didn't hear a car horn – but traumatized when I did. Mrs. S. returned twice and beeped her horn, but I did not open the door. I lay frozen in my garage with my ambivalent heart pounding in my chest.

At What Price?

I believe that it is true of all humans that our first sexual encounter helps to mould our full understanding of sex and leaves a brand on us for the rest of our lives. It is silly to try to analyse what it all meant. Nonetheless, my first experience was in many ways destined to repeat itself for the next thirty years in a series of clinical, physical encounters with no overtones of love and romance. If there is anything that I regret in my life – even after regrettable bouts with drugs, crooks, and failure – it is that somehow I have never found the formula to combine love and sex. My question is, Did Mrs. S. cause the seed of that particular tendency that was already within me to germinate, or did she plant the seed and thus affect me in a way that profoundly damaged my life?

7

The Ellen Burka Gallery

At the end of the summer of 1968, I stood poised at a crossroads. I was not making skating progress in Lake Placid, and I was at loose ends. I decided that there was only one person in the world who possessed the water-from-the-moon knowledge of how to train skaters properly, who felt an affinity with me, who understood me as an artist, and who also worked at the political epicentre of the Canadian skating world. That was Ellen Burka, the coach who had taken me behind the grandstand and encouraged me to continue after the disappointment of the 1968 Canadian men's championship.

I looked her up in the Toronto telephone book. At dusk on a lonely early September day, I went to a phone booth at the Olympic arena, dialled her number, and asked her to teach me.

In those days, there was a certain loyalty among coaches. If they taught a champion, they wouldn't immediately agree to take on his competitor (as some do today).

Ellen replied, "It is a possibility, but I would have to clear it with Jay Humphry." When she phoned me back, she announced, to my relief, that Jay had magnanimously agreed.

I returned to Baie d'Urfé, uncomfortably aware that I was taking the reins of my own life into my hands once and for all. Other young adults from literate families were heading off to university, while I was casting my lot with the fickle and uncertain world of figure skating.

My father dropped me off at the train station in Dorval, a suburb of Montreal. As I stood on the platform with my skate bag in one hand, my paint bag in the other, and very little else, it was a scene from *Fiddler on the Roof*: Tevye seeing off his daughter at a lonely railroad station. I had $50 in my pocket. My father didn't stay with me to wait for the train. He was an extremely nice man, but we shared no apparent bond beyond the accident of birth.

If I hadn't enjoyed a rich family life, however, at least I had known some sense of belonging. Now I was leaving behind the only life I knew and tossing myself to the wind like a piece of chaff.

Ellen had arranged for me to board with a widow who lodged me in a little cell and fed me widow's fare. Because of restless energy or frustration, I always felt hungry.

I was ejected from that boarding house and several others due to faux pas involving indelible art supplies. Finally Ellen, who had been married to an artist and did some painting herself, looked at my portfolio of fantastic, intricate, large, mad, disturbed, and tormented drawings. She was astounded at the spectrum of my work. It was probably some of the best that I have ever done. She saw me in a new light and told me that I could stay for a week in her basement, next to the furnace room.

I arrived with my skates and my paints. Ellen asked, "Have you had dinner?"

With Ellen Burka in 1991.

I replied, "Why no, I'm starving," but I had just eaten an entire bag of butterscotch chip cookies. We shared a delicious meal, and I moved into the basement.

Shaping Up

The bag of brushes and paints in one hand and the skate bag in the other became a ritual and a metaphor for my bifurcated life. I eventually painted and appeared on Broadway, painted and skated three shows a day with Holiday on Ice, and painted in hotel rooms when I travelled. In many ways that was madness – messy and exhausting.

During the fall and winter of 1968–69, I housecleaned my character. The gigolo thing did not play well with Ellen, a concentration camp survivor and former Dutch skating champion. She addressed that tendency of mine and counselled me about taking advantage of people. She set me on the straight and narrow path, taught me that hard work and excellence pay off, and showed me by example the value of independence.

One of the hardest lessons was practising my five-minute long program from beginning to end at the Toronto Cricket Skating and Curling Club. Ellen forbade me to stop in the middle, even if I passed out. Within the confines of my experience, no one ever did full run-throughs. One simply waited for the day of reckoning and hoped for good luck.

One day Ellen watched me nearly expire during one of my long-program run-throughs and said, "Look, I hate to tell you this, but it is going to take you three years to get into condition." That was not the assessment that I wanted to hear, but in many ways Ellen was right on the money.

During that painful period, I was so insecure, so reclusive, that I rarely ventured into downtown Toronto. I journeyed from my room in Ellen's house to the nearby Cricket Club, then back again to the basement. That was my life. In essence, I was attending reform school. Yet the artistic passion burned steadily, so I continued to paint.

Inching Higher

At the 1969 Canadian men's championship, I improved my position by one place by eking from fourth to third and ending up on the podium. However, the two people above me – Jay Humphry and David McGillivray – were so superior to me in conditioning and experience that my third was closer to fourth than it was to second. I did manage to advance to the North American championship in Oakland, California.

Tim Wood, who had already twice earned the U.S. title[*] as well as the 1968 world and Olympic silver medals, arrived in Oakland without a coach and won the competition, which astonished his competitors. The rest of us clung to our teachers, primarily because they held the keys to the car. Tim went on from North Americans to win his first of two consecutive world championships.

---

[*] Tim Wood would win his third U.S. title in 1970.

I skated an unusual program in Oakland. One or two people might have divined, at least in part, what I would become in the future. Nonetheless, I finished sixth out of six. So did my friend Hazel Pike, who joked that we came a "convincing" sixth.

Often the last-place finisher goes on years later to win gold. In her first world championship in 1962 in Prague, Gabriele Seyfert, a sturdy young woman from the German Democratic Republic who skated in Peggy Fleming's willowy shadow, came dead last. In 1969, after three silver medals, she finished on top, the first East German woman to do so. That and similar examples from skating history would give me a shred of hope during the months after the North American championships. I was nothing if not determined.

Meanwhile I flew back to Toronto while Ellen sallied forth with Jay to the world championships in Colorado Springs, Colorado. Providentially, I then made one of my most brilliant moves. With Ellen out of town, I returned temporarily to my family home in the Montreal suburbs.

Pictures at an Exhibition

Before leaving for Colorado, Ellen had suggested, "Why don't we put on a painting exhibition in my house during the spring so you can raise some money to pay your skating expenses?"

The agreement was that if I produced a lot of work, Ellen, her daughter Astra, and I would mount a joint exhibition.

Years earlier my family had hosted a foreign exchange student, Arun Kumar, an Indian prince. True, he was not a real prince, but he was wealthy, and he looked like a prince: beautiful and spiritual. Every member of our family fell in love with him in various ways, but my mother was the only one who went off to visit him in his native land. Several times during my adolescence, she flew to India in hot pursuit of the exotic Arun Kumar, leaving me alone in the suburbs.

When I arrived home in Baie d'Urfé, my mother had just departed on one such Indian pilgrimage. That suited me well enough. While my father was at work and my younger brothers were otherwise occupied, I could descend into the basement of our bungalow at 701 Dowker Drive and lose myself in my work. There I produced, in my obsessive-compulsive way, vast quantities of drawings, watercolours, and mixed-media paintings. I surfaced for air only long enough to take the bus into Montreal to buy art supplies. The works that I produced during that period were textured, meticulously detailed, and fraught with frustration and sexual tension.

As spring arrived, I did something unprecedented for a young man on the cusp of twenty. I went to a bank and talked the loan officer into lending me $2,500, which I used to pay for framing at the Montreal Framing Company on St. Lawrence Street. The framed works were then shipped off to Ellen Burka's home in Toronto.

Even though I had never been fundamentally entrepreneurial, I also commissioned prints of one of my elaborate drawings to coincide with the exhibition. Posters were popular in the 1960s. That was my first one, but over the years I kept a stack of various posters in Ellen's basement and sold them for $10 apiece. In a way, I was printing my own bank notes. Few days went by without at least one customer purchasing a signed poster.

Ellen made an extraordinary gesture when my paintings arrived. She removed every stick of furniture in her house, put it all in storage, and had the rooms professionally lit with gallery lights. Our paintings, which were beautifully hung, ranged in price from $25 to a staggeringly optimistic $250. We sent invitations to everyone in the realm.

The day of the exhibition arrived. The flowers were arranged. The house was clean. Everything looked splendid, but we truly did not know if anyone would attend our event. An hour before the scheduled opening, we became uneasy and anxious. Our misgivings were allayed by the tidal wave that followed – the arrival en masse of the entire Toronto skating world: judges, officials, Canadian champions, *tout le monde du patinage Canadien*.

The size and range of the art display astounded our guests. No skaters had ever produced anything like it. Ellen Burka and I were already viewed as the oddest couple in skating, but our exhibition cemented that reputation.

A number of people became quite drunk during the soiree, particularly Ellen on scotch. Admittedly the success of the event was heady. Every single one of my paintings sold.

Since there were no bedrooms left in Ellen's gallery, at 1 A.M. Jay Humphry and I retired to two cots in the furnace room. I remember counting my cheques and cash by the tiny pilot light of the furnace. On that one night, I went from having nothing at all to holding $5,500 in my hands. I felt exceedingly rich – even though I had to set aside enough money to repay the bank loan. Like Barbra Streisand in *Funny Girl*, I had won an Academy Award on my first time out. I knew even then that I had just achieved the greatest moment of my artistic life. Any future exhibition would pale in its light.

The economic triumph of the evening armed me with the comforting knowledge that I could continue to support myself as a skater. If I worked hard, somehow I would remain afloat through my art. Many years later, at a painting exhibition in Montreal, I grossed $130,000 in a single night. The thrill of that substantial sum was nothing compared to the youthful joy of counting $5,500 by the pilot light in Ellen Burka's furnace room.

8

The Truth about Strawberries

During the late spring or early summer of 1970, just a year after my first of several shows at the Ellen Burka Gallery, I was invited to California to skate an exhibition performance for the Glacier Falls figure skating club's end-of-the-season carnival in Anaheim.

As Salieri viewed Mozart – a master who regarded the virtuosity of a young upstart and was traumatized by it – I was penetrated by a dart of fear at the sight of Terry Kubicka performing at that carnival. Although I was the star of the show, and although I had placed thirteenth at my first world championship several months earlier at Ljubljana, Yugoslavia, and was actively engaged in forging my myth, I saw in that young Californian a raw jumping ability that exceeded my own. I pretended not to notice, but Kubicka was a cobra who, once full-grown, would have a bite as deadly as that of any in the jungle.[*]

Another skater at the Anaheim carnival who trained in California at the time was an unusual wrinkle in Canadian skating history. Karen Grobba (now Cahill) was born in Canada. She moved to California with her family at the age of five and trained with Nancy Rush for most of her competitive career. Mrs. Rush eventually left private coaching to take a job with the Ice Capades, so Karen switched to Barbara Roles.

Karen was a leggy teenage Catherine Deneuve with a certain artistic flair. In those days, school figures played a large part in competitive results, and Karen was an able practitioner. What is

---

[*] Terry Kubicka, 1972 U.S. junior men's champion, eventually won the 1976 senior title and placed sixth in the world.

more, she liked them. When she became proficient enough to qualify for national competition, she returned to Canada during the competitive season to train at Toronto's Granite Club with Osborne Colson and Donald Jackson. That was how she and I met and became friends.

Karen came from nowhere to place third as a senior lady at the 1970 Canadian championships in Edmonton. In that era, a skater was required to pay her dues: develop a following gradually as the judges watched her climb the ladder. It was next to impossible to enter a competition unknown and leave with a medal. Karen managed to do so.

Several months later, she invited me to stay at her family's house in California during the week of the Anaheim carnival.

A Doll's House

One day Karen took me to the home of her childhood coach, Nancy Rush. I was forewarned that Mrs. Rush was an eccentric, artistic woman. That was why I had been urged to meet her. I was also told that the remarkable Nancy Rush had built her own house – built it by hand with a hammer, nails, and a saw. The tiny, magical one-storey house, set in a wooded glen in Eagle Rock near Glendale, was as close as any house could be to Giselle's fairy-tale cottage. It was a doll's house built for (and by) a middle-aged doll.

Karen and I ventured inside. At first I didn't fully appreciate the monothematic environment. It didn't immediately register on my psyche. As I looked from one object to another, I realized incrementally that every conceivable decorative nuance in the house contained the strawberry image. The rugs were crocheted strawberries. The shower curtain was a field of beaded pink plastic strawberries. Strawberry porcelain bowls offered strawberry bonbons. Every print and painting on the wall evidenced a strawberry connection. There is a certain tedium in the description, but truly lampshades dripped with strawberries; ashtrays resembled concave strawberries; pencil holders held writing implements pocked with little strawberry imprints. I do not remember a single decorative touch that did not in some way refer to strawberries.

Such exuberance, I concluded, could only exist in California. There is a certain type of over-the-top Southern Californian who indulges in eccentricities that lack depth without lacking passion and conviction. A European might collect eighteenth-century etchings, for example, and exhibit the same passion, but those etchings would have far more artistic substance and economic worth. Only a brash new culture could spawn someone who worshipped the strawberry as Nancy Rush did. Sipping strawberry tea and eating strawberry bonbons, I thought to myself that I was witnessing a cultural phenomenon that could not occur in Eastern Canada.

The Strawberry Period

As I flew home to Toronto, strawberries pervaded my subconscious. The next work that I painted became the cornerstone of my strawberry period. I called it *The Great Strawberry Queen*. I had prints and posters made from that painting, so strawberries gradually infiltrated the global art scene. The painting became synonymous with my reputation as an artist. I don't know whether that was, on balance, more positive or negative. I sold *The Great Strawberry Queen* for $2,000. The last time I heard of it, it had been resold for nine times that amount.

I had not yet purged myself of Nancy Rush's strawberries, so paintings followed suit in rapid succession: *The Strawberry Patch*, *The Strawberry Tango*, *The Strawberry Sisters*, *The Strawberry Warrior*. Every subject in my artistic vocabulary sprouted strawberries. I have always subscribed to the maxim, "If something is worth doing, it is worth overdoing," but in the case of the strawberry theme, even I recognized superfluousness when I saw it. Strawberries overwhelmed my paintings like juicy red barnacles on a ship's hull: clusters and clusters and clusters, more and more and more.

The strawberry gouaches, my calling cards, were hot sellers. The more I sold, the better known I became and the more the demand increased for strawberry paintings. It was an endless, self-perpetuating cycle. The number of strawberries extant grew exponentially.

Most artists' themes, like Picasso's blue period or Dali's melting watches, run their course and vanish. Not so in the case of the strawberry, which never quite left my artistic vocabulary. Instead it assumed monumental implications and acquired secret symbolism known only to me.

When anyone works for long periods without communicating with others, he holds interior conversations with himself. As I painted vines of interconnected strawberries, I justified the time and effort by affixing the fruit metaphorically to the philosophy of the feminist movement. My vines of strawberries became young women sacrificing their virginity to rapacious agricultural workers.

It later dawned upon me that the strawberry was the only fruit I could think of that had seeds (actually, achenes) on the outside – a vaguely erotic revelation. In my mind, the fruit then took on a bisexual connotation. Its base was similar to the head of a penis, although the general configuration bore similarities to labia as well. I was intrigued by my new and thoroughly unscientific theory of hermaphroditic fruit.

The Fruits of Inquiry

After spending days on end executing nothing but strawberries, only a fool would fail to consider what a strawberry truly was and what it represented. I researched the subject and became the world's premier expert on the strawberry in the history of visual art and what the strawberry has meant historically to Western and Oriental culture. On two occasions I was a paid university speaker. I entitled my lecture "The Strawberry Revolution."

Strawberries, I learned, have traditionally been perceived as royal fruits. Strawberries Romanov was a favourite dessert of the Russian czars. Louis XIV of France invented a dessert of strawberries and cream consumed with a black-pepper garnish. It is still served today and tastes delicious.

The Ming tombs of China thrilled me. Their great oil-lamp urns that burned for one thousand years were encrusted with strawberries.

The Flemish painter Jan van Eyck adorned the foreground of his most famous triptych, *The Adoration of the Lamb*, with fields of wild strawberries.

At the Cluny Museum on the Boulevard Saint Michel in Paris, the celebrated "Lady with the Unicorn" Gobelin tapestries are not without their representations of the stemless members of the rose family. In medieval times, the fruit was viewed as a magic fertility talisman for childless women.

The classic colours of the strawberry have endured throughout the centuries and across many cultures. In the spectrum, no complementary colours are stronger than red and green. Some of the greatest interiors of the world have been decorated in variations on the strawberry-coloured theme. The red might tend towards burgundy, the green towards olive, but red and green have coloured such celebrated environments as the lobby of London's Savoy Hotel, the Brighton Pavilion, and many apartments of the Residenz in Munich.

The Rise and Fall of the Strawberry

My strawberry period lasted a decade. Fans presented me with strawberry objects that they had made or purchased. I developed such a great collection that I became more Nancy Rush than Nancy Rush. From shreds of hearsay, I know that Nancy is aware of her role in my art career, but there has never been a head-to-head meeting of the Strawberry Experts of the World.

Strawberries affected me in ways in which they did not affect Nancy, who simply collected them. They infiltrated films and inspired interior designers, greeting card companies, and porcelain manufacturers. In 1982, the Goebel company that makes Hummel figurines

One of the four Goebels plates depicting anthropomorphic butterflies adorned with fruit.

asked me to design a series of plates. One of my drawings for Goebel featured an anthropomorphic butterfly with strawberry wings.

The strawberries eventually found their way onto the ice, cementing my public association with the image. I wrote and choreographed one of the first visual fantasies on ice: "Strawberry Ice." One segment featured a strawberry court – king, queen, princess, and jester – costumed in the most innovative way by the Canadian designer Frances Dafoe. The 1982 CBC production won the Golden Rose of Montreux as Best Variety Show, the designation Best Television Program at the San Francisco International Film Festival, and Anik and ACTRA awards. It was sold for broadcast in sixty-seven countries.

During the early 1980s, in an upstairs room in my mad, overdecorated house on Carlton Street in Toronto, I slept in a king-sized bed with dozens of fuchsia, ruby-red, and magenta velvet strawberry pillows propped against the seventeenth-century, lime-green Italian screen that served as my headboard. That bedroom was duplicated as one of the sets of "Strawberry Ice" and was later reproduced for house and garden shows.

I was invited once to skate in a winter carnival in Trois-Rivières, a city on the St. Lawrence River, halfway between Montreal and Quebec. I entered the building and noticed a curtain across the ice. I had been behind so many similar curtains in so many Canadian towns – it could have been Yellowknife, the Northwest Territories, or Flin Flon, Manitoba – but behind the curtain in Trois-Rivières was a tribute to the glory of French-Canadian passion: twenty-foot-high scarecrow figures made entirely of strawberries. Huge production numbers featured children dressed as strawberries. The motif had passed gloriously to a new generation.

If one plays too long on the violin, the music becomes sour. When serious art collectors dismissed the strawberries as trite, I curtailed their production. From time to time, though, as I work on a decorative drawing, a strawberry pops out of nowhere and lands on the canvas.

9

Bratislava

In 1971, I ascended to the top of Canadian skating. David McGillivray had retired to concentrate on his medical studies. Paul Bonenfant led after the first three figures at the championship in Winnipeg, Manitoba, but I caught up, then easily surpassed him in the long program with a triple loop and a triple Salchow. I was on my way at last.

The following year I participated in my first Olympics. In Sapporo, Japan, I distinguished myself with a respectable ninth-place finish. Three weeks later, I devastated the world at Calgary (at least that is what I thought) by coming eleventh in school figures at the world championship, then pulling up to fifth by winning the free skating – at the age of twenty-two.

Capturing my first free-skating medal was a signal event in my life, but there was also something auspicious and magical about finishing in the top five, the circle of distinction in figure skating: it allows one's country to qualify a second team member for the next year's world championships. Though I did not climb the podium myself, I shook off a few other skaters, just as Midori Ito did in Calgary in 1988 by splitting judges with Elizabeth Manley, allowing Katarina Witt to win gold.

We skaters do not, as a rule, reminisce together about the world championships in which we have taken part. We absorb what happens to us – good, bad, or indifferent – but we do not discuss the incidents, power struggles, strategies, and performances after the fact. Each of us lives his own intense, personal experience. I ultimately competed at seven world championships, from 1970 through 1976.[*] The third and fourth, 1972 and 1973, were particularly important for my development as an amateur skater and with respect to my changing position on the international figure skating ladder.

My arrival in the top five of the skating world's elite boded well for 1973. I was on my way to becoming a world champion. Everyone around me was convinced of that, and I probably even believed it myself.

The First Time I Saw Vienna

The 1973 Canadian men's championship in Vancouver was a wonderful launching pad. I won my third consecutive title handily (over Ronnie Shaver and Bob Rubens) with blocks of 6.0s, including four for my *Sabre Dance* short program. A huge endorsement at home often meant that advantageous outcomes awaited abroad. Right or wrong, reputation was a factor that judges always considered.

In those days the Canadian team bound for the world championships flew to Europe three weeks early in order to acclimate to the six-hour time difference. All things considered, that was silly. It takes little more than a day to recover from jet lag and adjust to the time change.

Our 1973 training camp was in Vienna, the grand imperial city of the Hapsburgs. Vienna later played a significant role in my professional performing life. Although it offered such splendid hotels as the Imperial, the Inter-Continental, the Sacher, and the Bristol, we stayed in the moral and aesthetic equivalent of military barracks: a grey, dreary one- or two-star hotel overlooking the railroad tracks.

The Canadian team did not experience Mozart's Vienna of wine, women, and song. Instead we went to boot camp. We spent every waking hour practising in the Stadthalle in a bleak, freezing, horrid

---

[*] The results were as follows: 1970, Ljubljana, 13th; 1971, Lyon, 11th; 1972, Calgary, 5th; 1973, Bratislava, 5th; 1974, Munich, 3rd; 1975, Colorado Springs, 4th; 1976, Göteborg, 4th. During those years, Toller won three world free–skating gold medals.

little training rink. Ellen passed many of those hours condemning and humiliating me for the poor quality of my school figures (and not without reason).

If others trained for two hours, I trained for five. I could almost taste the medal I hoped to win.

Karen's Cloud

Training alongside me was my teammate and good friend Karen Magnussen, the Canadian ladies' champion. She was already the 1972 Olympic silver medallist. She wanted to leave Bratislava with a complete collection of world medals. To her bronze (1971) and silver (1972), she hoped to add gold. We were both so hopeful.

However, Karen was skating in Vienna with a cloud over her head. Her title-winning performance at Vancouver had been such that many observers thought she should have placed second behind Lynn Nightingale, a little-known sixteen-year-old up-and-comer from Ottawa. Lynn had placed ahead of Karen by one judge in the new short program and tied her with a spectacular long free-skating performance, but Karen won on the strength of a substantial lead in the figures. Lynn Nightingale and Cathy Lee Irwin accompanied Karen to Vienna as the second and third Canadian women on the team.

On to Bratislava

When it was time to leave for the world championships, we took a bus to Bratislava, Czechoslovakia, hometown of the reigning European, Olympic, and two-time world champion, Ondrej Nepela. The Czechoslovakian strategy was to star Ondrej as the conquering hero of the event. Nonetheless, the word in the skating pipeline was that Nepela was not the best skater in the field. There were several potential threats, including the Briton John Curry, the Russian Sergei Chetverukhin, the East German Jan Hoffmann, and me.

If Vienna had been a grand, glittering city, Bratislava was a sad, provincial, communist-grey workers' town close to the Austrian border. A red ski sweater or a brightly coloured team coat looked highly irregular in that dull cityscape.

We stayed in the only habitable hotel in town, the Carlton, a large, generic hotel that had probably seen grander days. The fare was infinitely East European: heavy, greasy, doughy, dumpling-type meals. The only gourmet element, one I think about often to this day, was the most splendid tomato soup served with floating lemon slices and piles of sour cream. That was the ambrosia on which I subsisted while I mounted my medal bid.

Stop the Music!

The competition opened with the pairs event, one of the maddest scenes that the skating world has ever witnessed. An incident on the long-program night transcended the rules of skating and became a show of political strength.

The new team of Irina Rodnina and Alexandr Zaitsev, who eventually won two Olympic titles, skated two and one-quarter minutes of their program. Then an electrical failure stopped their music. They continued to skate without it – in spite of emphatic negative signals from the referee.

Stanislav Zhuk, their grim Soviet teacher, stood conspicuously by the skaters' entrance to the ice with his arms folded over his chest. Irina frequently glanced at him while he indicated with his body language that she and Alexandr should complete the second half of their routine. Since skaters' marks must, according to international rules, reflect musical interpretation, the couple's win (the first of six for him and the fifth of ten for her) was highly controversial.

Immediately after Rodnina and Zaitsev's performance, a peculiar charade stopped the music again. The American pairs champions, siblings Mark and Melissa Militano, were an excellent team who occupied the interregnum between the two greatest American pairs: JoJo Starbuck with Ken Shelley and Tai Babilonia with Randy Gardner. The Militanos won their national title three times (1973–75) and twice finished sixth at the Worlds.

Fifty-two seconds into his long program, Mark went to the referee and complained that the music was playing too fast. He and his sister restarted their program, then stopped again at precisely the same point in the choreography. In a fit of pique, Mark picked up a small metal object[*] from the ice and tossed it at the referee.

Referees and judges were gods. One could not behave in such a cavalier way, particularly during a competition. Nonetheless, the referee allowed the Militanos to reskate their routine later that evening. Strangely, it seemed to me, their marks reflected no noticeable deductions for the prior mishap.

What Happened to Janet Lynn

Sometimes the most extreme figure skating competitors are nonskaters. Gloria Magnussen, Karen's mother, was a notorious "skating mother." Mrs. Nowicki, mother of Janet Lynn, was equally renowned. It appeared to me and to most other observers that the 1973 ladies' world championship would come down to a duel between their daughters. That fuelled Mrs. Magnussen's and Mrs. Nowicki's growing tensions.

American commentator Dick Button had aired an ABC television preview the week before the world championships. He had shown the American champion's magnificent four-minute performance in Minneapolis, Minnesota, for which she had received three perfect 6.0s and two 5.9s, contrasted to a short clip of the Canadian champion's only fall in Vancouver. Button then posed the rhetorical question to his viewing audience: "Now, which lady do you think

---

* According to Frank Loeser, writing in the May 1973 issue of *Skating* magazine, the object was "an elastic band with a metal pin." Joan Dean reported in the April 1973 issue of *Ice & Roller Skate* that Militano had found pieces of wire on the ice.

will win the world championship?" He baited Fate, and Fate would take her revenge.

Janet Lynn, it seemed clear to me, had a romantic interest in the American men's champion, Gordie McKellen. I cannot say so with certainty, because I wasn't her confidant, but Gordie McKellen certainly was in love with Janet Lynn. Rumour had it that Mrs. Nowicki found them not in flagrante delicto (Janet had immaculate religious scruples) but simply engaged in some innocent demonstration of affection. She excoriated her daughter until Janet dissolved into a puddle of emotional mush. Gordie received a severe reprimand as well.

What happened the next day was a tragedy. When Janet skated her short program (in the first year of the short program's implementation in world competition), she barely completed an element without error. She fell twice: first on the solo double Axel and then on the same jump during her combination. She finished that critical section of the competition, one that was designed expressly to benefit strong free skaters like Janet, in twelfth place.

Just as Elizabeth Manley would later rally at the Calgary Olympics because no one expected anything of her, Karen Magnussen skated a careful but flawless short program to Lalo's *Scherzo* and outpointed Janet overall – but narrowly (104.1 to 96.9). The judges had made sure that Janet would stay in the running.

The next night, in the way that true champions can dig deep and pull themselves together in unpleasant situations, Janet regained her composure, skated a magnificent program to the music of Claude Debussy's *La Mer*, and won the long free-skating competition hands down.

Karen also possessed an ability to dig deep. She skated a meticulously competent program to Rachmaninoff's Symphony No. 2 in E Minor and Third Piano Concerto, winning the coveted world title. Only days earlier, that would have been an entirely unexpected turn of events. Essentially Karen won on the strength of another competitor's misfortune, but that is often the nature of our sport.

A Strong Opening Bid

The next night was the men's short program event, again the first ever. I had arrived to win the men's world championship on something less than full steam, clearly having overtrained in Vienna. I was placed sixth after the figures event, though fifth in overall points. Ondrej Nepela led.

I opened my short program in a twisted Spanish pose that Arnold Gerschwiler did not like. The great Swiss coach had told me earlier, "I think that you are very good this year, but no man can stand at the beginning of the program like that. It is unmanly."

I replied, "I know what you are saying, but this man is going to do it anyway."

I skated the routine with my last bit of energy, won the short program, and pulled into fifth place. If I just held on, I could end up with a medal. Mathematically, that medal might even be gold if disaster befell the leaders.

The Firecracker Fizzles

I had known Ondrej Nepela personally for a very long time. Many people perceived him as handsome or even as beautiful. He evidenced an androgynous, Nijinsky-like quality. In physical features he reminded me of a Tartar from the Eastern European Steppes, with slanted Mongolian eyes yet light skin. He was small. He was fine. He was a steady, nerveless competitor, completely lacking in personality or finesse: a generic Soviet-satellite skater who had been browbeaten into becoming a fine technician – less fine in free skating and more precise or womanlike in the school figures.

Ondrej said little, but his glances, his telegraphed expressions, and his furtive manner seemed as erotic to me as they were exotic. That night after the short programs, at the Carlton Hotel over tomato soup with floating lemon wedges and sour cream, Ondrej Nepela, exuding overwhelming sensual energy, looked at me across the room. When you have been a sexually abstinent athlete for as long as I had been, the smallest spark of a suggestion ignites a fire. Ondrej lit the fuse of a firecracker that I did not know I had within me.

Even before the main course was served (boiled chicken and potatoes, the nightly fare), Ondrej and I had gone upstairs to my small room on the third floor.

The Carlton Hotel harboured one strange element that turned it into something like the set of an Ingmar Bergman film. The cleaning woman who looked after the third floor lived in the closet outside my room. She slept on a pillow in fetal position. Her body, although diminutive, was too long to stretch out in the closet. She survived on little buttered crusts that hotel guests left outside their rooms on their abandoned breakfast trays.

I mention this woman – whom I thought of as Carabosse, the evil fairy in *The Sleeping Beauty* – because she watched Ondrej enter my room. My eyes briefly met hers. I wondered whether she knew what was about to occur. I was not absolutely certain that she was corporeal rather than ghostly, but it disturbed me to have any sort of witness.

Within a minute Ondrej and I were lying on my bed. Within thirty seconds more our clothes were off – all new and different to me. What happened then was innocent enough in its simplicity. It was reciprocal masturbation, nothing more. Within seconds I experienced Mount Vesuvius. Before I had even reopened my eyes, Ondrej, who had not experienced a volcanic eruption or any reaction at all, was up, dressed, out the door, and down the hall past the vigilant, shifty eyes of Carabosse.

I never did return to the dining room for the boiled chicken and potatoes. I lay on my bed like the victim of a tsunami. I was spent. All the energy that I had stored during my celibate training life had dissipated in the blast that buried Pompeii.

The next day I slept until eleven o'clock in the morning and missed my practice session. I passed the hours before my long program in a somnambulistic state. Everything happened in slow motion. The simplest everyday challenges were too difficult for me to address. I had lost my edge.

Jockstraps and Skate Laces

Luck was not with me in any conceivable way. I had drawn to skate first. In those days, when we performed five minute long programs, it was dangerous, especially for the first skater, to sap one's stamina by expending too much energy on the warm-up.

That warm-up was the first occasion on which I skated in a jockstrap. (I usually wore a bathing suit or ordinary underwear beneath my costume.) The jockstrap fit poorly, so instead of concentrating on my jumps, I was distracted by the unfamiliar sensation. I felt as though I was skating naked.

In the middle of that unhappy warm-up, my skate lace came undone. That meant running off the ice, knowing that I was first to skate, knowing that the clock was ticking. I bent over and worked at the lace, but I could not undo the knot: a preview of Tonya Harding's pathetic mischance at the 1994 Lillehammer Olympics. My vision blurred, and I became dizzy. I relaced my skate just in time, but I tied it too tightly, and my toes went numb. That was when the announcer called my name.

My performance was a nightmare. Right before a triple Salchow, I zeroed in on the face of a strange Czechoslovakian peasant in the audience. The next thing I knew, I was sitting on the ice. I had completely lost my focus. I could not hear the music. My jockstrap was a constant irritation. In sum, the world championship that I had hoped to seize from under the nose of Ondrej Nepela in his hometown was not to be mine.

After my inferior performance, I went to the end of the rink where former world pairs champion Otto Jelinek was providing Canadian television commentary. Like a beaten dog that had failed its master, I watched my low marks come up.

The king is dead. Long live the king. What happened then was an interesting lesson. The man whose moment had arrived was the second Canadian man, Ronnie Shaver. He was as hot as I had been cold. I was forced to sit beside Otto Jelinek and listen to him extolling the virtues of Ronnie's program: exciting, inspired, flawless, and dramatic.* That was my penance, part of my punishment – my punishment for the sin I had committed the night before (although Ondrej Nepela's more devious sin must be judged the graver of the two).

A tiny sprite of a blond boy came to me with a few wilted Bratislava tulips. Years later, as the Canadian commentator in Copenhagen, I was interviewing the new European champion. That tall, handsome champion asked me, "Do you remember a little boy carrying two red tulips in Bratislava?" In a poetic twist of fate, Jozef Sabovcik had been that charming sprite.

When the men's event concluded and the final placements were determined, I had stayed in fifth place, fourth for combined free skating. Sly Ondrej Nepela had won. Sergei Chetverukhin had taken the second slot. Jan Hoffmann, who later won two world titles of his own (in 1974 and 1980), occupied the bronze-medal position, and John Curry finished fourth. Fifth was ignominious.

Afterwards I experienced a blackness and depression more intense than any in my past. I sat in the sanctity of my grey little room trying to determine what had gone wrong and why. There were many obvious answers and even more not-so-obvious ones. I had to live with the fact that I had failed, as the Canadian champion, to uphold the honour of Canada. That made Ronnie Shaver the new national heir apparent.

Cheering Up

By the end of the Bratislava run, Karen Magnussen could have opened a crystal shop. She received vast cauldrons and vases and crystal art objects of every description. At the awards presentation, I was given a

---

* Ronnie Shaver finished the competition in eighth place. The third Canadian, Bob Rubens, placed nineteenth.

small crystal wineglass that I did not pack in my suitcase. I left it in my hotel room for Carabosse in the closet to find and confiscate. I hope that she enjoyed that small gleam of luxury in her dull life.

I considered catching the next plane to Toronto, but I had been asked to go on the International Skating Union (ISU) tour, a grand series of performances throughout Europe. I said farewell to most of my Canadian teammates, who were going back to Vienna to whoop it up. I was on my way to Prague, the capital of Czechoslovakia, where Ondrej Nepela's countrymen would suitably acclaim him as the reanointed world champion.

Although Janet Lynn was perceived in some quarters as the uncrowned world champion, the Magnussens had Scandinavian roots. When we toured Scandinavia, Karen skated to national folk songs. If it pleased people in Sweden to think that she was Swedish, those in Norway that she was Norwegian, the Danes that she was Danish, and the Finns that she was Finnish, that was fine with Karen. It was at that point that I realized my sense of humour had returned.

We skated our last show in Cologne, West Germany. JoJo Starbuck, Ken Shelley, Janet Lynn, Mrs. Nowicki, Julie Lynn Holmes, and I had been told that we were to fly from Cologne to Brussels to connect with our return flight to North America. There had been a foul-up in the travel arrangements, and we didn't receive the tickets and boarding passes we thought would be waiting for us. The Lufthansa personnel informed us, "We're sorry, people, but you cannot get on this plane."

Mrs. Nowicki grabbed her daughter and dove under the cord, with JoJo Starbuck in hot pursuit. The three of them dashed out onto the runway and climbed onto the plane. A bystander overheard Mrs. Nowicki declare, "If we seatbelt ourselves in, they will never get us out." So the 1973 world tour ended with the hijacking of an airplane at a time in history when that crime was still unknown.

Ken, Julie, and I made ourselves such an embarrassment to Lufthansa that the airline paid for a taxi to drive us from Cologne to the airport in Brussels. We laughed all the way to Belgium with tears of mirth dripping down our cheeks.

I had come full circle, back to my old self, ready to ply my wares at the 1974 world championships in Munich where figure skating and I changed once and for all.

10

Munich: the Defining Moment

I had to wait for an entire year to wipe the slate clean of Bratislava. The new skating season, however, got off to an auspicious start. If ever there was a time in my life when I was trained to perfection, it was at the 1974 Canadian championships in Moncton, New Brunswick. I was twenty-four years old: the prime of skating life.

There was an early long-program practice one day. I habitually wore jet black to intimidate my rivals. I thought that I had to come across like the fourteenth century's Edward the Black Prince. I was first to run through my routine. After warming up for just three minutes, I produced a rock-solid program – at seven o'clock in the morning. That was an indication of just how ready I was to compete.

I won the figures over my arch-rival, Ronnie Shaver.

During the short program, I slid into the fourth dimension, skating flamboyantly and with emotion. Any concerns about technique became incidental to the overall performance. That has happened to me only two or three times in my life.

At a practice session in Munich.

The short program itself was unusual. My straight-line footwork included Rockettes-style fan kicks, crouching positions, and movements on multiple levels, like those that Canadian ice dancers Shae-Lynn Bourne and Victor Kraatz have recently popularized. In the middle of the two-and-one-half-minute program, my free leg flew too high on one of the fan kicks and I heard something pop.

Adrenalin allowed me to finish the program, but in the middle of the night I could not walk. The next morning I found that I could barely move, and I was unable to practise in the afternoon. Then I discovered the miracle of ultrasound treatment.

The long program was on Sunday afternoon. International referee Donald Gilchrist, a low-level Canadian skating diplomat, was a major Ronnie Shaver fan (as far as I was able to determine). When he heard about my injured muscle, he sought me out backstage and said, "Look, you really do not have to skate. Your short program was so good that you will be chosen for the world team anyway."

Mr. Gilchrist may have been entirely sincere. He may have understood my situation and wanted to help me, but I did not trust him. I suspected that Canadian officialdom might be setting a trap into which I risked falling. I had to skate injured.

There is no way of predicting what will happen when one takes the ice in pain. It is amazing how muscles sometimes react positively to adrenalin and applause. When the music started – Offenbach's *Le Papillon*, Drigo's *Le Réveil de Flore*, and some dynamic Greek dance music – my pain disappeared. I am sure the ultrasound had helped a lot. If I didn't received 6.0 from every judge, it was pretty damn close, and I won my fourth national title with an injured muscle.

One of the biggest problems for male skaters today – Elvis Stojko is at the top of the list – is that by concentrating solely on jumps, they forget the importance of developing flexibility. As a result, when they grow older, they are guaranteed groin problems. I blame the teachers who do not develop the skating moves that promote flexibility. John Curry knew what flexibility was. So does Rudy Galindo today. Because of the elasticity I had developed over the years through spin variations, Russian splits, and spirals, I was back in shape in time for the 1974 Worlds in West Germany.

A Sobering Start

Munich in March is as grey and bleak as any city in Europe. However, Ellen Burka, a European by birth and inclination, had glorified the city to such a degree that I was genuinely excited about visiting it. What I did not know at that point was that whatever exotic locale hosted the world championships – Paris, London, Milan, Geneva, or a one-horse alpine resort – I would have no time to sightsee. Therefore, Munich would not sweep me off my feet as it did years later when I returned as a professional skater. All its baroque Bavarian glory, its museums, galleries, and nightclubs, would wait for me in another incarnation.

As I passed though customs in Munich, I saw everything in slow motion. I looked at the various counters and deliberately chose number one, just in case passing through number five meant that I would finish fifth again. Because of my extreme paranoia, every action took on superstitious overtones. I chose to wear a yellow jacket, then fretted about whether yellow had a positive or negative portent. Did yellow stand for gold, or was the non-traditional colour choice bad luck?

Throughout my skating life, I was haunted by the frightening sense that everything I did – how I got on the ice, my numerical starting position, the colour of my costume, the way I laced my skates – was fraught with earth-shattering importance. If I made the wrong choice, everything would blow up in my face. I was tap dancing on a volcano. One wrong tap might activate the lava flow. Today I understand that such extreme sensitivity is, in part, the nature of a fine-tuned artist.

Our official hotel was the Holiday Inn on Leopoldstrasse, not far from the Olympiahalle, the Olympic site on the outskirts of town. A discotheque, the Yellow Submarine, adjoined the hotel. It contained an aquarium full of exotic fish, including some menacing twenty-five-foot sharks. Both the discotheque and our practice rink were part of the same complex as the hotel. We were obliged to walk through the Yellow Submarine each time we reported for practice.

In retrospect it seems silly, but I had brought with me an entourage: Ellen Burka as head coach; Brian Foley, choreographer and stylist; and Dr. Helmut May, a coach and former Austrian world and Olympic competitor (with a doctor's degree in economics), who calmed me down during the figures.

Because Ellen wanted me to shine whenever I practised, she pushed me to the max. Later Tamara Moskvina, a well-known

Russian coach, confided that the Russians had laughed at me. They knew it was foolish to be too brilliant in practice. Better to hold back energy for the performance that counts.

Watching competitors and friends on television before one's own competition is the worst thing a skater can do. It is better to hear the descriptions, opinions, and results second-hand the next morning in a neutral setting. Nonetheless, I watched the pairs in my Munich hotel room in the company of John Curry and a friendly, attractive waiter named Horst whom we never saw again. Apparently the Holiday Inn waiters were not allowed to hobnob with the clientele, no matter how innocent the circumstances.

My teammates, pair Sandra and Val Bezic, finished fifth in their event, an excellent showing. That put the pressure on me to hold up my share of Canada's honour.

On the morning of the school figures, I was tranquil and collected. My entourage of three was on hand to support me. I had come to think affectionately of them as characters from *The Wizard of Oz*. Ellen was the Cowardly Lion, Dr. May the Tin Man, and Brian Foley the Scarecrow. Those designations had more to do with esprit de corps than with any of my supporters' inherent characteristics. Somehow in that fanciful scenario I must have identified with Dorothy. As we waited for my turn in the Olympiahalle, the atmosphere was as murky, sombre, and silent as Kansas during the portentous calm just before the tornado that wrenched Auntie Em's house from its foundations.

Skating school figures was like engraving a perfect Fabergé design on a robin's egg – three times over. The shell could break at any moment and doom one's chances. At the time, those archaic tracings were still worth 40 per cent of total marks, although they had recently been downgraded from an even weightier 50 per cent.

Historically women have surpassed men in the art of skating figures. Their nerves have been better equipped to cope with the stress. The most macho man was a nervous filly in the figures event. Typical masculine attributes like strength, courage, and brawn had little to do with tracing figures successfully.

I pushed off to do a forward right outside counter, and something happened for the first time that later helped to dash my 1976 Olympic effort as well. Inexplicably, my eyes filled with tears. I remained surprisingly calm, even as I wondered whether I should stop and tell the referee, "I can't see. My eyes are watering." I did a terrible first figure, the largest ever skated in the history of the sport. I think that its ends may have touched (and possibly jumped right over) both boards. I placed an embarrassing seventeenth.

The Tin Man, the Scarecrow, and the Cowardly Lion, who had come to Munich to see me win the Worlds, sank into a dejected heap of tin, straw, and fur in the gutter beside the Yellow Brick Road.

There is one benefit of making a huge mistake right out of the blocks: it is very sobering. My next figure, a left inside rocker, was not exactly good, but it was infinitely better than the one that had preceded it. Perhaps I climbed as high as eleventh for the two figures combined. The last figure, the right forward outside loop change loop, consumed every ounce of energy in my body. My heart was willing, but my skating leg thumped in nervous frustration. The result was passable, and I found myself in eighth place overall. Eighth was a long way from the podium, but it was considerably more promising than eighteenth.

A Legend Is Born

For the short program, I wore a black jumpsuit with a deep scooped neck and an electric-raspberry and strawberry chiffon shirt that fluttered above the ice like a flame. The effect was almost psychedelic, as befitted the 1970s. I performed to Aram Khatchaturian's *Sabre Dance*, which had become one of my signatures, and I skated like a bat out of hell: so fast, so aggressively, and with such concentration that there was a standing ovation the moment the program ended. Two judges awarded me 6.0 for artistic presentation. One of them was Dorothy Leamen, a Canadian.

There was a tremendous stir in the audience, particularly from the enthusiastic Canadian contingent that regularly attends the Worlds. Although the building was not entirely full, a mild riot followed my performance. I climbed from eighth to fourth. That standing meant that if I performed the long program well, I would probably receive a medal. In truth, if you can believe it, I didn't give much thought to that possibility. I was entirely caught up in my skating.

My long program again was *Le Papillon* by Jacques Offenbach, a ballet piece. The performance was meticulous and emotional. By today's standards, it was hardly technically difficult. It contained two triple Salchows and one triple loop. That was good for its day. The total impression was such that I won the free skating (short and long) hands down by every judge. I also managed to move one place higher and win the bronze medal.

Sergei Volkov, a Soviet skater, placed second. Jan Hoffmann won the overall championship. Jan was such a consistent competitor that he eventually won medals at six world championships within seven years. Two of those medals were gold. (He sat out the seventh season with a knee injury.)

The German press, which is as wonderful and dangerous as any press in the world, in one night made my career and created a legend that has lasted my lifetime, even to this very day. The German reporters crowned me the unofficial world champion. They followed me. They interviewed me. They plastered me across every front page. I had completely redeemed my sins of Bratislava.

I didn't know it then, but Munich would be the summit of my career. The bronze that I won there would be my only world medal, and I would later view my Olympic bronze, tinged by frustration and defeat, as a badge of shame. Only that moment on the podium in Munich was one of unadulterated joy.

Putzi Hanfstaengl

The day after my long program, a strange, squeaky-voiced man phoned and announced himself as Putzi Hanfstaengl. He told me in perfectly grammatical English with a heavy German accent, "You are the Enrico Caruso of the ice. I must meet you."

I was wary. I agreed to meet Herr Hanfstaengl if Ellen Burka could accompany me. Ellen and I soon learned to our amazement that he was a famous German aristocrat whose family owned a prosperous Munich art-publishing business.

Born of an American mother, Ernst (Putzi) Hanfstaengl had known Franklin D. Roosevelt during their university years at Harvard. He had subsequently become a friend of Adolf Hitler, donated money to the Nazi cause, entertained Hitler with his practical jokes and piano virtuosity, and eventually served Hitler as the Foreign Press Department chief. Ultimately he had turned against Hitler and fled for his life.[*]

Ellen and I went first to the home of Putzi's sister, Erna, who lived in a tiny cottage outside Munich. In his callow days, Hitler had been in love with the stately young woman who later became the lover of a well-known German expressionist artist. Putzi and Erna, nonagenarians, bickered like three-year-olds while we all sipped tea and shared dainty little cakes.

We piled into Putzi's car and drove to the home of the Countess Arco von Zinnberg of the Royal House of Bavaria. That rang the magic bell for me. One does not meet many countesses in Canada.

We all then trundled to the home of one Doctor Reiss. He inhabited a large villa with gardens that opened onto the Isar River. There we watched a one-and-one-half-hour videotaped documentary about Putzi Hanfstaengl's life and escape from death. Hitler, turning against Hanfstaengl, had sent him to jump from an airplane, wearing a secretly sabotaged parachute. The pilot of the

---

* Putzi Hanfstaengl was ostensibly a prisoner of war under U.S. President Roosevelt. In fact, he did spend two of the World War II years in Washington, D.C., but he served his old university friend Roosevelt as "interpreter of German affairs and propaganda" (read spy). For Hanfstaengl's German background, see William L. Shirer's The Rise and Fall of the Third Reich.

plane, encountering turbulence, had landed it prematurely and had instructed his passenger to run for all he was worth.

The Hanfstaengl Company subsequently bought a large number of my posters and lithographs and exhibited them in the display windows of their Munich bookstore. I made a veritable fortune, thanks to my brand-new Putzi Hanfstaengl connection.

Dorothy Hamill's Catharsis

During the ladies' event at Munich, which followed the men's, something unfortunate happened to Dorothy Hamill, the American champion. Gerti Schanderl from West Germany preceded Dorothy in the skating order. Gerti could jump over the moon, probably higher than any other woman in the world and most of the men, but she was rather gauche and not at all artful. The home crowd rooted passionately for her, but the conservative international judges awarded her low marks, inciting the sort of riot that one might see at a soccer tournament. The judges feared for their lives. Fortunately a running track circled the rink and separated them from the hostile audience.

What happened then was an interesting lesson in psychology. When Dorothy twice went out to skate, she mistakenly thought the crowd was attempting to boo her off the ice. As Gerti waved happily to her adoring audience, Dorothy ran back into the arms of her coach, Carlo Fassi, and launched herself into a good, healthy crying fit. That opened a valve and released all her tension.

The referee asked the audience to settle down. *Will Miss Hamill please come back out onto the ice?* The Germans remembered their manners then and gave her a warm ovation. Dorothy was so fired up that she produced one of the finest performances of her life. An East German, Christine Errath, won the competition, but Dorothy became one of the sensations of Munich and earned a silver medal to take home to America.[*]

---

[*] Dorothy Hamill would collect a second world silver medal before striking gold in 1976, the year of her Olympic triumph. She won the U.S. ladies' title three times (in 1974, 1975, and 1976).

II

The Further Education of
a Skating Legend

Previous page: The Waddington's "Sale of the Century."

11

Supergroupie

If ever there was a country to appreciate me, it was Germany, East or West. The Germans demonstrate a profound understanding both of high drama and of kitsch, bad art sincerely wrought. I was a prime example of both.

A fan asked me if I knew what *Toller* meant in German. No, I replied.

"*Toll* means fantastic or terrific, so *Toller* means more fantastic or more terrific."[*]

As far as the Germans were concerned, my name was More Fantastic Cranston. It was like being the Amazing Kreskin, the Great Gatsby, or one of the Flying Wallendas. The artificial name played into my burgeoning myth.

The real climax of my Munich experience came not during the world championships themselves but on the day of the exhibition gala. I performed to what would become my definitive musical signature: "Vesti la giubba" from Ruggiero Leoncavallo's *Pagliacci*, sung by Luciano Pavarotti. That piece found its perfect audience in Munich. Art and sport met on an equal level. I had skated the

---

[*] That is perfectly true. *Toll* in German also means *mad* or *crazy*, so readers may choose their personal interpretations.

program in Canada without much success, but in West Germany the bouquets flew over the boards.

Invitations arrived from all around the world, from Australia to the Soviet Union: painting exhibitions, poster designs, skating shows, and even a recording contract. Willy Brandt, former chancellor of West Germany, summoned me to help him mount his political comeback.* Overnight, taxi drivers, shopkeepers, and café owners in every part of Germany recognized me, complimented me, and gave me goods and services free of charge. The German experience, the turning point of my amateur career, made my reputation. Hundreds of opportunities over the years can be directly and primarily attributed to one performance of *Pagliacci* in Munich.

Dorothy the Porcine Groupie

As fans sprang up like mushrooms in the forest, a certain brand of fanaticism emerged. Figure skating can claim some of the most peculiarly obsessive-compulsive fanatics in all of sport. Because the most extreme of those fanatics are women, male skaters, more often than females, are their prime targets. A certain mixture of masculine and feminine traits in a skater fascinates these supergroupies, perhaps because the groupies find such strong yet graceful athlete/artists more approachable than sportsmen who grunt like Tim Allen, the tool man on "Home Improvement," and exude maximum-strength testosterone.

The objects of supergroupies' fixations are not always conventionally attractive, nor are they necessarily heterosexual. Fans of heroes and mothers of children believe what they want to believe. They all belong to the mother lion club. That means that no defence of their beloved is too far-fetched.

The post-Munich fanaticism was personified by a woman named Dorothy. She was porcine in appearance (with an inch of

---

* Willy Brandt was chancellor of the Federal Republic of Germany between 1969 and 1974. Toller met with Brandt but fortunately did not become his political adviser.

space between her upper incisors), virtually omnipresent, but very kind. She made a foolish practice of driving too fast in her sporty yellow MG convertible. Wherever she could find me on the ISU tour that opened in Munich, then crisscrossed Europe, she brought me no fewer than three dozen red, pink, or yellow long-stemmed roses. Those were extreme gestures of affection. Oddly, Dorothy did not have the slightest interest in skating. I was sorry, yet not surprised, when I heard from German friends years later that Dorothy had been decapitated in an automobile accident.

The Role of Champion

The role and image of Olympic and world champion has changed drastically during the past half-century. Canadian Barbara Ann Scott, who won an Olympic title and two consecutive world championships in the late 1940s, captured the imagination of an entire nation as few others have done. During the mid-1950s, the American Tenley Albright, an Olympic and twice world champion, was a gracious and popular role model. Dick Button (Olympic champion, 1948 and 1952), brothers Hayes and David Jenkins (Olympic champions in, respectively, 1956 and 1960), Donald Jackson (1962 world champion), and Robin Cousins (1980 Olympic gold medallist) all transcended the medium of ice.

That is out of fashion now. Agents, money, and fame have so distorted the personalities in the sport that someone such as Nancy Kerrigan, who could have been the most charming heroine, lasted, for all intents and purposes, a scant six months.

Nancy did not possess the maturity to recognize that her narrow and controversial 1994 loss to Oksana Baiul at the Lillehammer Olympics was a gift from God, better than any gold medal. It gave her the opportunity to inspire youth and to positively influence a generation. Unfortunately she had no sense of her own destiny, no sense of her power. She did not play her role well, whereas the Tenley Albrights, the Barbara Ann Scotts, and the Peggy Flemings charmed themselves into decades of history and remain icons today.

One has only to consider how Peggy Fleming has used her survival of breast cancer to help others cope with their own illnesses. Likewise Fleming's fellow U.S., world, and Olympic champion Scott Hamilton, who, while beating testicular cancer, had a profound enough understanding of life to realize that negative energy could be harnessed and turned towards positive outcomes for himself and others.

The last major role models with larger-than-life personalities were Canadian Brian Orser and American Brian Boitano, the twin protagonists of the 1988 Calgary Olympics, the beneficiaries and victims of the "Battle of the Brians" media hype. There was an ethic to which such champions adhered. In public they invariably looked great, behaved impeccably, and treated everyone with equal charm. Today the American skater Michelle Kwan[*] is a member of that school.

Where it all began to go awry was with competitors like Christopher Bowman,[†] who turned to drugs and fast living; Tonya Harding,[**] whose husband and inept cohorts clubbed her archrival, Nancy Kerrigan,[††] on the knee; Nancy herself, who bore the injury stoically, then whined and pouted after winning the Olympic silver medal and a trip to Walt Disney World; Oksana Baiul,[***] who was convicted for drunk driving; and Oksana Grishuk,[†††] who dyed her hair blonde, changed her name to Pasha, and announced that

---

[*] Michelle Kwan finished second to Tonya Harding at the 1994 U.S. championships. She subsequently won four American titles, became the 1996, 1998, and 2000 world champion, and earned an Olympic silver medal in 1998.

[†] Christopher Bowman, 1989 and 1992 U.S. champion, won world bronze and silver medals before his lifestyle drove him out of the competitive branch of the sport.

[**] Tonya Harding, 1991 American champion and world silver medallist, was stripped of her 1994 U.S. title due to her role in the Kerrigan incident.

[††] Nancy Kerrigan, twice world medallist, won successive bronze, silver, and gold medals beginning with the 1991 U.S. ladies' championship. She withdrew injured from the 1994 event, then finished second to Oksana Baiul in Lillehammer.

[***] Oksana Baiul of Ukraine emerged from relative obscurity to win the 1993 world title and the 1994 Olympic gold medal. After turning professional, she was unable to sensibly manage her new American lifestyle.

[†††] With Evgeny Platov, Oksana Grishuk won four consecutive world ice–dance titles (1994–97) and two Olympic gold medals (1994 and 1998) before breaking up the team to pursue her acting dreams.

she was on her way to Hollywood. All those skaters possessed the correct credentials to be as great as any of their predecessors but abdicated as positive role models.

I learned early in my career that a note of encouragement to a young skater, a kind word from someone he admires, could be the very thing to push that athlete to fulfill his potential. It is dangerous for someone in an exalted position to forget what power and noblesse oblige come with the status.

As champions have changed, so – dramatically – have their fans. There has always been extreme fan behaviour, but never so much as in the years since 1988, when the skating culture changed in response to changes in the culture at large.

Why Me?

I do not know whether any of the skaters who have been victimized by overwrought groupies are aware of the precise reason for their own appeal. It would be naïve on the part of, say, Brian Boitano to think that his fanatic followers (reputedly among the most rabid) were interested only in his skating. The hook is not the skating per se. Who knows what it is?

The most obsessive, mad attentions are lavished by lonely social misfits (many of whom are significantly obese). Perhaps there is a certain safety in their lifestyle. They can show their feelings, give of themselves, travel to the ends of the world to see their heroes, but never in the normal way that a young girl would show her attentions to a young man. The giving has a selfish side. *What emotional reward can I reap in return?*

The reward might be momentary attention; inside information; the verbal equivalent of a pat on the head; or access to a skater's inner circle, however briefly – perhaps an "accidental" meeting in an elevator or a chat with a member of his family. In the end, the groupie's behaviour is theatre of the absurd. Conquest cannot be anything more than an impossible dream.

The RCMP, in the way that a police organization may use a psychic to help find a murderer, should hire over-the-top groupies to ferret out missing persons. With the tiniest whiff of a scent, they will get their man. The tracking seems at least as interesting to them as the ultimate contacts with the objects of their desires.

One cannot reason with such a mind. *You are hurting me. Can you leave me alone? You are disturbing me. You are upsetting me. You are embarrassing me.* All protests fall on deaf ears. When an extreme groupie chooses someone as an object of her fixation, he becomes an integral part of her life, a part of her inner fantasy world, whether he likes it or not. He has no choice.

Enter Janice, Stage Left

My own number-one obsessive-compulsive groupie is as unusual a case as has ever existed in skating: first because of her tenacity; second because, like Dorothy, she is not the least bit interested in figure skating; third because of the seemingly insuperable challenges posed by my lack of accountability. Even my manager, accountant, and publisher cannot track me down. Janice can.

If many skaters can claim an egregiously zealous groupie, wouldn't you know that mine would be a mental patient? Janice is an American from Pontiac, Michigan, who has been in and out of institutions for many years. I believe that her diagnosis is schizophrenia. She must have first chosen me as the object of her obsession during the early 1970s, and Munich certainly fanned the flames of her adoration. Her fanatic devotion persisted for more than a quarter-century and continues today. Although I am prone to exaggeration, hundreds, thousands, and maybe even tens of thousands of letters have found their way through the postal system and landed on my doorstep.

Janice would be sorry, I suspect, to know I no longer read her letters. I found them to be so sexually explicit, so deranged, or so off-the-wall that it disturbed me to absorb the information. Even friends who have literally stumbled upon the piles of letters on my doorstep have chosen instantly to discard them.

Though I have been selfish by not reading Janice's letters – at least not for many years – I imagine that I am still the recipient of her emotional confidences as a diary would be for somebody else. She pours out her life as though I were her best friend, speaks in a familiar manner, invites me to events on her schedule, and tells me everything.

I do not know whether Janice has ever threatened me overtly. Several times the contents of certain letters disturbed Marietta de Aubrey, who oversaw my property in Mexico for many years. I asked Marietta, "Please don't tell me about them. I do not want to know," so she kindly kept the upsetting information to herself.

I once arrived in Stuttgart, West Germany, to perform with Holiday on Ice. The manager, as he showed me to my dressing room, noticed a mountain of fan mail. "How does it feel to be so famous?" he asked.

I took one look at the prodigious mound of small white envelopes and banished the manager from my dressing room on the pretext of needing to rest. I didn't want him to know that every one of those hundreds of letters was from Janice.

There was a point at which Janice crossed the line. Her fixation became more disturbing than irritating. No matter where I was – it could have been on Broadway, in someone else's home, or in my private residence with an unlisted telephone number – she found the number and dialled it. If I slammed down the receiver or begged, "Janice, please don't phone me," that was in no way a deterrent. It was gas to her fire. Perhaps my rejection was the impetus for trying harder the next time. Janice certainly wouldn't have considered rejection a reason to break off our relationship, because the relationship existed within her own mind and did not depend upon our interaction.

Janice stopped at nothing to track me down. I don't know precisely how, but I can imagine the scenario. In the late 1970s and

early 1980s, she would have phoned the main Holiday on Ice
number in Amsterdam.

"Where is Toller Cranston?"

"Oh, he's with the Blue show."

"Where is the Blue show?"

"It's in Paris."

"Where is Toller staying?"

"I don't know. I'll give you the office of the Blue show."

"Hi. I'm Toller Cranston's cousin, phoning from America."

A secretary would have answered the call, and she wouldn't
have been warned not to talk to Janice.

Janice must have run up thousands of dollars' worth of long-
distance calls to Europe. She also sent me a multitude of gifts – for
example, videotapes of movies that she thought I might enjoy –
most of which I threw away unopened. Such waste is tragically
sad, especially since I surmise that Janice has lived her life on
public assistance.

Several times Janice cajoled the switchboard operator at the
Toronto Cricket Club into revealing my private telephone numbers
by pretending she was related to me and needed them for urgent
family business. There was no knowledge that Janice could not
somehow glean.

The First Visitation

There were two truly memorable occasions when I met Janice in
person, and only three occasions in all. The first meeting occurred
while I was living at 1 Metcalf Street in Toronto after the demise of my
Broadway show, Toller Cranston's The Ice Show, in 1977. I had rented
a $550-a-month apartment in Cabbagetown where I licked my
wounds, strategized, and healed from the enormous financial, legal,
and emotional debacle that I described at length in Zero Tollerance.

My doorbell rang at eleven o'clock one night. I had two doors,
one that led into the hall from my apartment and one, with a square

of opaque glass, that led to the street. When I opened the outer door, I knew instantly that the person on my doorstep, a sloppily dressed young woman of medium stature with pasty-white, unhealthy-looking skin (the kind of skin seen in hospitals), was none other than Janice, my intrepid pursuer. It is odd how one can sense such things.

It was inevitable. There had been so many letters, so many phone calls. Sooner or later I was going to meet Janice in the flesh.

Her hair is streaked with grey now, but in those days it was chestnut brown. People with her particular kind of mental imbalance – I have seen this many times – often allow their hair to fall over their faces so that they peer between their tresses with one eye. It is a type of protective disguise.

As soon as the door was open, Janice ran at me. There was a scuffle, like two cats in a hissing match, front paws flailing and slicing the air. I ran through the inner door and slammed it just as Janice pushed her hands through the narrowing gap. Her disembodied arms, free up to the elbows, reached into my apartment and grabbed at my hair as I leaned against the door to keep her out.

Somehow Janice extricated herself, or perhaps I released her. I locked my door, went panting upstairs to my bedroom, and instantly dialled the police. I glanced out the window just in time to see Janice turn the corner and trundle along the sidewalk, a crooked shadow on Carlton Street.

"Do you know who I am?" I asked the officer who answered the phone. "I am Toller Cranston, the figure skater, and I have just been attacked by a mental patient from Michigan."

"Did you open the door?"

"Yes."

"Did she hurt you?"

"No."

The recently vivid incident took on a certain pallor. To the police, it was not a very big deal. I could understand their point of view, but my adrenalin-charged heart still thumped against my rib cage. It was midnight. I had absolutely nobody to whom to tell my fantastic tale, and I was too keyed up to fall asleep. Thus Janice became the catalyst for one of my greatest cinematic discoveries: the Japanese version of *Macbeth* on a late-night movie channel.

Her Moment Onstage

Several years later, I had moved down the block to a four-storey house at 217 Carlton Street. For a downtown dwelling, it was remarkably spacious and secure from intruders, or so I thought. The walled back garden contained a freestanding studio where I worked late one fine spring afternoon. At about 6:00 P.M., I put away my paints and brushes and returned to the house. I had left the back door open, but now it was locked. When I used the key that I kept hidden under a flowerpot, the lock released, but I saw that the door was chained. I did not need to be a rocket scientist to figure out that someone who should not have been there was inside my house.

The structure had an unusual floor plan. In order to get to the back of the house, one had to enter by the front door, climb a flight of stairs to the second floor, cross the full depth of the house, and descend the back staircase. People to whom I have told this story have found it strange that I immediately entered the house, knowing that an intruder lurked within. I liken the situation to the case of a victim chasing a pickpocket down the street. Maybe the thief has a gun or a knife, but the victim, in his outrage, just does not think about that at the time.

I felt a certain expectancy. My heart raced. I knew that I was about to find something unusual, but I had no idea what it might be. I crept down the back stairs, investigating as I went, and eventually peered into the kitchen. Janice was lying on her back on my kitchen floor – on the Paddy-green and white diamond-patterned tiles – stark naked but for one poetic touch. She had carefully arranged candy-floss-pink rose petals over her vagina to make it more inviting.

Strangely, Janice didn't react to my arrival. She remained in languid repose. Her head never left the floor as she answered my queries with monosyllables.

I summoned the police. They walked in through the front door, up the front staircase, across the house, back down again, and into the kitchen. I had the impression that they were used to such occurrences. I most certainly was not, but to them it was just another familiar beat in the daily rhythm of Toronto.

Janice's arrest was nonviolent. She was starring in her own life, and she savoured her time onstage. The officers led her, naked and serene, up the back staircase. Then she vanished from my view.

I am not quite sure what two uniformed policemen do with a naked young woman. Do they march her right into the patrol car across the street? Do they offer her a jacket? Are handcuffs and leg irons applied? I did not find out. Janice's nude silhouette on my upstairs landing was the last that I saw of her that day.

I had summoned my former coach, Ellen Burka, who lived across the street from me at the time. She was privy to the scene as well, so I had a witness to support my testimony. After that, I took it upon myself to request a restraining order. Janice was no longer allowed to cross the Canadian border. As far as I know, she returned to Pontiac, Michigan, and never sang "O Canada" again.

That legal manoeuvre did nothing to diminish the ardour with which Janice pursued me. Her arrest was little more than an incidental bump on the long, winding road of groupiedom.

Bad Energy

The third and final time I saw Janice – and this was so many years later – I had grown older and so had she, but there was absolutely no doubt in my mind as to her identity. I was skating with Stars on Ice in Muskegon, Michigan, just across the Lower Peninsula from Pontiac.

Stars on Ice is a touring skating company featuring Scott Hamilton. I had performed with the group during its maiden season and continued to do so from time to time over the years, particularly in Canada.

I do not know how Janice was able to discover the company's schedule nor the address of our hotel. She disturbed my fellow skaters with her odd behaviour and her omnipresence in the lobby, then managed to sneak into our rehearsal. Rather than make a scene, I asked Byron Allen of International Management Group (IMG), producers of Stars on Ice, to let her stay as long as she wasn't doing any real harm. Instead of pretending not to notice her, I approached her and said hello.

On the night of the show, like Dorothy before her, Janice was truly not interested in the skating – even in *my* skating. She would have preferred to sit backstage, watching the cast's comings and goings. The last time I saw her, she was following our van to the Muskegon airport, peering through her tresses as she barrelled down the four-lane highway.

Most extreme fans eventually mature. Their ardour and obsessiveness cool over time. That was not so with Janice. When I returned to Toronto from Mexico in the fall of 1998, there were twenty letters waiting for me. A friend asked to open one of them, and we read it. It was neatly handwritten in blue ink on lined white paper.

Dear Toller,

I don't know where to buy a Sweetest Day card. I don't know what date it is, or if it changes every year like Thanksgiving.

Anyway, Happy Sweetest Day. (You said you didn't like my cards.)

Love,

Janice

Yesterday was a perfectly fine day for going out, but the ACT[*] *team never came out. I waited all day for them. They never showed.*[†]

12

My First and Last
Hollywood Shindig

During the turbulent period after the 1976 Innsbruck Olympics, I fantasized about attending a genuine Hollywood shindig. I was still licking my bronze-medal wounds – how great that gold medal would have been, but I would have settled for silver – even though I was busy mounting Toller Cranston's The Ice Show, a production that I hoped would take Canada and then Broadway by storm. Elva Oglanby, my manager at the time, received a phone call from Elliot Roberts, the manager of the global legend and folk icon Joni Mitchell, a brooding singer and songwriter from the Canadian

---

[*] ACT stands for Assertive Community Treatment, a team approach that provides a variety of treatment and support services to those with serious long–term mental health problems.

[†] Accompanying the letter was a carefully clipped Associated Press article dated October 11, 1998: "Letterman's stalker's death puts human face on schizophrenia." The story from Hotchkiss, Colorado, began with these chilling words: "To the world, Margaret Mary Ray was a joke, the daffy celebrity–stalker who kept breaking into David Letterman's house. . . . Usually her antics ended in her arrest. But to those who knew and loved her in this valley high in the Colorado Rockies, Margaret Ray was a good mother, a compassionate friend, a genial, creative and intelligent woman. Obsessed stalker? Kindhearted pal? That she could be both illuminates the struggle with schizophrenia, the mental illness that consumed her. Last Monday, around midday, she walked to the edge of this little town and stood at a railroad track, stepped in front of a train, kneeled down and died." The unkindest cut of all is to know exactly who and what you are but be unable to change.

Prairies who had defected to the more lucrative sprawl of Los Angeles. Among her hits were "Both Sides Now," "Big Yellow Taxi," "Chelsea Morning," and "You Turn Me On (I'm a Radio)."

Joni had taken a shine to me (as a result of the Olympic television coverage, I imagine) and felt that I would be the perfect specimen to adorn her newest album cover. The album was entitled *Hejira*. Living in my hermetically sealed frozen fish bowl at the Cricket Club, I might have known who Johann Strauss was if he had phoned me from the grave, but with anyone in the pop/rock department I was clueless. I told my panting, exhilarated manager, Elva Oglanby, that I would be most happy to shoot the photograph with Ms. Mitchell if Ms. Mitchell would kindly come to where I was at the moment. Ms. Mitchell agreed to do so.

You Sing, Don't You?

We shot the cover in Buffalo, in the northwestern corner of New York State. My show was previewing there prior to its gala Toronto opening and subsequent initial Canadian tour. I shoehorned Joni Mitchell into my busy schedule late one afternoon. In perfect Hollywood style, a black limousine longer than a city block arrived at the rather grand hotel where I was staying with the cast of The Ice Show, not far from the now-razed War Memorial Stadium where we performed. Another Ice Show cast member, Canadian ex-beauty queen Barbara Berezowski, was to play a cameo role in the cover shoot as well.

I joined Joni and Barbara in the passenger cabin of the limousine, instantly ruining my image. I opened the door for myself, broadcasting naïveté. I did not know that I was supposed to wait for the driver to open it for me.

To engage Joni in polite conversation, I made a rather gauche remark: "You sing, don't you?" At the time she already had recorded eight best-selling albums, but she took my kindly intended pronouncement in her stride. As we chatted, I tried to demonstrate how well informed I was. I actually did come up with a half-baked version of the title of one of her songs. I felt that our ride would be that much smoother if I could show some evidence of knowing who she was.

We drove to an absolutely frigid hockey rink somewhere in greater Buffalo. Our session was more teeth-chattering than glamorous. I, in my famous peacock costume, the costume that never fell down, was required simply to assume an elegant pose. Barbara Berezowski had been asked to please rent and wear a bridal gown. I did not understand how the photo layout was going to work, nor did I really care. I wanted only to rush back into the heated dressing room and change out of my chilly peacock costume.

Joni Mitchell laced up a pair of black skates. In her long black skirt, black beret, and voluminous, flapping black cashmere cape with dozens of sable tails edging its rim in a thick fringe, she reminded me of a fairy-tale raven.

In time the shoot was *fait accompli*, thank you very much. As I recall, I received little or no payment, but Joni made the most glamorous and stunning gesture that any Hollywood star could bestow upon someone who craved stardom and glamour. At the moment of her farewell and parting hug hug, kiss kiss, she suggested, "You really must come to Los Angeles, Toller. We should get together. And why don't you just take my limousine for the weekend? Be my guest."

Thus did Joni Mitchell introduce me to the fine art of riding in a limousine. When I arrived in Toronto after my Buffalo preview, I remember swelling with pride and experiencing a sense of celebrity as I careened down the Gardiner Expressway in my chauffeured weekend gift. Let's face it, nobody can be a real celebrity unless he is riding in a limousine. I have many times since come and gone in limousines, but each time I am thus conveyed along the Gardiner Expressway, I think of Joni Mitchell and how she turned me on to the joys of that kind of luxury.

The Wolf of Bel Air

True to Joni's word, during the New York City run of The Ice Show at the Palace Theatre on Broadway during the spring of 1977, Elva Oglanby received a second phone call from Elliot Roberts. *Would Toller like to attend a party at Joni Mitchell's house in Bel Air this weekend?* The invitation was kind, and I accepted it – on the condition, of course, that Joni fly Elva and me to California on first-class tickets and put us up in the swankiest hotel in town. All terms were accepted.

A residue of winter still lingered in the New York air. I had recently acquired a wolf coat that virtually dragged on the ground. I deplaned at the Los Angeles International Airport in my trailing wolf as travellers in shorts passed me on the concourse. Palm trees sprouted in profusion beyond the plate-glass windows. I tried not to acknowledge how ridiculous I looked. After all, it might get quite cold in Los Angeles after dark. Anyhow I was a star, and didn't stars wear wolf coats?

I marched past the Bel Air Hotel's swimming pool where bronze women with facelifts sunbathed in bikinis. I inspected my suite, palatial by any standards. The living room was like an enormous summer cottage with Laura Ashley chintz all around and wallpaper that matched the upholstery. Next to the bed – double king size – was a mound of chocolate-covered strawberries. I wasn't sure whether Joni had known that strawberries were my particular trademark or whether the hotel had simply made a lucky guess.

The party was to take place the same evening. What I wore is embarrassing to describe. To be discovered in Hollywood, I felt that I needed to stand out. I might be cast in a movie that very night. I donned a white satin Russian shirt with voluminous pleated sleeves and pearl buttons that marched across my shoulders, the same get-up in which I had recently stunned the patrons of a Montreal discotheque. I tucked the shirt into my white shantung knee-length bloomers. Then I neatly tucked the shantung bloomers into my high-heeled, oxblood riding boots. Satin and shantung are a chilly combination, so of course I had to suffocate the ensemble in my furs.

As our limousine swept along Bellagio Road in Bel Air, two people on foot flagged us down and asked our driver whether they had the correct address for Joni Mitchell's party. The woman was a teeny, sparrowlike blonde creature with a full bottom lip. She walked beside a tall, dark-haired man with a rather weak chin but nicely capped teeth. I noted by the cut of his pants that he had absolutely no ass.

The sparrow was Julie Christie, star of *Doctor Zhivago*, *Darling*, and *Shampoo*. I decided that Julie, who had played a sexual siren in *Doctor Zhivago*, was just too short and slight in the flesh to be taken seriously as a temptress. The assless gentleman was Warren Beatty, Julie's companion and oft times costar. Joni Mitchell's house was in sight, so we pointed it out to the celebrated couple but did not offer them a ride.

Elva and I knocked on Joni's door, and I swished through the entrance in my furs. Whatever I had been expecting of that fancy party for which I had been flown from coast to coast, the reality was its absolute antithesis.

The Mitchell dwelling, as I recall, was a large small house. Its most memorable feature was a spacious breakfast area that adjoined the kitchen. The hostess was nowhere to be seen, so I was not greeted with a tremendous "Darling, it is so good to see you!" As a matter of fact, my entrance, as dramatic as I thought it was, was entirely forgettable (if not invisible) from the point of view of the other guests. It dawned upon me after the butler relieved me of my furs that I must look frighteningly overdressed to the casual crowd in jeans, T-shirts, and running shoes. But hey, I was a grand star from New York.

Perhaps it is a great lesson in humanity that, no matter who people are, even if they are movie stars, moguls, or record producers, when they mix with their peers, they seem pathetically human. I started to meet my fellow guests. There was an unwritten hierarchy that depended on one's level of stardom. An A-class star could not initiate a conversation with a B. The B had to speak first – or, in my case, the D. I would have been rather lonely if I hadn't approached the As, Bs, and Cs. They would never have spoken to me first.

A pleasant fellow, Jimmy Webb, broke the alphabet rule and approached me like a friendly spaniel. He had written "Up, Up and Away," "By the Time I Get to Phoenix," "Wichita Lineman," and "MacArthur Park," the latter popularized in the skating world by JoJo Starbuck and Ken Shelley.

Jack Nicholson was in the room, but he did not drop by to have a word with me. Various starlets fluttered past. Bob Dylan buzzed around in sunglasses with minuscule lenses but didn't speak a single word to anyone, as far as I could tell. An invisible fog seemed to accompany his mute movements.

There was a sumptuously appointed buffet: as much as one could eat; as much as one could drink; and probably as much as one could smoke, and I don't mean Marlboros. The main centre of action – as it invariably seems to be, whether the party guests are kings and queens, movie stars, or the great unwashed – was the kitchen. That was where the party guests ended up. The hostess still had not been sighted, but reliable reports placed her in her bedroom.

That was where I eventually reintroduced myself to Joni Mitchell. The prevailing atmosphere of her bedroom was dark and shady. Restful forest green dominated the colour scheme. It was a large room with a four-poster bed and a fireplace surrounded by chairs, ottomans, and sofas. An overwhelming scent of cannabis wafted through the air. I was offered some but did not partake.

I went back to the Bel Air Hotel feeling rather deflated. I had not been discovered. My John Barrymore profile had not been admired. There were no Hollywood contracts in my agent's office waiting for my lawyer's scrutiny. The next morning I conspicuously underdressed. I carried the wolf coat over my arm.

On the way to the airport, Elva's and my limousine passed a billboard promoting the album *Hejira*. The design was a black-and-white photomontage with Joni in the foreground, flying around on an outdoor pond just like an exotic bat, beret askew, hair blowing in the breeze, with a road in a country landscape superimposed upon her lower torso. I was recognizable but infinitesimal in the background, striking a pose in my peacock costume. Barbara Berezowski, the bride, was little more than a demure upright white ant in the distance. That album cover was a work of great originality and mystifying cleverness, but it had absolutely nothing to do with a freezing hockey rink somewhere in Buffalo, New York.

I entered the first-class cabin of my airplane with my tail between my legs. Then I returned to New York, where at least a few people knew and understood me.

13

Wayne and Me

As I approached the age of thirty, the signpost of decrepitude for a figure skater, I continually looked for new ways of promoting myself, different venues in which to star. I had already skated past the average out-to-pasture milestone. With the fear of impecuniousness hovering on my horizon, a nagging interior voice urged, "Do just about anything to make money!"

It's not that I wasn't earning money on a fairly regular basis, but I managed it irresponsibly, spent it profligately, and realized that neither skating nor art offered long-term security – let alone a retirement package.

That is why, without a moment's hesitation, I agreed to compete on the "Superstars" show, a televised invention of Dick Button's Candid Productions, immediately after finishing a three-month stint in Holiday on Ice at the Palais des Sports in Paris. The producers selected well-known sportsmen who then went to glamorous locations and competed in sports completely unrelated to their own. I was on my way to Nassau in the Bahamas.

Toller Cranston Superstar

Other "Superstars" competitors travelled with their wives or girlfriends. I brought along Ruth Dubonnet, the eighty-three-year-old dowager socialite who was my improbable sidekick, travelling buddy, and entree into the European social stratosphere.

We were met at the Nassau airport by a limousine that already contained several athletic luminaries: Doug Collins, a six-foot-six professional basketball guard who had starred at the 1972 Munich Olympics; Earnie Shavers, an American heavyweight boxer; and another boxer whose name I've forgotten who looked like the missing link. Ten minutes out of the airport, our limousine was involved in an accident. I briefly considered claiming whiplash in order to collect my fee and leave without competing.

By osmosis I learned how to talk jock talk, affecting the image of the athletes against whom I would compete. I had a shrewd idea that feathers, sequins, spandex, and stage make-up would not fly with the superstars. Nor would sophisticated conversation. A rather simple wrestler missed an entire event because he could not find clean underwear. In confusion, he locked himself in his bedroom. I have never known a figure skater to do that.

I sensed that my inability to perform with even moderate credibility in some of the sports could work to my advantage if I made a joke of it. I began the competition with the swimming event and did remarkably well: fourth out of ten. After that, my performance level declined in increments from respectable to bad to worse. By the time the obstacle race came along – the final televised event – I was so not into it, so bored by it all, so certain that the millions of dollars I had planned to reap were beyond my reach that, instead of leaping over the hurdles, I ran under them.

That was my first "Superstars" competition but not my last. Trans World International, the television arm of IMG, sponsored a competition for Canadians. By then, inferior athletes had started hauling home the prizes. Instead of playing one sport professionally, they trained year-round specifically for the "Superstars" events. I viewed that as legal cheating.

My performance as a Canadian superstar was among the most tragically pathetic athletic accomplishments of my life. The event did not have the glamour or international flavour of the Nassau experience, and I felt superior to the other athletes – with the notable exception of Wayne Gretzky. My enthusiasm was further dampened by a soccer player named Brian Budd who trained full-time in the "Superstars" sports in order to beat those of us who hadn't trained a day of our lives in those specific events.

Brian, with manufactured glee after handily winning the rowing competition, leapt into Lake Ontario in front of the crowd and television cameras on what must have been one of the chilliest days of late April. After he won the overall competition, I never heard of him again.

Wayne Gretzky was very young in those days – definitely pre-Great Gretzky, a star but not a superstar. He was a phenomenon who had sprung up in the WHA and showed great promise.

Cycling, the event that I thought would be my forte, almost turned out to be my death. With my piston thighs and my superior cardiovascular conditioning, I felt that the burned-out hockey players would not have a chance against me. I was almost right.

The race began. I was ahead. On the third turn, in my ardour to win, I made a final sprint towards the finish line. My bicycle slid out of control across the track, throwing Wayne Gretzky and his newly insured million-dollar legs into the ditch.

While Wayne lay in one ditch, I lay on the opposite side of the track, thinking that even though I had not won the race, the accident had been noble. It would certainly be featured on-camera. That was not the case. The man with the million-dollar legs emerged as the child of the moment. Lying in the mud, I was forgotten.

14

My Sherika

I met Sherika Bakova (a pseudonym, my pet name for her) in 1982 in connection with "Strawberry Ice," the first in my series of fantasy skating specials. The CBC had asked Sherika, a top-notch, Emmy-winning hair and make-up specialist, to go to my house on Carlton Street to style my rather difficult hair before the day's taping. I met her in the kitchen. There was instant chemistry between us, a sense of already knowing one another. I felt that I was meeting a member of my own tribe, someone whom I would know for the rest of my life.

It did not occur to me at all that Sherika was a transsexual. I failed to detect the slightest indication that she had ever been a male. In fact, I have never thought of her as anyone other than the woman I met that day.

Over time, I learned her history. Special friendships include elements of trust, discretion, and respect. Our mutual exchanges of intimate memories were part of the glue that kept our friendship together.

Sherika was born in Hamilton, Ontario, my own birthplace. We entered the world within a year of one another. Hamilton spawned other notable Canadians during the same period: among them, Brian Linehan, a well-known commentator, and Karen Kain and Frank Augustyn, celebrated ballet dancers.

Sherika Bakova, né Bobby Graham, was anatomically a boy at birth. I do not know much about the earliest part of her life, but it was similar to mine in some important respects. We both sensed that we did not fit into our highly conventional worlds. We were born different. Rather than living as lobsters and clams, we were hermit crabs, trying to fit into other creatures' shells.

Teenage Angst and Then Some

Sherika experienced an emotional revelation when she was thirteen or fourteen. Her mother mentioned that she had read a magazine article about people who had changed their genders through surgical procedures. To Sherika, that news was a lightning bolt from the blue. Something that had been unimaginable became her festering *idée fixe*. Perhaps it was possible to right a congenital wrong, to redress a divine injustice. Perhaps her body could some day be in tune with her psyche.

Sherika's family life was tragic. Her father, a chronic spouse-abuser, had eventually left the family, but Sherika's brother followed his father's example. One day, when Sherika's brother was home on leave from the army, he swung a rifle at their mother. The gun went off accidentally, and he fatally wounded himself.

A police officer went to Sherika's school, took her out of class, and told her, "You won't be returning to school this afternoon. Please come with me." She spent two hours at the police station before officers told her what had happened. Her mother had picked up the rifle and ended her son's suffering. Then she had turned the weapon on herself and shot off half of her face – events that lend a brand-new dimension to the term "dysfunctional family." By comparison, mine was the Brady Bunch.

Sherika's mother survived for twenty years after the accident, serving as the subject of a variety of psychiatric experiments. Sherika still has nightmares about visiting her mother in mental institutions, viewing the disturbing after-effects of electroshock therapy.

During Sherika's years as a boy, older males molested her. At fifteen, she made up her mind to undergo sex-change surgery. In the early 1960s, changing one's gender was something that the average person could not imagine, let alone contemplate doing. Because the procedures were hit and miss, patients became guinea pigs. Atrocious acts were committed, in the name of kindness, on their internal organs. Sherika, with no familial support, jumped off a cliff without a parachute.

A Drastic Solution

Gender transformation surgery is particularly complicated and grave because it is more than a physical procedure. It involves one's chemical and psychological make-up as well. Michael Jackson or Ivana Trump could happily have half a dozen operations to alter their exteriors, but Sherika tinkered with her insides as well. Transgender surgery changes behaviour and one's entire sense of self.

There were potent drugs to alter her hormonal balance, hours of counselling to help her fit into society, and dozens of operations over a period of many years. The undertaking was monumental.

Many men who become women through surgery later turn to lesbianism. One's emotional equation can become so unbalanced that hateful twists of fate occur. Transsexuals are no longer the people they were born to be, nor do they ever truly become new individuals with fresh identities. They land between a rock and a hard place. That is the cruellest irony. A few young men who underwent the same procedures became Sherika's friends through the bond of common experience. She watched most of them, one by one, turn to lives of prostitution and crime.

Afterpains

Sherika was cut from a different cloth. Her professional ambition had always been to serve at a high level as a hairdresser, and she was gifted. While working on hairstyling and make-up for television and movies, she managed to be on hand for most of my important professional ventures. She met and worked with many of the top skaters in the world.

Over the years she continued to be my sounding board. She elicited and reinforced instincts and feelings within me that I might not have been aware of had I not met her.

Sherika possessed a total understanding of stardom and aesthetics, as one did in the Hollywood of old. She pushed the envelope of perfection, and she encouraged my own sense of theatre in appearance, clothes, and image on and off the ice. We invented a certain conversational style that mixed lies, exaggeration, and truth: fantasy dialogue in which two children might engage, more chemical or electrical than verbal.

Sherika fell in love with a handsome man. On the day after their marriage, he left her to move in with a gay lover. Like everyone else, Sherika had wanted to belong, to be loved, to have a home, to fit into life's mainstream. Instead she lived like an unconvicted criminal, looking over her shoulder to see if anyone had guessed her terrible secret. Insensitive friends and strangers alike humiliated her.

An obsession with becoming thin was one of Sherika's hang-ups. She had a doctor wire her mouth shut, which meant she could ingest only liquids through straws. She carried a pair of wire cutters in case of emergency and talked like a ventriloquist. In time, she shrank into a skeleton. Such are the extremes some people will go to in order to achieve their heart's desire, but at what price and to what effect? Inevitably Sherika's weight mounted up again.

Because of rumours that envious professional competitors spread about her medical history, there was a time when Sherika was blacklisted as a hairstylist within the show business community and ended up virtually without work. She had bought and renovated a charming house in Baltimore, Ontario, primarily because I owned the house next door. (I had purchased it as a country house, and I stayed there periodically with Krystyna, my house manager, and my dogs.) The trauma of being unable to earn a living paralyzed Sherika emotionally. She couldn't keep up her mortgage payments, so she lost that wonderful house and its garden.

Sherika suffered a nervous breakdown and went through more than a year of intensive psychiatric rehabilitation. She climbed a psychological Mount Everest, then scaled every other peak in the Himalayas.

Because of the mistakes that Sherika's original doctors had made, there was a chance years later that she would die of complications from the surgery. Government health insurance paid for a trip to London, England, where the operation was redone.

Sherika returned from that painful, degrading surgery when I was about to begin a run with Ice Capades at Maple Leaf Gardens. She came to the arena to make sure I looked my best. Meanwhile she was required to perform an excruciating follow-up medical procedure using a metal instrument to ensure that the tissues of her new vagina didn't grow back together. Like the soldier she was, she religiously performed the procedure at home between shows and still managed to take care of me. Who else would have the fortitude to pay that terrible price, a price that will never be paid in full?

Today Sherika's fires have been extinguished, although there will be flare-ups when she least expects them. She is solvent, successful, in demand as a movie hairstylist, and at a level of tranquillity that many others would aspire to and envy. Nevertheless, Sherika told me, the price she paid to achieve that level was too great. It would have been preferable to live with her false male identity.

15

Nina Simone

The greatest contributors to a particular medium – dance, music, skating – are often neither the richest nor the most famous. Among their peers, however, they are the most highly respected. Such was the case with Nina Simone, an eclectic jazz, rhythm and blues, and soul singer-pianist whom I encountered during the early 1980s.

A black American born Eunice Kathleen Waymon in Tryon, North Carolina, Nina had been classically educated through a scholarship to the Juilliard School of Music in New York City. She had become an important female singer, no less important than her contemporaries Sarah Vaughan and Ella Fitzgerald. Those women were the collective voice, soul, and poetry of black America. When John Lennon gave an interview to *Playboy*, the last important interview of his life, he cited Nina Simone as one of the two major musical influences in his career.

Unlike her contemporaries and equals, however, Nina Simone did not become a household name in America. Embittered by early encounters with racism, sexism, and other perceived social injustices, she was outspoken in her anti-government views of America's involvement in the Vietnam War. She paid a nasty price for speaking out. She was blacklisted. That meant fewer record deals, engagements, and paycheques.

In such circumstances, one can either evaporate into the unknown or leave the hostile environment. Nina abandoned the United States and plied her wares elsewhere: in Liberia, Barbados, Trinidad, and throughout Europe. She eventually returned to

North America, but her career here never quite bounced back. That was due to her notoriously prickly personality and to her penchant for saying exactly what she thought. Sometimes she even chastised her audiences.

Of Wolf Coats and Wolfman

I happened to be performing with Ice Capades in Montreal when a good friend of mine, Thom Hayim, in an unprecedented display of largesse, decided to throw a party for me there. Ultimately, however, the party was dedicated both to me and to Nina Simone, whose birthday it was.

The gala took place in Thom's third-floor apartment at 4508 Saint Catherine Street West. That particular area of Montreal was precisely at the midpoint between a chic neighbourhood, Westmount, and the most sordid gutters. The party's unique location was reflected in its wide range of guests.

Thom was normally not particularly sociable. He was more an observer than a director of action, but in this case he extended himself. In addition to Nina and me, he had invited an array of guests that included rock singer Corey Hart's rather gorgeous, glamorous mother and some strange, exotic nightclub and dance people who hadn't achieved anything of artistic consequence but were colourful. To that he had added a collection of soft crooks.

One particular guest never actually entered the living room. Wolfman was the most hirsute black man I had ever seen. His body hair was no less thick and dense than his beard and the thatch of hair that topped his head. Although Nina and I were the stars of the party, Wolfman was a serious side attraction in the kitchen. Everyone wanted to see him, and to see as much of him and his hairy body as possible.

Midway through the party, Nina came right up to me, grabbed me by the arm, and firmly sat me down on the couch. We had our first but not our last intense conversation. I don't believe that she

Childhood friend Thom Hayim.

really knew who I was, because she had just come from Paris, but she told me she was a genius of the highest order and felt that I was a genius as well. We did not have to sit there and listen to the stupid, ordinary people at that party. We were above it all, and we didn't have the time to waste. She whispered sweet words that were all too credible to me. I concurred with every point she made.

Several times when people approached to speak with one or the other of us, Nina dismissed them with a wave of her hand and no charm whatsoever. She was the Queen of Hearts. *Off with your heads!*

Nina related to me bits and pieces of her textured, difficult early life as the sixth of eight children in the rural south. Her voice was infinitely more masculine than feminine, yet it resonated with conspicuous nobility and sagacity.

Although she had forty albums to her credit, she was intensely bitter. The world, she felt, did not understand her genius. Getting to Hollywood, home of the music establishment, was an important goal for her. There she could make the money she deserved. Montreal was merely a stepping stone.

Nina struck me that evening as unattractive. Her hair, however, completely dazzled me. Curtains of braids swished and flew whenever she turned her head. Years later I figured out that she had been wearing hair extensions.

I can't remember what Nina wore to the party, but I had dressed like a star. I had arrived in one of my many fur coats: the wolf coat with fifty wolf tails all lined up like little soldiers along the boa. No notes could have struck a more sensitive chord within the breast of Nina Simone. Her life's fantasy was to own such a coat. If she tried it on once, she tried it on twenty times. At the height of the party, she sat encased in wolf tails – mine, to be exact. Although cannabis and similar delicacies were consumed, causing events to take on a certain dreamlike quality, my eyes remained focused on that fur coat. It would not leave the room without my notice.

I planned to spend the night at Thom's apartment, so I had no need to go scurrying out into the night. Nina, *au contraire*, was searching for someone who might scurry away with her. At that particular party, there weren't too many eligible specimens. Most of the men were younger than Nina, and half of them were gay. Nina's eye eventually zeroed in on a French-Canadian man of her age, and he made a mistake that groupies often do. Because he was in awe of Nina's talent, he behaved in an overly kind and affectionate way. Nina completely misinterpreted his gestures and decided that he would become her date that night.

The French-Canadian gentleman, with his artificial, permed hair and a fluffy raccoon coat, was decidedly effeminate. Even had he been heterosexual, he did not possess the mettle to take on the likes of Nina Simone. As Nina moved in, the man realized he had given her some serious miscues. He said goodnight and ran down three flights of stairs to the street. Nina followed him. I joined the chase, because Nina was still wearing my coat.

Montreal is extremely cold in the winter. The three of us ran down the street towards the gentleman's car, Nina in my coat, the man in much less of a coat, and me in no coat at all. The dénouement took place atop a snowbank. The scene was complicated and bitterly frigid. Somehow we agreed that the gentleman would drop Nina off at her hotel, and my wolf coat would be restored to me.

Reformed and Recidivist

Nina Simone went on to make huge waves in Montreal: turbulent, disturbing waves that never brought her any closer to the golden shores of fame and fortune. She was the kind of performer who arrived at a sold-out club, then threw a prima donna fit and demanded more money from the promoter.

Nina's God-given talent was far greater than the shoulders that supported it. She was ultimately ousted from her Montreal hotel for nonpayment of bills and left the city in a cloud of the sort of controversy and negativity that were completely consistent with the prior course of her life and career. She had caused a sensation but had not scored points. Nina had a great talent, a unique personality, but was destined to fail because of flaws in her character that she simply could not transcend.

Three or four years later, I was skating in Los Angeles in something called "The Big Show." I had flown in from Berlin to work on the television set when I received a phone call in my dressing room. It was Nina Simone. She was performing on Sunset Boulevard at a famous club where aspiring musicians appeared in order to be seen by record producers. Although I was busy, tired, and soon to fly

back to Berlin to continue performing with Holiday on Ice, I did go
to see Nina at that club.

I have virtually no recollection of her performance, but the
prickly, temperamental, arrogant prima donna whom I had met in
Montreal was not at all in evidence that evening. Nina was on her
Sunday-school-best behaviour. She had finally reached Los Angeles,
and that was where she wanted to make her name. Ironically, Nina
was so well behaved that she came across as saccharine. She didn't
have that old edge. She didn't make an impact. Nobody picked her
up for a record deal, as far as I know.

I went backstage for a warm reunion, and I remember noting
one poetic detail. There, on a hanger, was a sad, narrow, tailless
version of my wolf coat. Although the coat wasn't voluminous or
glamorous, Nina had indeed arrived in Hollywood and had acquired
the coveted symbol of success.

I believe that Nina felt deeply insecure and lonely. I was a shard
of her past that she remembered with pleasure. She wanted me to
go out with her that evening, but she terrified me on too many
levels. She was too strong, opinionated, sexual, and demanding, a
veritable emotional octopus. With just one of her tentacles around
me, I would never escape. I had seen what had happened to the
French-Canadian gentleman, and I saved myself just in time.

It is true that somebody in her entourage took me home and
seduced me in the car. By the time I arrived at the Hyatt Hotel on
Sunset Boulevard, I was quite happy to be there by myself, away
from any further Nina Simone influences.

I encountered Nina one more time in my life. She was in
Toronto, and the buzz filled the air. Everyone I knew planned to
see her perform at an ex-dinner theatre on Sherbourne Street in
Cabbagetown, an unusual venue and a somewhat cafeterialike
environment. The large hall had a jerrybuilt stage for the 3:00 P.M.
Sunday matinée.

After keeping the audience waiting for an hour, Nina Simone appeared onstage, made no apology, and reverted to type. I felt that I was seeing a detoxified drug addict hit the street again, running. I don't know if Nina was drunk, high, or just so bitter that she couldn't contain herself. She resumed the financial argument she had been having with the promoter. Her lids drooped over her eyes as she vented angst and spleen. One sensed that if her tongue should protrude, it would be forked.

From time to time, Nina began to sing and play the piano, then stopped mid-phrase to rage again in a continuing diatribe. It was a tour de force of mad, avant-garde theatre, a brilliant one-woman show. No one left the room. The performance was riveting. However, I chose not to go backstage afterward.

I never heard from Nina Simone again, but one day I did find her album *Baltimore* in the $5.99 bin at a used record store on Yonge Street. I had a feeling that something wasn't quite right, so I attempted to distract the proprietor at the cash register by presenting it to him with a second album from the same bargain bin.

"There has been a mistake," the shopkeeper told me. "This record is a collector's item. It sells for fifty dollars." I had met someone who, like me, knew the true worth of Nina Simone. Unfortunately I had to leave without making a purchase.

16

Taxi to the Toilet

Today society takes an open, casual view of sexuality in a way that has filtered down, to a certain extent, to the exceedingly proper world of figure skating. If Rudy Galindo[*] can fly out of the closet with the proud proclamation of his homosexuality, and if the scandalous off-ice antics of certain heterosexual skaters are met with a wink of approbation, that just proves how much society's mores have changed. There was a time, however, when a skater's wholesome public image was just as important as his on-ice talents.

I was at home on Carlton Street in Toronto when Thom Hayim phoned me from Montreal and meekly asked whether I knew about my unscheduled appearance in an award-winning German porno film. Often, in times of shock, one emits a shriek, but my silence on the phone that day was infinitely more deafening.

As it turned out, my highly recognizable image had been inserted into a gay dramatic comedy called *Taxi Zum Klo: Taxi to the Toilet*.

The very next day I flew from Toronto to Montreal wrapped in a bulky trench coat, believing that such a coat was *de rigueur* for a trip to the theatre to see a porno flick. At the airport I hailed a taxi, noting the ironic overtones of choosing that mode of transportation. I went straight to the Strand Theatre and took my place at the end of the queue. I was heavily bundled to avoid recognition. With the

---

* Rudy Galindo won the 1989 and 1990 U.S. pairs title with Kristi Yamaguchi. In 1996, he became the first openly gay man to win the U.S. men's singles title. See *Icebreaker* by Rudy Galindo and Eric Marcus, 1997.

scarf around my neck covering most of my mouth, my voice sounded muffled as I ordered my ticket. *Un billet, s'il vous plaît.*

Viewing the Evidence

The film was in German with French subtitles. My heart palpitated uncomfortably from the first strains of the music as I wondered exactly how I was going to figure into the film. I had no idea when and in what vulgar context my image would appear.

The plot intrigued me in spite of myself. It was the story of a talented young Munich schoolteacher who encouraged children to be creative and free, and to mature into textured and broad human beings. In the meantime, in his private life, he lived a sordid, Jekyll-and-Hyde existence. His darker dramas were generally played out in public toilets.

The title of the film derived from the fact that when the teacher was hospitalized for an unrelated ailment, his raging libido drove him to extreme behaviour. He jumped out of bed, ran along the corridor in his hospital gown, exited onto the street, and flagged down a taxi. Then he made the rounds of his favourite public toilets, where he engaged in sexual encounters with other men. Suffice it say, the film was X-rated, yet it had garnered a certain respect in the international film community. There was marginally more substance than depravity.

Midway through the film, the schoolteacher picked up a man in one of the toilets and took him home for what can only be described as a Robert Mapplethorpe scene. Various instruments of sexual titillation were in evidence. At, shall we say, *le moment critique*, one of the partners urinated into the mouth of the other.

Just then the camera panned to a larger-than-life television screen in the teacher's bedroom, and my moment of truth arrived. There I was, in a scene from the CBC's televised "Toronto Symphony On Ice," resplendent in glittery peacock blue, leaping about to Franz

A strenuous Russian split jump.

Lehàr's *Graduation Ball*, with a heavy emphasis on dramatic split jumps. The characters had used that fantasy image of my skating to become sexually aroused.

I remember that my head and my heart pounded in perfectly synchronistic downbeats, but I also remember – and I never admitted this to anyone – being absolutely thrilled beyond words at seeing myself life-size on the silver screen. I was slightly disappointed that my little vignette had not lasted just a bit longer.

I could say that I immediately ran out of the theatre in disgust, but that would be untrue. I stayed until the last credit rolled. The film had a rather poignant dénouement, highly unusual for X-rated movies. Although the teacher was well regarded by the school administration, and although the children he taught would be quite sorry to see him leave, he was summarily fired. One of his taxi-to-the-toilet escapades had been reported.

I did not pass Go. I went straight back to the airport. As my plane neared Toronto, I became more haughtily flummoxed. I definitely had a bee in my bonnet. I had seen the evidence. I could imagine how that filthy film was going to destroy my career. Something had to be done about it. Alert the lawyers! Alert the CBC! Do *not* alert the media! I wanted my cameo appearance excised from the film.

The producers had no right to use pirated footage. Worse still, they weren't paying me royalties.

The CBC assured me that its legal team would get right on the ball and solve the problem.

Even the greatest porno films – with the exception, perhaps, of *The Devil in Miss Jones* and *Deep Throat* – do not enjoy long runs. *Taxi Zum Klo* had its little flicker in Montreal and, as far as I know, was not seen again. I never heard of anyone else who witnessed my cameo: either because the film was so poorly attended or because the filmmakers really did cut me out of it.[*]

If a similar crime were perpetrated against Elvis Stojko or Philippe Candeloro today, maybe he wouldn't like it, but what would he care? He could laugh it off. For me, that film was the absolute antithesis of everything that I aspired to in my professional career. At least in my mind, I was a serious classical artist. My portrayal in the film, the environment in which it occurred, was a radical departure from everything that I was and that I believed in.

The More Things Change

That was many years ago. Perhaps it was an early indication that certain personalities within the skating world were beginning to

---

[*] Although *Taxi Zum Klo* (1981, Germany), directed by Frank Ripploh and starring Frank Ripploh and Bernd Broaderup, is available for purchase on the Internet, the authors did not order a copy for research purposes for fear that the transaction might generate an avalanche of mail in plain brown wrapping.

capture the imagination of people outside that world. Katarina Witt recently appeared nude in *Playboy* magazine,[*] and nobody seemed the least bit put out by that.

In modern Germany, nude beaches and nudity in communal saunas are part of being natural and sporty. Katarina Witt, with or without her clothes, is always a lady. She has a naturally healthy appearance, an athletic body, and a wholesome image and personality that will not be compromised.

Katarina was proud of the photo layout, and she should have been. She looked great. She also became richer because of it. *Playboy* paid her more than $100,000. What I once perceived as unthinkable and potentially devastating to my career had become, years later, a business opportunity.

17

Krystyna

During my early thirties, I was flying quite high, living excessively above my means in my enormous house on Carlton Street in Toronto. I was alone with my beloved English setters, Lapis and Minkus. I had a cleaning woman, but it occurred to me one day that I needed a live-in housekeeper to organize my chaotic, débris-strewn environment.

---

[*] The ten–page photo layout, shot in Hawaii, appeared in the December 1998 issue. According to a *Playboy* spokeswoman quoted by CNN/*Sports Illustrated* (cnnsi.com), Witt was the first [professional] athlete to pose nude for *Playboy*.

Choosing a live-in housekeeper is almost as serious as choosing a wife. It means selecting a stranger who will live under your roof, eat meals with you, and become an integral part of your life. She will go straight from zero to your inner sanctuary.

The Parade on Carlton Street

I found a listing in the telephone book for an employment agency just down Carlton Street that provided domestic help. My phone call triggered a Fellini-esque parade that encompassed the full range of the human gene pool.

A young Filipino girl knocked. I opened the door. The first words that came out of her mouth were "How much money will I make? How many days off will I get per week?"

"Don't phone me. I'll phone you" was my polite response.

There was a French-Canadian valet, a middle-aged man with a certain warmth but raggedy social edges. He announced that he really was great at his job. He loved dogs. He loved my house. But he did have a drinking problem. And he smoked in bed.

There was a Scottish housekeeper who looked like a distant relation to Mrs. Claus. She was charming and sweet like a little brown wren, but she arrived half an hour late through the back entrance. She told me that she was tardy because she couldn't find my front doorbell.

A German *Putzfrau* sailed in like the Titanic. Before she sat down to discuss her potential employment, I had already sensed that at any second she would want my heels to click together, and I would be obliged to salute her. She was overpowering.

There was an au pair girl who was too soft and colourless. She was not the sort of person who would have taken control of my household. She would have become irritating, like bad wallpaper.

The list went on. Maybe hiring a housekeeper was not such a brilliant idea after all.

With Krystyna Miedzinski.

How Soon Can You Start?

Then the telephone rang. It was a cold, wintry late November day. Snow was softly falling. The clerk at the employment agency told me optimistically, "There is a woman here who would be perfect for you. She is Polish. Could she come to see you right now?"

Ten minutes later, my doorbell rang. I opened the door to an apparition of beauty in a chocolate-brown cashmere coat with a sable collar that exactly matched her warm, soft deep-chocolate-brown eyes. Her honey-blonde hair and facial features were no less lovely than Grace Kelly's. With them came an aura of refinement, breeding, and intelligence.

I blurted out incredulously, "Why ever are you applying for this job?"

Krystyna Miedzinski's English was not perfect, but that was part of her charm, and I learned that she spoke five other languages. As I led her upstairs to the living room, in my mind I had hired her on the doorstep. I served her tea in my ruby-red lacquered living room and conducted a brief interview.

Krystyna had been visiting her daughter in Paris when martial law was declared in Poland. She considered the dangers of returning to her homeland and decided not to risk going back. She could not stay in France with her daughter because of employment restrictions. She had once lived in Canada for a short time and had worked for the Creeds, the Bloomingdales of Canadian high-end clothes. As one often does in times of strife, she had gone back to the place where she had been relatively happy.

I told Krystyna, "You are welcome to accept the job. I will treat you as an equal member of my family. There are no rules. There is no schedule. There are no specific hours to keep. All I ask is an organized household."

She agreed. We shook hands, and she promised to move in the next weekend. That very night, she went to the home of some Polish friends for dinner and told them about her new job as a house-keeper. As seems to repeatedly happen in my life, a remarkable coincidence occurred. As Krystyna sat watching television with her friends, one of my skating specials aired.

The Un-Housekeeper

Krystyna moved in and quickly became part of my life, part of my environment, part of my comfort, and part of my pleasure. At first I relegated her to a downstairs bedroom, but soon I moved her up to an imperial chamber with a six-foot-long chandelier and a hand-painted Chinese bed. She had an entire floor of the house to herself.

Because of her beauty, taste, and fastidious appearance, Krystyna became, in that mad, flamboyant house, my most prized and valued *objet d'art* – equal only to Lapis and Minkus (which flatters them all). She was a fine Arabian filly, sensitive and gentle. In any other age, she would have been a great hostess or a lady of leisure. I included her in my social gatherings, although she never presumed to join in unless I invited her. Her sense of etiquette was flawless.

I sometimes threw swanky, absurdly extravagant black-tie dinner parties for eighty or ninety guests, catered by chefs and liveried servants. Krystyna presided impeccably and became friendly with my circle of acquaintances. At breakfast the day after such a soirée had been staged, we reviewed the guest list so that Krystyna could make recommendations for the future. With her judgment and sense of character, she held the reins of social power in my household.

She was embarrassed about one deficiency that I found perfectly charming. At first she could not write English. When she left telephone messages for me, she spelled them out phonetically. There was never a time, however, when we did not communicate perfectly. If she couldn't say something in English, she said it in German, Italian, French, or Spanish. Somehow I always understood what she meant.

Nobody in the world arranged flowers better than Krystyna. My house generally looked as though a professional florist had decorated it, which contributed to the kind of environment in which I liked to live. Krystyna was the only person I ever allowed to make painting suggestions. She was my clothes consultant, my social adviser, and my classically trained pianist and music expert. She often selected skating pieces for me.

I quickly concluded that housecleaning was beneath Krystyna's station in life, so I suggested that the housekeeper hire a housekeeper. When I employed a Polish cleaning woman, Sylvia, I came to think of my house as the Polish embassy.

Lady Melania

When Lapis died, I decided to get another dog to keep Minkus company. I didn't want a puppy that Krystyna would have to train, so I phoned an English setter expert, Sally Vertulia in Milton, Ontario, who told me that a stray female was available. I had never owned a female dog, but I went to see that one.

Minkus was the most handsome dog in the world, a masculine, liver-spotted champion. By contrast, the dog I saw in Milton was ugly, skinny, and almost colourless. She did not even look like an English setter. I turned on my heels and went back to Toronto.

Sometimes in life one has to dig deep to help a creature in need. In the middle of the night, I woke up and decided to adopt that needy dog.

Krystyna christened her Lady Melania after a blonde Polish courtesan she had read about. With Krystyna's love, healthful food, and grooming, that unattractive dog became Krystyna's canine counterpart. They were the two most gorgeous creatures in Toronto, two blondes with deep brown eyes.

The Little Black Cloud

A little black cloud hung perennially over Krystyna's head and followed her wherever she went, like Pigpen's cloud of dirt in the comic strip *Peanuts*. While we lived on Carlton Street, men – and they could have been grocers, gypsies, tramps, or thieves – chased her down the street. That amused me, although it was the bane of her existence. She had been unsuccessfully married twice in Poland and continued to form unsuitable attachments in Canada. The men in her life consistently behaved in the same execrable way: they tried to dominate her. She eventually rejected each of them.

Krystyna was smitten at regular intervals by bad luck that left her in a chronic state of melancholia. Not long after her arrival at my house, she slipped on my back doorstep and broke her ankle in five places, an injury from which she never fully recovered. The rehabilitation period was difficult for both of us. I had to become Krystyna's maid, a job for which I was remarkably unsuited.

Eventually I decided to move. I wanted to collect more stuff, and I needed a bigger house in which to store it. I could not afford a bigger house in a better area, so I was forced to buy a bigger house in a worse area, one of the great catastrophes of my life.

When people told me that the secret of real estate is location, location, location, did I know what that meant? I learned a lesson when I later tried to sell that 5,000-square-foot mansion in Toronto's most unsavoury prostitute- and drug-infested area.

Krystyna moved with me to Pembroke Street. There she resided in an apple-blossom-pink bedroom with a dressing room, an enormous bathroom, and a private living room with hand-painted ceilings.

May I Join You?

In March 1987, I went to Cincinnati, Ohio, to provide CBC commentary during the world championships. When I returned to Toronto, Krystyna told me that she was leaving me.

"I met a man. He is Polish and very wealthy. He has offered to buy me a condominium, and he has given me this."

This was a pigeon-egg-sized sapphire ring with diamonds dancing around the perimeter.

"I don't have to sleep with him," she informed me. "I only have to converse with him once a day for an hour."

I immediately asked if I could go in on the deal.

The Worst Luck of All

Krystyna moved out of my house, but we kept in touch. Although she possessed a certain amount of money, she was unhappy. The wealthy, unattractive, rather primitive sapphire-purchaser was madly in love with her. She continually fought off his attentions. Eventually she terminated their arrangement.

During the late fall of 1997, on the eve of my tribute show at Varsity Arena, a friend phoned to say that Krystyna had tripped on a loose carpet and had broken her neck. She was paralysed from the neck down. I was horrified. Visiting her in the hospital was as frightening as studying the David drawing of Marie Antoinette going to her execution. I had to spoon-feed Krystyna her dinner.

"Things will get better," I said, though I didn't really believe it.

Through months of exercise and heroic hard work, Krystyna rehabilitated herself. At the end of two years of torture, she had learned to walk again and had resumed a semblance of normalcy.

I don't have many outlets for emotion or affection in my life. Where do the currents of emotion flow when one doesn't have a husband, wife, or lovers? In my case, they flow to close friends such as Krystyna who have never, ever deviated in their loyalty to me.

18

Escape from the Circus

During my mad Munich days of the mid-1980s (chronicled in *Zero Tollerance*) when I mounted a one-man painting exhibition, pulverized Joan Collins on the Thomas Gottschalk talk show, stirred up the nightclub scene, and generally became the toast of the Stadt, I received a highly unusual invitation. A German businessman phoned me and asked whether I would like to star in a new show called Fantasy on Ice. His words were a symphony to my ears. First I thought *star*. Then I thought *money*.

I met the refined businessman, and we dined at the Opera Hotel. He looked dapper yet professorial in a long, navy-blue, cashmere Loden-Frey coat. His ice show was revolutionary, he informed me. Instead of playing in buildings, it played in tents. For some reason, business was not brisk. He needed a major star. Would I be interested?

As a lion tamer in a childhood ice carnival. Life comes full circle.

Bring on the Lion Tamer

I was flown to Brussels, Belgium, the very next day and driven to Rotterdam across a lugubrious, grey Dutch landscape. There in the middle of the City Square was a great, shabby, circular, striped enclosure that looked suspiciously like a circus tent.

I noticed a poster in the square on which were breathlessly imprinted the words, "And special guest star Canadian legend Toller Cranston." In another life, at another time, I would have complained about the flagrant false advertising, but the show's manager assured me that the error had been innocent, and we both made light of it.

The environment inside the tent was unlike anything that I have seen in skating. The small ice surface, a Holiday on Ice kind of tank, was rectilinear, although the show was presented in the round. The wooden bleachers were circular. The atmosphere was half circus, half nightclub.

I later discovered that the manager indeed sprang from a circus background, a particular circus that, for whatever reason, had gone bankrupt. With Fantasy on Ice, the German promoters had attempted to duplicate the circus format on ice. In short, circus people were trying to put on an ice show.

The ushers, snack bar attendants, and ticket-takers were all from the circus mould: strange dwarves and swarthy gypsies. I distinctly remember passing a dwarf smoking a joint. The hairs on the back of my neck told me that I would not be starring in Fantasy on Ice.

Something disconcerting happened to me then. I asked whether I might visit the men's room.

"Just through that curtain," I was told.

I walked out through the curtain and entered a little johnny-on-the spot, doorless in the open air. Colourful and rustic took on a primitive quality. As I sat on the toilet, I looked up and noticed that residents of the adjacent apartment building were watching me as though I were on television. I had never before entertained an audience under quite those circumstances. I waved and blew kisses. That seemed like the correct thing to do. Today I might compare the scenario to *The Truman Show*.

Dusk had arrived, so I went to my seat in the tent. The tiniest sprinkling of an audience had started to arrive, and the reefer-smoking dwarf showed people to their seats.

The manager came to sit with me, and we chatted before the show started. He told me things that mystified and thrilled me. In fact, his narrative was the highlight of my evening. He had been a lion tamer with the circus before it went under, and he regaled me with advice about the psychology of the great cats. I was riveted in particular by the gruesome tale of a lion mishap that had cost him a part of his genitalia. I just managed to prevent myself from asking him to show me the scar.

Fantasy on Ice was a tawdry show with little artistic substance beyond what Kirk Wyse and his masterful Charlie Chaplin act could provide. Otherwise it was a C-quality circus hybrid of Holiday on Ice. One charming thing happened. The cast members skated their hearts out for me. I appreciated that. Still it was clear that Fantasy on Ice and I were not meant for one another. But how was I going to bow out gracefully?

At intermission, the lion tamer-turned-manager asked me, "How are you enjoying the show?"

I said, "More than you can ever know," and that was true. Bad theatre is more enjoyable to me than anything mediocre or quite good.

The manager was under the mistaken impression that I would be performing in the next city. I was the saviour who was about to stave off bankruptcy. In essence, it was all up to me. Could I rush back to Munich to get my skates?

Running Away from the Circus

My companion and watchdog wanted to go out after the show. I said I was tired and asked him to drive me to my hotel. He took me to a one-star establishment in the most sordid part of Rotterdam. I quickly realized that it doubled as a bordello. There were red lights in the windows and terrifying prostitutes at the bar – old prostitutes with bleached hair.

My host wanted to buy me a drink. We could eat dinner at the hotel, then have some fun (whatever that meant), but I declined and went straight to bed. There was something in the air that made me nervous.

The man was to return to pick me up in the morning and take me to the Brussels airport, but I tricked him. I arose at 2:00 A.M., grabbed my bag, crept furtively into the deserted streets of Rotterdam, and vanished into a taxi. I went straight to Brussels and sat in the public safety of the airport, waiting for my seven o'clock flight to Munich.

Once back in Germany, I felt strangely energized. I rushed to the Vier Jahreszeiten hotel, where I consumed a sumptuous lunch to celebrate my escape from Fantasy on Ice.

The show eventually limped off to Piraeus, Greece, where it ground to an ignominious halt when the local promoter stole the entire bankroll and left town.*

19

The Dorian Gray

As a result of my continuing popularity in Germany, I received a telephone call one day in 1986 inviting me to stage an art exhibition in Frankfurt. I flew from Canada to West Germany and stayed at my favourite local hotel, the Hessischer Hof, ready to perform my *grand artiste* act. I was extremely nervous about such events. I didn't know anyone in Frankfurt (including the sponsor), and I wasn't sure that a single soul would attend my show.

As an artist, I have never been salaried. Perhaps people who receive paycheques every two weeks find it difficult to imagine the angst that fact implies. Not only does my livelihood hang precariously on the whims and tastes of the buying public, but I invest large sums in canvas, paints, advertising, and especially in framing and shipping. I simply can't afford a disastrous show.

The exhibition was to open at 5:00 P.M. During the mid-afternoon, I went to the building that was to house it. There was no

---

* See *Robin Cousins* by Martha Lowder Kimball (1999).

gallery. There was no showroom. There was nothing more than a huge empty space that looked like Saddam Hussein's bunker, with grey cement floors and walls and many paintings in crates. I was stupefied. I started to uncrate my work, but I didn't know why I was bothering. I was standing in the middle of a garage.

Little by little, people of various descriptions trickled in. First came workers in overalls. Then a truck driver delivered tables. Fake walls and partitions appeared. Special effects sprouted like exotic mushrooms. In the period of an hour and one-half, the bunker was transformed into the most fabulous showroom Frankfurt had ever seen. The man who was sponsoring the show, it turned out, was the owner of a famous nightclub and discotheque, housed in the Frankfurt airport, called the Dorian Gray. He was connected to the local glitterati, and he knew how to give a party.

I left and returned to the Hessischer Hof, relieved but still not quite getting the full picture. Playing my hand to the max, I dressed in a general's jacket with ten leather belts wound around my waist like spaghetti. I took a circuitous route back to the exhibition site. I did not want to make my entrance too early.

When I arrived, the place was jammed with guests. Champagne flowed. Fake trees and tremendous pots of lilies and roses adorned every niche. Waiters wearing white jackets and gloves served heaps and piles of juicy red strawberries. The paintings looked good.

I stood and talked, stood and talked, but no one bought my work. I had come a long way from Toronto, and nothing was selling.

A scant five minutes before the exhibition was to end, there was a tap on my shoulder. "You must meet Mr. so-and-so from Dubai." Mr. so-and-so from Dubai, a beturbaned, bemoustached sheik in a business suit, bought ten paintings – six-by-six-foot oils, the biggest and the most expensive – and dropped $30,000 in an instant.

I scurried back to my suite and flopped into bed, not the least bit tired. As relieved as I was that my expenses were covered and my studio rent could be paid, I was equally charged up about the clothes that I was going to buy the next morning with my new-found wealth. The exhibition was saved, and my wardrobe was soon to be replenished.

20

A Day at the Bank

Financially I have always flown by the seat of my pants. I have never in my life balanced my chequebook. I simply hope, when I try my luck with an ATM as though it were a Las Vegas one-armed bandit, that there will be a few pennies left in my account so I can pick up my dry cleaning.

One morning some fifteen years ago or more, I was particularly jittery. As I lined up in the queue at my regular Toronto bank to inquire about my balance, I expected "Go directly to jail. Do not pass Go." I suspected that my account was overdrawn again.

I approached an East Indian teller and meekly asked whether she could tell me the balance of my chequing account. She returned from her computer and announced crisply, "Eleven thousand dollars."

"That is impossible," someone else might have replied. "I really don't think that I have any money at all." Instead I blanched, said thank you very much, left the bank, and hyperventilated on the sidewalk.

I went back inside and lined up a second time. I chose a smiley, dreadlocked Jamaican teller and said, "Excuse me, madame, could you please give me the balance of my bank account?"

Back she came. "Eleven thousand dollars."

This time, instead of turning white, I turned red. My adrenalin was pumping and the blood was coursing through my veins. I left the bank again.

After regaining my composure, I turned around and entered the bank a third time. I went to a portly Caucasian bullfrog and said, "Kind sir, could you please tell me how much money is in this account?"

He gave the same answer: "Eleven thousand dollars."

"I should like to withdraw ten thousand five hundred."

"That is a lot of money. You will have to wait."

"Waiting is not a problem. I will be glad to."

The transaction took a bit of time. When it was completed, I walked out of the bank with $10,500 in cash. It was difficult to wipe the smile off my face.

I knew that something was gravely wrong, but for once the gravely wrong had ended up on my side of the ledger. What should I do about it?

I strolled down Carlton Street, walked straight past my house, and fantasized about what I might buy with the windfall that had landed on my lap. Then I set out on my rounds. I didn't hail a taxi. I thought that it would be pleasant to walk the streets of Toronto enjoying the unaccustomed feel of a substantial wad of money weighing down my trousers.

I visited Holt Renfrew on Bloor Street West, Ronald Windebank's antiques shop and the Chinese flower market on Avenue Road, and Mitsuma, a Japanese designer shop in Yorkville. Then I treated myself to a delicious lunch à un at the Four Seasons Hotel. In an afternoon, I dropped the entire wad. I blasted every single dime.

I thought, in my imaginary dialogue with the bank examiner, "Look, you made a mistake. You gave me a false impression of my balance, so it is your fault. Yes, I will pay it all back over time, but I will not pay interest!" I had already strategized my defence.

Then I went home and waited for the phone call. I waited for a prim, crisp, official voice to announce, "Mr. Cranston, I believe that we have a problem."

I am still waiting.

21

The Last Days of Liberace

The most exciting little rink in which to perform is the one at Rockefeller Center. It is unique on the planet, in part because it is at the world's hub. The essence of New York City is captured in that one small piece of real estate. The art deco buildings that surround Rockefeller Center exemplify America when it was the New World – the New World that Dvořák hailed in the symphony that I skated to with such disastrous results, and the bustling new world that the Gershwins immortalized in song. The sunken rink beneath the golden Prometheus statue is a New York landmark of the first order.

Rockefeller Center is the staging ground for many New York spectacles: the lighting of the famous Christmas tree, major charity events, and previews of new Broadway shows. The annual rink opening, marking the beginning of New York's winter season, means exhibitions by world-renowned skaters. Most of the top skaters – the likes of Robin Cousins, Scott Hamilton, Peggy Fleming, Dorothy Hamill, and John Curry – have performed there and always with pleasure. There is never a paid audience: only the tourists and natives who congregate daily to enjoy the activities of the moment.

The New York-area skating community invariably arrives at the rink opening, making the occasion a class reunion of sorts: a chance to catch up on gossip, see old friends, and bond again for an afternoon. After the exhibition, everyone gathers in the adjacent restaurant for a wonderful New York lunch.

A non-skating celebrity is chosen each year to head the bill. It might be Liza Minnelli or Lily Tomlin, but in 1986 it was Liberace.

Liberace could not tinkle away on an outdoor grand piano, so he made an appearance, Santa Claus-like, in a sleigh. He took two laps around the rink before the skating show began.

Lunch with Lee

The show came and went. I do not recall my own contribution, so it must have been neither particularly good nor particularly bad. The perk for the skaters was to have lunch with Lee – that was what his friends called him. Because I was the featured performer, I was permitted to sit next to him. On his other side was the catamite of the moment, a man very much cut from the same cloth, a young Lee, equally artificial.

Although we skaters did not wear our costumes to lunch, Lee continued to sport his Louis XIV regalia. His clothes were well made, conspicuously expensive and detailed, but bordering on the grotesque. He wore a diamond ring on every finger. One of them was the famous grand-piano ring with 260 diamonds set in gold and piano keys made of ivory and black jade. I presume that all the stones were real, but the settings struck me as a cut below the most tasteful that Woolworth's could offer.

As though playing a perverse parlour game, I tried to find one patch of Liberace's body that was not unnatural. He wore the most horrifying toupee, far thicker than normal hair. His extensive facial plastic surgery had turned him into a gargoyle with a permanent grimace. Like the red shoes that could not stop dancing, his face could not stop smiling. Every tooth in his head appeared to have been capped at least twice. His skin was a coarse grade of sandpaper covered by a half-inch of pancake make-up. His lips were glossed to look naturally moist, but the layers were apparent. If there was any fascination in studying him, it was in the fact that I had never seen anyone who had been taped, glued, strung, nailed, and thumbtacked together to quite such an extent. If his life in the entertainment business had been war, he was the human rubble that remained.

One learns from *Beauty and the Beast* and Victor Hugo's *Notre Dame de Paris* that it is possible to be charmed by unattractive people if there is something genuine in their make-up. In Liberace, I sensed, that element had long ago been cast away.

The legitimate show-business legend did not for one moment stop performing. He took not one step out of character. There was not a "Can we talk?" or "How do you really feel?" While he sat at the table having a bowl of soup, his eyes worked the floor, looking to see whether anyone recognized him – or whether there was anyone in the room more important than I, to whom he should shift his attention. It was a Radio City performance for six rather than for three thousand: no human emotion, no true dialogue. He held court.

An effective way to communicate with stilted, self-absorbed people is to cut to the chase, act irreverent, and be a bit flip: let them know that you are not taking them seriously. That technique did not work with Liberace.

Lee and I discussed the plenitude of his wardrobe. He told me that it occupied warehouse after warehouse. That day he happened to be wearing knee-high, fawn-coloured, doeskin chamois boots with perfect little beaded tassels. I asked him whether I could please have one of the tassels as a souvenir. He was not amused.

Lee's farewell and exit were in keeping with his entrance: another show, silly in its superficiality. The very next day the great Liberace, with sold-out houses, cancelled his upcoming dates due to fatigue. I later learned that fatigue had not prevented him from performing. He was suffering from AIDS.

Maybe, to be fair, his personal performance at lunch that day had been heroic, one of his greatest efforts ever to pull himself together. Perhaps every moment had been torture. He died a few months later.

The death from AIDS of Hollywood star Rock Hudson in 1985 had already made international headlines. Liberace's death followed somewhat anticlimactically three months after our lunch at Rockefeller Center. His greatest fear, I read in a magazine, had not been death, but that his fans would think he was gay. Was there anyone who could have thought otherwise?

Liberace departed without a trace. Few members of today's younger generation now recognize that glittering name that once was so prominent on neon marquees.

22

The Drug Smuggler

I was asked through IMG (although my management agency had never before been involved in anything related to my painting) to produce a portrait of Britons Jayne Torvill and Christopher Dean, the 1984 Olympic ice-dance champions, for the 1988 Olympic souvenir program.

I had a month to paint it before the deadline, but for numbers of reasons I didn't quite get around to it. I accept any offer that involves money without necessarily considering what it will entail. The realization slowly dawned that what the officials who had commissioned the

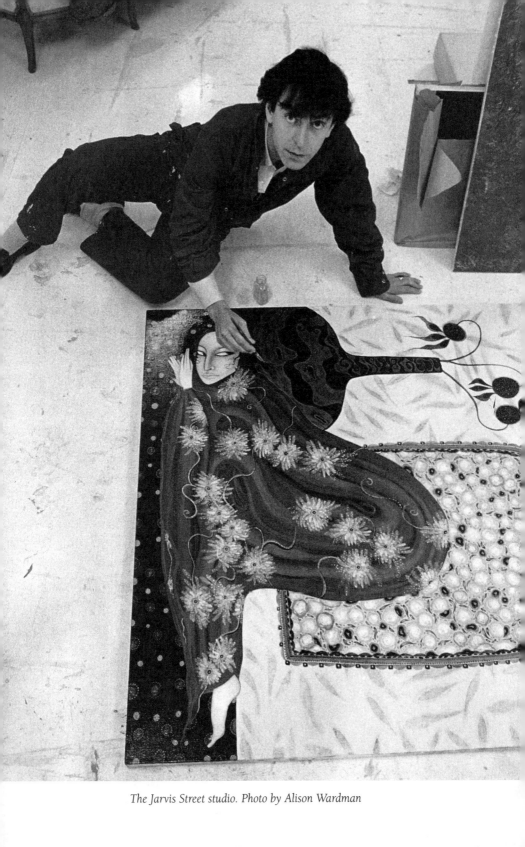

The Jarvis Street studio. Photo by Alison Wardman

work probably had in mind was a lifelike rendering of Torvill and
Dean – impossible for me to execute. My work is much more abstract
than literal. I accepted the $2,000 fee and spent it, but the days went
by without so much as a brush stroke on the canvas.

I happily went off to perform with Stars on Ice in the northwestern United States. Then I received an unwelcome phone call
from Jan Warren of IMG. If the Torvill and Dean gouache was not
completed within the next two days, I would have to return the
$2,000 (that I had already spent).

The Stars on Ice cast had a short break, so I flew back to Toronto
on a Friday. That left me a single Saturday to complete the project that
should have taken weeks. Deadlines usually bring out the best in me,
so I had figured out by then that instead of producing a Kenneth
Danby-style photographic rendering, I needed to create in a design
format the essence of Torvill and Dean's lines and movement.

True to form, like a petulant child, instead of getting up on
Saturday morning and going straight to the studio that I was then
renting on Church Street, I went shopping. Next I ate lunch in a
restaurant and went home. It was not until three o'clock that
afternoon that I decided to slouch down Pembroke Street towards
my studio.

Anti-Fungal Pills

I realized that I was in for a long day and an even longer night.
My landlord, who promoted rock groups, was a member of the
respectable demimonde (if that is not an oxymoron). He had once
given me a large, clear plastic pill bottle full of amphetamines: speed,
to be precise. Although I had not yet fallen prey to cocaine, I cannot
say that I was lily-white in the drug department. Nonetheless, speed
was not my drug of preference. The bottle had remained untouched
for quite some time.

Knowing what Herculean labours lay ahead, I took the bottle of
speed with me to my studio. I uncapped a few jars of paint, selected

some clean brushes, and set to work. Until nine o'clock at night, everything went as planned. The painting shaped up rather well. When I felt fatigued, I dipped into the bottle of speed and revved into action, finishing off about three-quarters of the work. At one-thirty in the morning, I dipped into the bottle again. By five-thirty the gouache was finished, but my eyes looked like two bull's-eyes. I was stoned out of my gourd.

Secure in the knowledge that the painting would be ready whenever someone came to call for it, I strolled merrily home. Along the way, I noticed with avid interest that many people had saucer-shaped bull's-eyes exactly like my own. Later in my life I became all too familiar with the idiosyncratic characteristics of Toronto's night culture, but that dawn I encountered its denizens for the first time.

I showered quickly, drank a cup of strong black coffee, threw a few possessions into my skate bag, and rushed to the airport. Terminal One was in the throes of a major construction project. Workmen in hard hats carrying two-by-fours mixed with the travellers to create a disarmingly casual atmosphere. The customs area seemed less formal than usual.

The official who examined my passport was a mannish woman, gaunt, brusque, and professional. She reached into my black leather skate bag and asked accusingly with a *ha!* in her voice, "What is this?"

Then she pulled out the plastic bottle containing fifty tablets of speed. I must have accidentally knocked the bottle into my skate bag as I rushed to pack my belongings. Fortunately I was still ripped out of my mind, so I did not react in the normal way, which would have been all-out panic. Instead I slid slowly into a controlled state of shock.

"Oh! Those are anti-fungal pills for my feet."

The officer replied, in a quiet, deliberate tone, "They look like speed to me."

The horror of what was about to happen kicked in. Carrying drugs across the border, especially in that quantity, meant being blacklisted and prevented from ever working in the United States again. Then the inquiry would generate enough bad publicity to instantly end my Canadian career as well – assuming that I didn't go straight to jail.

I held on to my last shred of hope and persisted with the anti-fungal story. There was a logical reason why the words *anti-fungal* had popped into my head. Two years earlier, I had indeed contracted foot fungus. The pills that a doctor prescribed for me then were similar in shape and colour to the flecked, light-blue amphetamines in the bottle that the customs agent was holding in her no-nonsense hand. In any case, I knew that I couldn't just pass off the tablets as common aspirin.

"Who is your doctor?"

"Dr. Barry Long."

"Where is his office?"

"On Danforth Avenue."

"Just a minute. I'm going to phone him."

While tribal war dances drummed in my head to the rhythm of my pounding heart, the customs officer phoned Dr. Long.

"Do you have a patient named Toller Cranston?"

"Yes."

"Does he have a problem with foot fungus?"

"Yes."

"Did you give him a prescription for it?"

"Yes."

Had she asked only one more question – "What do the pills look like?" or "When did you write the prescription?" – I would have been finished.

She returned to her counter, handed the bottle back to me, and admonished me sternly, "Never travel with unmarked prescription drugs."

I crept into the departure lounge, realizing that I might have only seconds in which to dump the pills. I sensed that I was being watched. All I needed was for the official to return and say, "You know, give me one of those pills. I think we'll just have it tested."

If I disposed of them in the airplane lavatory, there might be a way (however unpleasant) to retrieve them. Better to let them stay in Canada. I reached into a garbage bin and pulled out a *Globe and Mail*, simultaneously dropping the bottle of pills among mustard-stained napkins and banana peels. At least I no longer had the evidence in my possession. As I boarded the plane, I imagined the alert agent recovering the bottle from the trash bin, then chasing me down the Jetway.

Quite the Loveliest Flight Ever

The flight was uneventful until I was about to deplane in the United States. Then there was an announcement on the intercom: "Would Toller Cranston please report to the customs agents at the end of the Jetway." I felt fairly composed as I made my way along the aisle. I had spent an hour and one-half rehearsing an alibi. Two agents met me at the gate and asked for my passport. Then they handed it right back to me, saying, "Have a nice trip."

"What was that about?" I asked them.

"Oh, we just pick travellers at random and check their passports."

I swallowed the heart that had leapt from my chest into my mouth.

Then I endured a three-and-one-half-hour wait for my connecting flight to Denver. Once onboard, I was stuck in a bulkhead seat between a 350-pound woman and a child of eight. The woman's pointed elbow jabbed at my upper arm. The child, in mid-flight, vomited on me. (A flight attendant kindly cleaned up the mess, but the odour lingered.)

Byron Allen of IMG met me at the Denver airport. "How was your flight?" he asked conversationally.

After managing against all odds to enter America without criminal prosecution, I told him, "Byron, it was quite the most divine flight of my life."

23

Reflections from a Bejewelled Bed

There was a time when I was always waiting for large, clearly legible writing to appear on the wall. *Toller Cranston, you do not have to skate any more. You will become a great actor – or a great designer, a great painter, a great teacher.* Anything! I was forever trying various projects that might lead me into a new career. Sometimes I was unsuccessful and failed; sometimes I was very successful and still failed.

By 1988, I had moved my painting studio to the ground floor of a derelict house at 354 Jarvis Street, close to the CBC, where I produced a tremendous amount of work. I was to mount an exhibition at the now-relocated Beckett Gallery on John Street in Hamilton, Ontario. I decided that the point of view of that exhibition would be that I, the artist, was lying in bed imagining all the images in the paintings.

I went to my friend Duncan McLean of Waddington McLean & Company and told him that I needed a fabulous, elaborate Victorian bed frame – headboard, footboard, and slats – so that I could paint and decorate it as the centrepiece of the Hamilton exhibition. He found me one immediately. It was a solid-mahogany pillared bed with a massive headboard and posts with balls on the tops. It reminded me of the Disney film *Bedknobs and Broomsticks*. It was just what I wanted, quite incredible, and remarkably inexpensive – perhaps $500. I took it to a decorator and had it lacquered black with rectangular gold-leaf insets.

As soon as the lacquered pieces arrived at my studio, I spent several weeks adorning them with painted jungle plants and mad Doctor Doolittle-style animal designs. Then I went to a store that sold ovals of clear glass that artisans used for stained-glass work. With a certain type of glue that I absolutely swear by – it is called Goop – I covered the bedknobs with jewelled ovals the size and shape of small river stones. A well-known psychiatrist named Edward Kingstone stopped by with his wife, Barbara, who was a friend of mine, to see the bed. He assured me that I was a genius, and that the bed belonged in the Louvre in Paris.

The bed, sans mattress, was placed in the middle of the Beckett Gallery. If one stood within the bed frame, dazzled by the gold leaf, jewels, jungle flowers, and mystical animals, the images in the paintings seemed to flow psychically from the decorative magic of the bed.

One can never count on anything in art, but the exhibition was quite a huge success. A week later, someone from the gallery phoned and told me that the bed itself had been sold for perhaps $7,000. Even more interesting than the fact of the bed's sale was the information that the person who had bought it, John Howard, was a wealthy client of the Beckett Gallery and a personal friend of the owner, Tom Beckett. Mr. Howard wondered if I might be persuaded to decorate ancillary pieces. That was exactly the question I wanted to hear.

At the time, my house at 64 Pembroke Street, half museum and half bordello, Disneyland gone terribly wrong, was at the height of its opulent decadence. As pretentious as it sounds, I threw a swanky black-tie party in my red-lacquered *grand salon* with its jewel-studded ceiling. There were oceans of flowers. Incense wafted heavily through the air. That was one of the last galas of its kind.

I had invited the prospective client, John Howard, to my party, and he came. Mr. Howard was a divorced man of average height with regular features and short salt-and-pepper hair. He had sold his high-tech company for millions of dollars and had retired. My living

room, which must have seemed to him like an extension of the jewelled bed, catapulted him onto the halcyon planes of Euphoria. He
was transfixed by the house, the paintings, the atmosphere, and the
thousands of *objets d'art*.

Vineland

At the time, Leanne Pockar, skater Brian Pockar's sister, was living in
my commodious house. John Howard invited Leanne and me to
come to his home in Vineland, a place then unknown to me, just off
the Queen Elizabeth Way not far from Saint Catharines. Since
Leanne and I did not have our own transportation, an artist friend
named Chris Williams, who specialized in jungle flora and fauna (he
was particularly heavy on parrots) offered to drive us to Vineland
and thus became enmeshed in our soon-to-be enterprise.

John had barrels of money. He had taken courses in the history
of art at Oxford, and he wanted me to inspect his Norman castle
with a view to providing him with pieces of furniture to complement the bed he had bought.

Until I saw that house, I had no idea what John meant by
Norman castle. It was simple in design with a flat roof, not magical at
all from my point of view. It made no architectural sense and was
falling apart at the seams. John had designed the house himself and
had built it on a shoestring at a time when he had considerably less
money than he had amassed by the late 1980s. Now he was interested in major redecoration. I was beginning to picture myself
launching a new career and becoming the world's greatest interior
designer. *Au revoir*, skating.

There was a twenty-five-foot-square sunken living room with
water marks on the walls and falling plaster; a slightly raised dining
area off the living room; a minute modified galley-style kitchen; a
metal staircase leading to the second level; two bedrooms upstairs;
and a small office housing state-of-the-art computer equipment. The

Chris Williams (left) and John Howard.

bedroom of his divorced daughter, the room that was to accommodate the jewelled bed, was interestingly round but derelict.

John was perfectly charming and obviously proud to show me his home. I was in shock. I said, in a polite and professorial tone, "Had you considered razing this house to the ground? Is that a possibility?"

John's birthday-party smile collapsed under the weight of such candour. I realized that one should be careful about speaking the truth, especially when emotional attachment (to a child, a pet, or a prized possession, for example) is involved.

Not being entirely insensitive, I started to tap dance. I extolled the irregularity of the house, which was truly its appeal. Even as I tried to remove the barb of the harpoon that I had carelessly tossed, I knew that the point had been unnecessarily sharp.

Carte Blanche

Somehow we got back on track. John was about to leave for Europe. He told me that he would be away for two months. During that time, he wanted me to redecorate the house in any way that I saw fit. Money was no object. He gave me a pile of signed blank cheques and told me, "Just furnish the house as you would for yourself." Those words were only slightly less dangerous than dropping the bomb on Hiroshima.

When I am flush, or when there is the prospect of a lot of money in my immediate future, I am ridiculously generous. In the car on the way back to Toronto, I appointed Leanne Pockar the financial chairman of a three-way equal partnership. Chris Williams and I would collaborate on the artistic work. What the three of us had before us was part decorator's dream job, part fantasy, and part madness. We couldn't have been more stupid in how we approached it.

Castle Howard had to be completely finished by October 1. John Howard had offered it to the Hamilton Opera Company for the staging of a medieval feast. I decided that the controlling decorating scheme would be forest green and white. I would ground the twenty-five-foot-square living room, the only room with any real panache, with a floor of forest-green marble covered by a large oriental rug. All the furniture would be upholstered in dark-green velvet in the identical shade.

It is embarrassing to mention what I did next. All day long I painted in my Jarvis Street studio (with resident rock stars on marijuana upstairs). Then between 4 P.M. and the shops' closing time of 6 P.M., I cruised my favourite haunts. It was a shopaholic's fantasy come true. With a snap of the fingers, I bought anything that I wanted myself, even though I knew, alas, that it would end up in Castle Howard, not Castle Cranston. I didn't dicker. *I'll have it. Wrap it up! Send it immediately!* My taste was eclectic, my shopping habits extravagant. I dropped thousands upon thousands of dollars.

To be fair, I bought some unique and clever objects. Numbers of those items probably increased in value over the next few years. There were fabulous rugs, including a strawberry-coloured Heriz; a large collection of modern glass; mad, strange ceramic monkeys from Nancy Poole's Studio; interesting Arts and Crafts lamps; and an entire collection of valuable Cylla von Tiedemann photographs. The objects that I chose were intended to dazzle, thrill, terrify, and amuse their new owner.

I purchased an Italian glass dining-room table with a base of carved fish. Its green-and-gold-leaf chairs, adorned in varying shades of mother-of-pearl, had slats that were reminiscent of the scalloped shell in Botticelli's *Birth of Venus*.

The round bedroom with the jewelled bed and complementary pieces was done in *eau de Nil*, a pale turquoise. Over that I painted, like filigree work, a tangle of transparent pastel gardens that integrated with the bed and grew up onto the ceiling. I had the room's Chinese furniture upholstered in strawberry-pink moiré. The visual images were like those of an exotic fairy tale.

I bought works from every painter whom I had ever patronized, creating an instant art collection. I sold several things from my own collection – at a fair price, but still it meant more cash for me. I also commissioned myself to do a fabulous painting for the red-lacquered den with green velvet furniture. At the same time, I commissioned Chris Williams to create the *chef d'oeuvre* of his life, a fifteen-square-foot surreal painting of a river with dozens of parakeets flying to heaven.

As we came down to the wire, with the medieval feast hovering on the horizon, I was up on scaffolding, producing Miró designs on the living-room ceiling: flying geometric shapes in black and primary colours against a red background.

We all had a wonderful time spending John Howard's money. Something makes me think that we might have dropped a quarter of a million dollars in two months. The house should have made the cover of *Architectural Digest* as Canada's maddest interior. Such eclecticism was so natural in my life that I ceased seeing the environment with other people's eyes and saw it only with my own.

John tried to be enthusiastic when he viewed the final effect. He was diplomatic, almost ambassadorial. It didn't enter my head that he might not like it. Why wouldn't he like it? It was Castle Cranston II, and more. In truth, Mr. Howard, though he had thought that he wanted an environment like mine, deep down inside most certainly did not.

Does Somebody Live Here?

The most telling moment, which struck me as odd and later began to haunt me, occurred when the rather humble Hamiltonians arrived for the medieval feast that was to transpire in a tent in the back garden. A portly, middle-aged Tom Jones wench stuck her head through the doorway of the living room but didn't follow it with her feet. She asked rather timidly, "Does somebody live here?"

That remark mushroomed in my mind, and I saw my creation with different eyes. When the medieval feasters toured the house, it was with a deep reverence, as though they were going through an odd historical site. They did not sit on the chairs or in any other way take over the environment, as they surely would have in a real home.

A large photograph was subsequently made of John Howard sitting in his house. That photo appeared in the *Hamilton Spectator*. Years later I realized how incongruous John looked, perched there within the Toller-esque décor.

Quite a number of outstanding bills remained, so my corporation invoiced Mr. Howard. At that point, he blew the whistle on us. The affair ended on a sour note that coincided with the general downward spiralling of my life (including troubles with Christopher Bowman, drugs, and depression). I personally got stuck paying the balance of $15,000 in order to avoid being sued by the furniture restorer. Don't ask how I paid it. I really don't know.

When the *Titanic* went down and I had my big household sale at Waddington's, I sold a number of items that had belonged to Chris Williams, notably a painted table. I applied the proceeds of the sale to what I viewed as his third of the deficit. He never spoke to me again.

Leanne Pockar soon went home to Calgary. In 1999, when I had an art exhibition there, she brought me two serious buyers, so I felt that our score had been settled – a decade late.

Some years after the medieval feast, I revisited Castle Howard. A traditional decorator had redone the premises. There was now a baronial bedroom on the third floor, outfitted in what looked like deluxe Laura Ashley chintz, with a bed on a raised dais. All exotica had been discarded. The result was Vineland, not London or Paris, but I learned that you can't comfortably wear someone else's shoes.

With the rise and more particularly the fall of Castle Howard, I was forced to continue to skate. I did so for another full decade.

24

Katia and Sergei in Torontoland

Contrary to legend, the professional career of the sublime Russian skaters Ekaterina Gordeeva and Sergei Grinkov did not take off like a rocket. Although Ekaterina and Sergei were the 1988 Olympic pairs champions, Canadians Barbara Underhill and Paul Martini defeated them at Landover, Maryland, in December 1990.

Gordeeva and Grinkov, who were married the following April, had entered the International Management Group fold. In an effort to put everything right, IMG hired me to choreograph their 1991 Landover technical program.

At the time, I was teaching Christopher Bowman, and my life was simultaneously imploding and exploding. I realized to my great distress that I would somehow have to work with Gordeeva and Grinkov during the same two weeks for which the agency had booked me on a tour.

Ekaterina and Sergei arrived in Toronto and immediately felt vulnerable and alone. They were living in a modest apartment-hotel on Jarvis Street.

Late on two consecutive nights, on top of teaching Christopher and preparing for the fateful, memorable, and horrendous tour through British Columbia and Vancouver Island that would forever after be known to me as the Tour from Hell, I had to choreograph the number that would remake Gordeeva and Grinkov's career.

With that particular pair, the work was easy. They could do anything. I did find Sergei to be infinitely Russian, however. He was academic. He did what he was told, not with an attitude but without any apparent pleasure. He was doing his job.

I had chosen the Grand Pas de Deux from Tchaikovsky's *Nutcracker Suite*, music that is eternal. Sergei and Ekaterina immediately liked it. I did not have the chance to design their costumes for the program, something I would have liked very much to do. Nor, with only two nights, could I follow through with the development of the number, as I would have liked to. After I had cut the music and laid out and choreographed the program, I gave it to Ellen Burka to hone and fine-tune. I then trudged off reluctantly to join the Tour from Hell.

Stop! Police!

During Gordeeva and Grinkov's visit, as usual, I had no means of private transportation. After practice the first night, Thom Hayim, who was visiting from Montreal and staying at my house, offered to drive Sergei and Ekaterina to their hotel. It was one o'clock in the morning.

Something happened that was surreal, funny, and horrific at the same time – and acutely embarrassing for me. At the intersection of Yonge Street and St. Clair Avenue, three police cars careened

Sergei Grinkov and Ekaterina Gordeeva. Photo courtesy of IMG

towards us and forced Thom's car to the side of the road. The officers jumped out of their vehicles and pulled their guns. The incident happened like lightning: one, two, three.

Thom cooperatively rolled down his window, but the officers opened the driver's side door and pulled him out of the car at gunpoint. Then they laid him over the hood.

Stunned and somewhat timid, I spoke up. "I am Toller Cranston. These are the Olympic champions in the back seat."

The officers snapped, "Shut up. Don't open your mouth."

Luckily I was not splayed across the hood, but I was removed from the passenger side of the front seat. Consistent with Murphy's Law, John Wang, a Cricket Club teacher who happened to live on Yonge Street, strolled by just then. He saw Gordeeva and Grinkov cowering in the back seat, Thom over the hood with a gun to his head, and me frozen next to the car, unable to open my mouth to explain the situation. That wrinkle in the scenario compounded my considerable angst.

The black clouds passed quickly when the facts became clear. During the time when we were all skating at the Cricket Club, burglars had entered the parking lot and had removed Thom's licence plates, exchanging them for those of a stolen car. The police had seen the licence number and had presumed, not unreasonably, that the occupants of the vehicle were the car thieves. It was all a terrible mistake.

Since Sergei's English was next to nil and Ekaterina was tired, afraid, and in shock, it was difficult for me to make light of the situation, explain it to them, or assure them that such events were really quite rare in North America.

What should have been a high watermark in my career ended up in rat shit. I was a loser in two respects: without the full opportunity to work with Gordeeva and Grinkov and doomed to go on a tour that was one of the most difficult of my life.

However, Gordeeva and Grinkov did win the World Professional Pairs Championship at Landover in 1991, the first of many triumphs for them and the beginning of a spectacular professional career that sadly ended, at its very height, with Sergei's premature death.

25

Winterlude

As one slides ever further down the ladder of fame and desirability, the employment opportunities become less attractive. Eventually a skater is no longer paid for his name and his abilities. He is awarded hazard pay for surviving hostile conditions: hence my frigid engagement at the Ottawa Winterlude at the age of forty-three.

Winters in Ottawa are so horrifyingly cold that celebrating them doesn't pass the laugh test. Laughter freezes in one's throat. Some skaters perform outdoors without difficulty. I am not one of them. Hard outdoor ice is inhospitable to my best jumps, the Salchow, loop, and Axel (with take-offs from edges rather than from toe picks). Invariably I slide off my edges. Had I been born a decade earlier, in the era of outdoor competition, I would never have become a figure skater.

One of the last outdoor championships occurred in 1963 at Cortina d'Ampezzo, Italy. The last men's competitor took the ice after 12:00 A.M. The weather was so cold, from all reports, that the spectators could not have left if they had wanted to. They were frozen to their seats.

Anyone could win the Worlds then with a double Axel. Canadian Don McPherson (whose father, according to legend, cashed in an insurance policy to send his son to Italy) triumphed that year for two reasons. One, he was the only skater who consistently remained standing. Two, the political machinations were such that nobody earned a majority of first placements. At the age of eighteen, Don garnered the winning majority of seconds and became the youngest men's world champion in history.

If the skaters endured torture at Cortina, the judges endured more, so they sounded the death knell of outdoor world competition.

Marching Home from the Russian Campaign

Some of my favourite Canadian skaters joined me in the Winterlude cast: Norman Proft; Michael Shinniman; Christine and Dion Beleznay, a husband and wife adagio team; and Karen Lopez, the diva of all divas, a truly great unknown. The show included musical acts, a master of ceremonies, and a French-Canadian singer, Véronique Beliveau, with whom I became friendly. Véronique, a native of Quebec, was a pop recording star of national repute.

At the finale, the musicians were to play, Véronique was to sing, and I was to improvise for five and one-half minutes at a temperature with wind chill of -45°.

Instead of telling myself, "Maybe I should wear a sweater under my costume," I allowed vanity to prevail and appeared half-naked in sequined spandex.

One reached the ice via a canopied passageway that led from a tent backstage. Along that passageway, someone had planted kerosene heaters in the snow. The heaters burned brightly but offered no comfort. At -45°, they were decorative props surrounded by circular pools of melted snow. I wondered whether dying in flames was as unpleasant as it sounded. If my fur coat caught fire, my life would have a glorious ending. There are accounts of Napoleon's frozen soldiers, retreating from Moscow during the War of 1812, setting themselves on fire and laughing at the flames before incinerating.

The ice was the sort that one finds in an old-fashioned icebox: neither true ice, nor chalk, nor frost. When Véronique sang, swathed in a faux leopard-skin maxi coat with matching hat and woollen gloves, I skated in my gossamer spandex. Frozen, I cut my repertoire to the bone. I feared that at any moment one of my limbs might snap off and shatter like glass.

I looked out into the audience and saw an ocean of Eskimos enveloped in heavy winter clothing with narrow eye slits above the bridges of their noses. A multicoloured sea of jujubes with little eyeballs peered in my direction. Those eyeballs were filled with the kind of bewilderment that Eskimos might exhibit while watching tropical fish in an arctic aquarium. The scene made no sense.

Since I could not jump, and I could not spin, I fell back on creativity. I slid onto one knee, then lay dramatically on the ice, a favourite trick in any weather. What I had not foreseen was that I would stick to the surface like the tongue of a child who has foolishly licked a metal railing. My sequins and beads adhered as though superglued. As I pried up my costume, my hands stuck. I expected to see palm-shaped patches of skin embedded in the ice.

When the music stopped, I fled along the canopied walkway straight into the dressing room, a glittering apparition streaming past like headlights in a slow-speed photograph. The producers of the show, Debbi Wilkes and Mel Matthews, assured me, "That was great! That was wonderful!"

I muttered to them through blue lips, "At what point is being professional being stupid?"

I ran like an arctic fox to my favourite Ottawa hotel, the Château Laurier. I remember streaking along the sidewalk past a mother consoling her crying child. I called out to her, "Don't you know that he's crying because it's so *cold!*" When I reached my room, I just managed to squelch the impulse to jump into a scalding bath without removing my furs.

The following weekend, the cast performed seven shows on Saturday and another seven on Sunday. Christine Beleznay and I developed frostbite on our hands. The only consolation in such extreme discomfort was company in one's misery, a bit of camaraderie to ease the pain. It also helped to joke, swear, and rant.

I toured the Parliament complex during my free time, on the correct assumption that the government buildings would be well heated. The Beleznays and Norm Proft wrote me a cheery message in the snow in front of the clock tower.

I left Ottawa secure in the knowledge that if I could survive Winterlude, I could survive anything that life threw in my path. For some reason, though, the Ottawans have not invited me back for a return engagement.

26

Skating with an Elephant

I was contacted by the casting director of the "Sharon, Lois, & Bram's Elephant Show," a Canadian children's television program featuring three adult hosts whose bucolic songs and childlike enthusiasm captured an international market.

My piggy bank was empty as usual, so I accepted the offer that was put to me: how would I like to skate with an elephant? My mind did not exactly register the word *elephant*. I was more focused on the sum of money that was mentioned. The show was to be filmed at the Moss Park Arena in Toronto, a convenient stone's throw from my house on Pembroke Street.

On the day of the taping, I worried about two things. An Elizabeth Manley commercial had just been filmed in the arena, and the people involved were still milling around. I was afraid that I would meet a prestigious member of the skating community and have to explain myself. Second, I had begun the process of breaking in a new pair of boots, and they were stiff. My feet hurt, and I wasn't skating particularly well.

Even though it was a spring day, the rink was frigid. I wore an electric-yellow spandex costume with a black faux vest and white collar. The elephant, with its costume's thick grey synthetic growth, had substantially more protection against the dank chill.

I was supposed to skate in circles around the elephant to a Latin musical beat, dance with it, hug it, and pin a medal on its furry chest. All that would have been relatively painless. Unfortunately, the elephant had a huge ego. When anyone paid attention to me, its pachyderm feelings were hurt.

What particularly slowed the pace of the taping was the elephant's propensity to overheat. The elephantine head had to be removed at frequent intervals so that cool drinks could be poured down the human throat residing inside the costume.

Subsequently the "Sharon, Lois & Bram's Elephant Show" became even more wildly popular and even more widely distributed. There was no clause in my contract that limited the number of times that my episode could be rerun. As far as I know, it is still being played today. People who see me in the supermarket or pass me on the street are forever telling me, "Hey, I saw you the other day. You were skating with an elephant."

27

Magical Salzburg

I accepted with unsuppressed euphoria the request (tendered sometime during the early 1990s) that I replace Katarina Witt in an exhibition for the Special Olympics in Salzburg, Austria. I suspect that every other desirable skater was otherwise engaged.

I had to leave for Austria that very night and perform the next day. When I arrived in Salzburg, I was driven straight from the airport to the chilly practice arena outside Salzburg proper. Old skating friends became reacquainted in a veritable orgy of hugs and heartfelt greetings. The head choreographer was my friend and compatriot Sarah Kawahara. The cast included numbers of people with whom I had previously enjoyed working: Scott Williams, a U.S. medallist and producer of professional skating; Charlene Wong, Scott's wife, a Canadian medallist; Jamie Isley, an American choreographic genius; Stephanee Grosscup, a fine American artistic skater; Tai Babilonia and Randy Gardner, U.S. and world pairs champions; Catarina Lindgren, a former Swedish champion; Catarina's husband, Tom Dickson, an American men's competitor; and an American dance team, Kristan Lowery and Chip Rossbach.

At the exhibition, I presented medals to Special Olympians whose event had just concluded. It is always humbling to cross paths with people who share with you the common denominator of skating but who, for whatever unfair reason, were given unequal gifts in life. Those competitors, despite their various handicaps, radiated a conspicuous and enviable joy in their accomplishments.

Rita Moreno

I finally checked into my hotel, the Oesterreichischer Hof. Although I had been up for forty-eight hours, I got my second wind and didn't feel the least bit tired. Rita Moreno, along with her husband and manager, Dr. Lenny Gordon, and their daughter, Nandy, who works in Hollywood, invited me to join them for dinner. Skaters and Broadway gypsies have a lot in common. Whenever we sit down to a meal together, it is a gathering of old friends. Caustic, outrageous humour and intimate chit-chat are part of the conversational mix, no matter how long it has been since our last encounter.

Years earlier, Rita, Eli Wallach, and I had dined together at the Peasant Larder in Toronto. On that occasion, I told Rita some of the stories that eventually appeared in *Zero Tollerance*, in particular my Broadway tale of woe involving Dennis Bass. Both Rita and Eli stopped eating their enchiladas and tacos and assured me that they had never heard stories like those in all their years in the theatre.

By a strange coincidence, when I sat down to dinner with Rita and her family in Salzburg, I had just finished reading the biography of Marlon Brando's first wife, Anna Kashfi. In that book, Kashfi claimed that Rita had climbed the garden wall to perpetuate a long-time affair with Marlon. I asked Rita if the story was true. It was.

The Glory of Feather Beds

After dinner, I toddled off to bed. Only international travellers can fully appreciate the glory of the bed linens in fine Swiss and Austrian hotels. At the Oesterreichischer Hof, a sumptuous five-star hotel on the River Salzach, bed linens hit the heights. I careened into a soft, white eiderdown, a foot deep in feathers, suffocating in its luxurious depths. With chocolates on the fluffy, down-filled pillows and vases of fresh roses blooming in the early-spring chill, everything was simply perfect.

You can marvel at Salzburg, you can be enthralled by its detail, but no foreigner can ever truly become part of it. There is a sanitized, civilized lifestyle that exists only in Switzerland and Austria, exemplified by the postage-stamp gardens in which each flower seems to have been planted under a microscope and by hedges trimmed within millimetres of perfection. Where my hotel room was concerned, though, I was happy to enjoy excessive attention to minutiae.

Fine Weather for a Rehearsal

The Special Olympics had ended, so the next morning we skaters went on to our second assignment, the filming of a live show for American television. Eunice Shriver was the chairwoman of the very fancy event, and although we did not meet or even catch sight of him, Arnold Schwarzenegger was there in an official capacity as well. Just the possibility that we might spot him sent a frisson through the cast.

On a stage five or six feet above the ground, tank ice had been installed in the Residenzplatz beside the magnificent Dom, the church where Mozart once played the organ. Our practice session went on for hours and hours, thanks to Sarah Kawahara's Austrian-style perfectionism. I went through my skating routine several times, but the most important consideration was to somehow avoid falling off the platform and killing myself on the ever-so-picturesque cobblestones below.

I was determined to complete the elusive double Axel that I had missed in the exhibition the night before. Meanwhile, on that early spring day, every known form of weather conspired against me. Stephanee Grosscup and I were the only skaters who seemed to notice that the weather changed at half-hour intervals. When the rehearsal began, so did the rain. Then the skies pelted us with hail. Suddenly the most enormous snowflakes in the history of Salzburg floated down from the sky like fluffy white *Lebkuchen*[*] and the air developed an arctic sting. When the clouds parted, the atmosphere

---

[*] A special German Christmas cookie coated with confectioner's sugar.

became so tropical that we had to remove our jackets. Each time something new and different happened, Stephanee and I burst into fits of laughter. The special effects of nature went beyond anything that movie magic could have conjured.

Look Out Below

With the first notes of the overture, we found ourselves in a Cinderella environment. I couldn't help but revel in how fortunate I was to have been invited to Salzburg. To the lilting tunes of Strauss waltzes, horses, carriages, and cloaked and plumed aristocrats set the tone of the evening as they thundered down the cobblestone streets in eighteenth-century regalia. It was like a page out of a two-hundred-year-old history book, mystical and wonderful.

The live show featured Munich opera singers, a full orchestra, and the vocal talents of Rita Moreno, the special star. Sarah Kawahara's well-rehearsed corps executed an exceedingly detailed skating routine. It floated above the heads of most people in attendance, but I appreciated its complexity. Tai and Randy, who were used to the small tank ice of Las Vegas and Atlantic City, performed well in that environment.

Then my big moment came. No matter what happened, I intended to prove to the American viewing public that the old dog really could still do a double Axel. I managed to squeak one out on that tiny ice surface. I also gave birth to a single flip and nearly catapulted off the stage into the picturesque tableau below.

Somewhere Going Nowhere

As the program ended, Rita appeared in a bobbed Leslie Caron wig to sing "Somewhere" from *West Side Story*. The accompaniment dragged so badly that she waved the conductor away and directed the orchestra herself. Although the number was delivered with great enthusiasm and energy, the evening ended on the discordant note of a "Somewhere" that wasn't going anywhere.

We all walked back to the hotel through the twinkling fairy-tale town with its glittering pastry shop windows and cosy cafés. Rita went to her room, changed clothes and wigs, and came back down to the hotel restaurant wearing haute couture that looked like a cross between Bob Mackie and Chanel. The deep slit in her skirt revealed incredible legs.

I complimented Rita on her necklace. Without batting a false eyelash, she coolly informed me, "Oh, my husband gave this to me for my sixty-second birthday."

I thought, "Boy, you are the real thing. A phony would have lied about her age."

Then I said goodnight, went upstairs, and plunged into my eiderdown with dreams of Salzburg dancing in my head.

28

Welcome to Charles Schulz's Santa Rosa

The legendary Christmas show at the Redwood Empire Ice Arena in Santa Rosa, California, for years was choreographed to perfection by Karen Kresge, a ten-year Ice Follies alumna, and subsidized in the most extravagant way by Charles Schulz of *Peanuts* cartoon fame. The 1992 show was called "A Christmas Portrait."

Charles Schulz, a die-hard skating fan of the first degree, built his own rink in 1969 for figure skating, hockey, and community events. Each Christmas season he mounted a mini-Ice Capades with a budget that ran to hundreds of thousand of dollars – a mere drop in his overflowing bucket of wealth generated by *Peanuts* comic strips, books, videos, television specials, and licensed merchandise. Schulz retired at the end of 1999 after fifty years of drawing Snoopy cartoons. Eerily, his death coincided with the publication of his very last work. When Charlie Brown died, so did his corporeal embodiment.

The December Santa Rosa show offered employment for professional skaters who had not made the cut for Dick Button's exclusive and concurrent World Professional Championships in Landover (recently relocated to Washington, D.C.), with its handful of elite competitors. At least that was true for me. My last Landover appearance was in December 1987. The next year Brian Orser and Brian Boitano, fresh from the Olympics, supplanted Norbert Schramm and me in the field of just four men.

If Dick Button didn't want you any more, Santa Rosa was a viable alternative, although you really had to dance for your money. There were two shows a day over a period of nearly three weeks rather than only two performances at Landover.

The Second Border Skirmish

Somehow I left for Santa Rosa without a U.S. work visa. Two days before the show was to open, I was involved in another border incident with a perceptive customs official as I was about to change planes for my second flight.

His question was simple enough: "Why are you going to California?"

I probably should have said, "I am going to skate in an ice show in Santa Rosa," but I didn't want him to know that I would be working without the correct papers. Instead I told the agent, "I am going to visit a friend."

"Who is the friend?"

I had cleverly anticipated that question. The friend I cited was a woman I had met in San Miguel de Allende, my second home high in the mountains of central Mexico. She had invited me to stay at her house in Santa Rosa during the run of the show, although I had no intention of doing so.

"Where does she live?"

That was the moment at which I recalled Sir Walter Scott's observation, "O, what a tangled web we weave, When first we practice to deceive." Oddly, I did not know my friend's phone number. I did not know her address. Nor did I have a return plane ticket for Toronto, because I was planning to fly straight from California to Garmisch-Partenkirchen, Germany, to perform in a New Year's Eve special.

"Come with me."

The customs official was barking up the wrong side of the right tree. He knew that something did not add up, but he couldn't quite analyse the math. My story was that my friend would pick me up at the airport, obviating my need to know her address and telephone number. Then we would drive together all the way to San Miguel de Allende (considerably more than one thousand miles, I imagine), where I owned a house.

The official could not come to terms with that scenario, especially since I had a pair of skates with me, a bag of make-up that included false eyelashes, and a dozen glittering costumes.

Customs officers make you dance a very agile jig. As your plane is boarding and ready to taxi, you are still in their holding tank, but if you evidence any impatience, you will be there all day. I was careful not to show my irritation. Luckily I was released. I am not sure why, since even I did not believe my far-fetched story.

Mind Your Manners

I was met at the San Francisco airport by Cory Gilman, an intimate friend of Laurence Owen, a celebrated artistic skater who died in a 1961 plane crash en route to the Worlds at Prague, Czechoslovakia.

Cory's and Laurence's mothers had been friends, and the girls had skated together in Boston, developing their own special bond. I

The Santa Rosa cast, standing, from left to right: Cassandra Litz,
Eric Harryman, Toller, Nicole Lesh, unidentified, Terry Pagano.
Front row: Jill Schulz, Karen Kresge, Kimberly Navarro, Paige Carroll,
Jerod Randolph, Christopher Nolan. Photo courtesy of Karen M. Kresge

had always wished that I could have known Laurence Owen, so the trip to Santa Rosa passed in fascinating conversation. I asked Cory if I could read the letters that Laurence had sent to her in the course of their years as young friends. She kindly let me do that during my time in California.

The Santa Rosa show was mounted on a reduced ice surface. The surrounding set was like a glamorous Parisian nightclub with tables on three sides and a curtain across the fourth. Every detail was carried out to perfection. Thanks to Charles Schulz's bank account and enthusiasm, the rink even housed a costume department.

The principal skaters, who (besides me) included Cindy Stuart, Robin Cousins, and Terry Pagano and Tony Paul, a talented adagio team, were lodged at a motel. Normally I do not like motels, but it was a very California place to be. Then we went to work. Truly I had not laboured that hard for years. After breakfast at the motel each morning, we sauntered to the rink for an intense, competitive practice. Then we began preparations for the first show. We were required to be at the arena each day between approximately 11 A.M. and 11 P.M. That was difficult. Fortunately Karen Kresge kept the champagne chilled and ready for thirsty performers.

At the time, I was positively intoxicated by Fahrenheit cologne. I sprayed it on liberally before my first number and asphyxiated the entire cast of "Snoopy's Scottish Games." The skaters came off the ice in their kilts, accompanied by the wail of bagpipes, just as I whooshed out of my dressing room in an aromatic Fahrenheit haze.

Charles Schulz took great pleasure in arriving between the first and second shows in order to dine with the stars. That sounds innocent enough unless you knew Charles Schulz and his rules governing dinner conversation. If one did not adhere to them, I was told, one might fly out the door. I wanted to ensure that my two-and-one-half-week run remained intact, so I studied those rules most diligently.

One was never to mention Walt Disney, the man who had rejected Snoopy. Out the door!

One was never to encroach on forbidden creative territory by proposing potential scenarios for Snoopy and his pals. Instant dismissal!

One was never to suggest adding a new character to the *Peanuts* gang. Off with your head!

Above all, Garfield the cat was taboo. Alluding to Garfield, Snoopy's feline arch-rival, was the very worst thing that anyone could do.

I later learned that it was particularly helpful in understanding Charles Schulz, the man, to realize that he *was* Charlie Brown.

The Toller Cranston Interpretive Competition

The show that year was phenomenal. The headliners were Robin Cousins and I, although Robin outranked me in pedigree and took his bows last at the finale. We were joined by Cindy Stuart (magnificently choreographed by Jamie Isley to Debussy's *Rêverie*); Doug Mattis; and Christopher Nolan, another Canadian without a work visa – all splendid performers and genuine artists. The chorus consisted of artistic wannabes, so we ended up performing for each other.

As a patriarch of skating, an elder statesman, I have always felt an obligation to entertain and enlighten the troops. I realized that Santa Rosa was the perfect setting for the Toller Cranston Interpretive Competition. First, it would break the tedium of the weeks of two-show days. Second, that cast was unique in its passion for the artistic side of the sport. I thought that it would be thrilling for the relative unknowns to compete against, and potentially defeat, Olympic medallists such as Robin and me.

I drew up a list of rules and posted it on the wall. Anyone who wanted to participate in the two-night event was welcome. It would take place after the second show of the day. Male and female skaters would compete in the same field, each skating to the same obscure piece of music (which Karen and I selected for the first night). Everyone would dress in black and perform under full theatrical lighting. I would donate original drawings to the top three and lithographs to the rest of the competitors.

The event almost didn't take place. Charles Schulz, dressed in his Charlie Brown hat, looked at the poster and objected with a perfectly straight face.

"But somebody might lose!"

That remark stunned me. I carefully explained to Mr. Schulz that everyone would win at least a lithograph, and the event was more a creative skating exercise than a competition.

The thing that disappointed me most was that, for reasons that I have not been able to precisely determine, Robin Cousins did not want to skate. I thought that it would be wonderful for former chorus skaters in their rocking chairs to be able to tell their grandchildren, "I competed against Robin Cousins." Cindy Stuart, who was suffering from the flu on the first night of competition, believes that Robin may have been under the weather as well. In any case, two pivotal skaters who could have taught the cast a great deal did not participate. Nor did Snoopy. I will have more to say about the beagle later.

Many others turned out on the first night: Karen Kresge, Doug Mattis, Christopher Nolan, Terry Pagano, Cassandra Litz, Jill Schulz, Kimberly Navarro, Paige Carroll, Jerod Randolph, Eric Harryman, and Nicole Lesh. Each contestant was allowed to watch the others interpret two and one-half minutes of music. We drew for skating order. The judges I chose for the first night ranged from the wardrobe mistress and the Zamboni driver to Jo Cousins, Robin's mother.

By the second or third skater, the pot was boiling. The lesson to be learned was that technique was incidental to passion. Although everyone tried hard to do a Toller Cranston imitation, when the results were tabulated the real Toller Cranston placed a convincing fifth. Doug Mattis was so phenomenal in his interpretation that had he competed at Landover that year against Brian Boitano, Brian Orser, Paul Wylie, and Victor Petrenko, he would have left them all in the dust. The audience was hypnotized. Doug won, and I trundled off to my motel to sip something a hirsute truck driver had recommended to me: decaffeinated peppermint tea – only in California!

The next night even Charles Schulz himself showed up for the final round. Robin and Cindy could not skate because they hadn't previously qualified, but they took it upon themselves to choose music and judges.

They spliced two unusual cuts, one from Vangelis's *Mask* album and one from the movie soundtrack of *Wings of Desire*, in an attempt to challenge the competitors' ingenuity. Cindy also served as a judge, along with Rick Samuels and Lorene D'Adam.

I realized that I had made a fundamental mistake the night before by interpreting the music in skating vocabulary, not in emotion. When my turn came, I announced to the audience exactly what my second interpretation would represent. A sane person (me) would be followed on the street, then accosted and forced into a mental institution. There was a loud clang in the music that I imagined as the gates closing behind me, sealing me in. Then the abnormal would become normal. Eventually I, too, would go insane.

I have had hundreds of skating experiences all over the world, sometimes in front of audiences of thousands, sometimes on live television. Rarely have I entered what I think of as the fourth dimension, a dimension without time, space, and sound. That night I definitely entered the fourth dimension. Others might call it an out-of-body experience, but I view the phenomenon as internal. I entered my soul.

I ended my interpretation by sliding on my back under the curtain with my legs in the air like a dead housefly. I remember lying there, partially under the Zamboni, as though I had just awakened from anesthesia. I was not at all sure where I was. I appeared from behind the curtain to a standing ovation. The applause was deafening. It was an unforgettable moment. When I distributed the awards, I didn't give myself the lithograph that I had planned to receive. I simply disqualified myself for being too brilliant.

After that, "A Christmas Portrait" lost a bit of its steam. The climax of the run had been the interpretive competition. When the final show arrived, I had little energy left. I failed to skate as well as I had hoped to.

Ode to Joy

It was someone else who hit her apogee on closing night: Joy Brown, the wardrobe mistress, a woman with a theatrical background. Joy was a butterfly who had flown too far north, an exotic specimen in a mundane habitat. She gravitated towards me right off the top, recognizing one of her own species.

Joy's particular specialty was beading headdresses, although she would happily bead anything that didn't move. For more than a decade, she constructed accessories for the Santa Rosa shows and served as a dresser for the performers.

During the two and one-half weeks of the 1992 show, Joy's apparel accelerated from moderately aberrant to completely mad. Her look relied heavily upon flowing skirts, voluminous capes, and unusual headgear. I believed that she was dressing especially for me. If she had walked down Fifty-seventh Street, New Yorkers would have applauded. In the rather bucolic bedroom community of Santa Rosa, she was viewed at best as a harmless eccentric.

In Dr. Seuss's *The 500 Hats of Bartholomew Cubbins*, each time Bartholomew takes off a hat, the one revealed beneath it is more exotic and flamboyant than the last. In the same way, Joy's appearance on each successive night became more extreme. At the final show, she wore a crown topped with burning candles.

Poor Snoopy!

Judy Schwomeyer Sladky and her now ex-husband, Jim Sladky, were famous ice dancers in their day. They placed second at the world ice-dance championship in Ljubljana, Yugoslavia, in 1970, but that was the year when Ludmila Pakhomova and Alexandr Gorshkov first dominated the scene, changing ice dancing dramatically. The good old American technical style paled in the face of Russian artistry and theatre.

At the opening of the Redwood Empire Ice Arena in 1969, Judy donned a Snoopy costume and played that role on ice for the first time – the first of thousands. During the subsequent decades, she gradually assumed Snoopy's persona. She began talking in the beagle's voice and referring to herself as though she were actually Snoopy.

Judy's 1992 run ended traumatically when Snoopy broke his leg. There was a great scene at the hospital when Judy absolutely would not allow the doctors and nurses to cut Snoopy's costume. *Snoopy wouldn't like that!* But how else would they extricate Judy and repair her genuine human broken leg? I believe that she had to be heavily sedated before someone could amputate Snoopy's furry white cloth limb.

The 1992 Santa Rosa show also marked the first time that Snoopy ever took a drink in public. When he became a trifle tipsy after drinking a root beer during the square-dance number, dozens of letters of protest arrived in the mail, proving as usual that truth is stranger than fiction.

29

Partying with the Mob

One of the best friends of my youth, a supporter from the time when I was twelve or thirteen years old, was a fellow Montreal skater of about my own age named Donna Hart.

Donna was the daughter of Mindy Hart and her husband, Bert, a Montreal real-estate tycoon of the 1960s. Donna's brother, Corey, became an international rock singer who sold ten million albums and had several number-one singles by the time he reached his mid-twenties. The Harts helped me with my early skating expenses, and I greatly appreciated their generosity.

Donna's father vacated Canada to undertake some tremendous real-estate projects in Nassau in the Bahamas. Eventually the rest of Donna's family moved to Florida, where she married a fellow Canadian, Howard Obront.

Donna and I lost contact with one another until about a decade ago when she and Howard moved from Florida to Toronto. Donna and I rekindled our friendship, and I helped her to get a job as a skating teacher at the Cricket Club.

Howard Obront's father had been involved during the 1960s in a notorious tainted-meat scandal, so the family name was well known in North America. For reasons that were not spelled out for me, he was subsequently incarcerated in a prison in Lake Placid, New York. I have never paid much attention to family reputations. I accept people based on how they treat me, and Donna and Howard scored 99 per cent in that department.

The relocation from Florida to Toronto had included Howard's brother, Allan Obront, and Allan's wife, Andrea. We all became close friends, lunching and dining together. Although I knew that the Obronts lived in luxury, I wasn't sure what they did for a living. Ignorance was utter bliss.

The Obront brothers, I subsequently learned, had become involved in telemarketing jewels to Americans. My dear friend Donna, who had always lived high on the hog, started to live even higher. That hog was enormous. Donna wore a $250,000 diamond necklace with its clasp welded shut. When I asked Howard, "Isn't it a bit ridiculous for Donna to go to Loblaw's to buy cornflakes in that necklace?" his answer stopped me in my tracks. "Well, who would ever think that it was real?"

Howard eventually abandoned the jewellery business. Brother Allan continued in telemarketing.

The Invitation

Allan Obront was perennially full of energy, with an eye out for the luxuries that money could buy. I was stirred out of my torpor one day in the early 1990s, a black period in my life, when a mile-long limousine arrived at my door. The chauffeur hand-delivered an invitation topped with white orchids. Would my guest and I be so kind as to grace with our presence Andrea's surprise birthday party? The event was to take place in a specially rented loft on Adelaide Street. *Répondez, s'il vous plaît.*

Knowing that the party would be one of the supreme extravaganzas of all time, I ran to the telephone to invite my guest. I chose Janice Kussner for the honour. She and I had skated with Donna Hart at the Town of Mount Royal arena. It would be fun to bring that circle to a close.

I also took it upon myself, though I know that it was gauche, to invite two additional guests: my old friend Thom Hayim, and a good friend of Donna Hart, a society writer for the *Toronto Sun* named Barbara Kingstone.

The four of us met on the night of the party at my house on Pembroke Street. We had drinks and discussed our party strategy. There was great anticipation. Normally we would have decried any appearance of social and economic excess, but as Elizabeth Taylor said about oversized diamonds, they are totally vulgar unless you are wearing them yourself.

Janice had arrived in an understated faux Chanel suit. Barbara, a savvy international woman, was chic as usual. Thom's attire was nondescript. That was perfectly fine. I made up for both of us by wearing a Michael Jackson-style grand hussar jacket purchased at a Toronto flea market. In my case, I believed that overstatement was what would be expected. I lashed ten silver belts around my waist.

Keep Your Eye on the Exit

Janice, Barbara, Thom, and I arrived in a taxi. That was a faux pas right out of the starting gate. The valet was miffed that we had no Mercedes for him to park.

We ascended in the elevator and entered what we discovered was normally a dance studio with labyrinthine chambers, all rather sparse. Each room offered a particular style of cuisine. One chamber contained a sushi bar presided over by Japanese chefs. A second featured a seafood bar with seafood chefs. The third contained an Italian bar attended by Italian chefs. French chefs presided over the dessert bar laden with pastries. In each room a live band reflected the character of the fare being served.

The guests were elaborately dressed, mostly in black. Andrea Obront arrived in haute couture: a short, sleeveless black satin dress splotched with huge fake jewels. Someone panted in my ear, "The latest from Versace!"

The lighting was unnaturally bright, and I soon realized why. At every turn in the labyrinth, someone videotaped the proceedings. Each time the cameras rolled, guests assumed artificial body language and behaviour. We all comported ourselves like animated catalogue mannequins. Dancing instantly triggered the lights, which in turn triggered more artificiality and cooled any spontaneous ardour.

I joked to Barbara Kingstone that we ought to keep an eye on the exit just in case a police raid occurred. Our plan was to consume as much lobster, oysters, pasta, sushi, and anything else that we could stuff into our salivating mouths, then dash for the door as quickly as we could. Hit and run. In one hour, we had eaten our fill.

"Let's use the fire exit," I suggested. "We don't want to be in the elevator when the police arrive."

We scampered out the fire door and onto the street, out of view of the supercilious valet parking attendants. Then we hailed a cab going in the opposite direction.

The Party's Over

There is an old Chinese proverb that maintains, "No feast lasts forever." The Obronts' feast came to an abrupt end in 1994 when the Royal Canadian Mounted Police, the Metropolitan Toronto Police fraud squad, the U.S. Federal Trade Commission, and the U.S. Postal Inspection Service concluded a joint undercover investigation. A web of individuals and corporations, mostly from the Toronto area, had systematically defrauded American gem speculators by offering to represent and sell the gems in the Americans' collections, then duping buyers with inferior stones. Allan and his telemarketing company had been a small cog in a very large machine.

A federal grand jury in Harrisburg, Pennsylvania, handed down dozens of indictments. The charges included wire and mail fraud and conspiracy to commit fraud. According to the *Hamilton Spectator*, an industry watchdog agency named Toronto the "gem scam capital of the world." Approximately one thousand victims had been bilked of an estimated $48 million.

Before his trial, I met a much-subdued Allan Obront at a Corey Hart concert. Although the scandal had been played up in all the newspapers, Allan, in true Bill Clinton fashion, had ventured out in public with his head held high.

I shared a few words with Allan at that concert. With his slightly bulging blue eyes full of wonderment and childlike amazement, he explained, "It is all a mistake. The detectives don't know what they are doing. I'll get off. Don't worry." He refused to acknowledge the inevitable. Andrea, living in her own pink and purple jewel-studded world, concurred that the indictment had been nothing but a bureaucratic slip-up.

Allan Obront was convicted and sentenced to eight months in jail. The story made front-page news in the *Toronto Sun*, the *Toronto Star*, and the *Ottawa Citizen*.

The fantasy existence that Allan had lived was not too different from one that I once enjoyed, although his was on a much more affluent level. Interestingly, though, his bottom line was the same as my own. We both wanted to be loved by others. We wanted to be respected and appreciated. What Allan did not know – what I had already learned – was that extreme largesse only turns other people against you in the long run.

It would be interesting to know how many of the guests who consumed Allan's lobster, sushi, and champagne subsequently visited him in jail. I suspect that few, if any, were sufficiently grateful or solicitous to make that uncomfortable pilgrimage in the name of friendship. I know that I did not.

30

Too Many Georgias

Earning one's livelihood as an artist requires two antithetical qualities: a suspicious nature and the willingness to take enormous leaps of faith.

In the spring of 1994, at the very moment when I was emerging from the shell shock that accompanied the dénouement of my CBC lawsuit, I agreed through my trusty friend and art agent Paul LaPointe to mount an exhibition in Vancouver at the Harrington Gallery on Georgia Street. With a bit of due diligence, Paul learned that the gallery was legitimate, enjoyed a good reputation, and occupied an excellent location. We discovered a little later that the Harrington Gallery had been, in fact, all that it purported to be, but that it had changed hands.

The new owners were Terry and Georgia (like Georgia Street) Tremaine. Paul sent mountains of artwork to them in huge crates at great expense on Canadian Pacific. I arrived with a portfolio of loose drawings. Terry Tremaine met me at the airport. He was a weedy-looking guy close to my own age with an air of trying to recapture a misspent youth. There was a whiff of hippie about him. His hair was rather long, and he wore casual pants, a sweater, and moccasins.

At the Harrington Gallery. Photo by Jim Harrison

Terry was chirpy and cheery. I wanted to dispel any preconceptions that I was a temperamental artist, so we chirped away at each other, picked up my luggage, and drove to the Georgia Hotel on Georgia Street. The Georgias were starting to pile up.

The owner of the hotel was a friend, so I was given a lovely room at an attractive price. Then I sauntered to the gallery and was happily surprised. It appeared to be a high-quality gallery, my work had arrived safely, and Georgia (a peppy, middle-aged blonde who could have been a distant relation of actress and celebrity Ann Jillian) seemed competent and upbeat.

"Leave the hanging of the show to me," she said. Although I virtually never relinquish control of the hanging of a show, I allowed myself, for once, to go with the flow.

I hired Paul Douglas, an ex-skater and long-term friend, as a cover for publicity and interviews in the event that the Tremaines did not come through. Paul is a smart, groovy guy who certainly had his finger on the pulses of the trendiest residents of Vancouver. Better to be safe than sorry.

Paul began to get a different slant on the situation. The gallery and the Tremaines that I had seen were not at all the gallery and the Tremaines that Paul Douglas informed me about. Paul reported that when Georgia spoke to him, she was curt, rude, nervous, arrogant, and did not want our help. There was a tiny little rain cloud in my sky.

I agreed to do as many interviews as I could. To date I do not believe that I have ever done as many for a single show. The opening came and went. It dawned upon me that, had Paul Douglas not invited the trendy people of Vancouver, I would have been sorely disappointed at the turnout. The Tremaines themselves and the Harrington Gallery accounted for little more than a fifth of the attendance.

I Smell Trouble

There were minor sales. The show went on and on. It was certainly well attended over the long haul. With another batch of drawings that I sent from Toronto after the opening, total sales, on paper, came to slightly under $30,000. Then the trouble started.

Paul LaPointe and I both tried at various times to contact the gallery to arrange for the payment of our share of the proceeds – without success. I told Paul, "I have a long, pointed nose, and I smell smoke." Paul assured me that I was imagining things. If I stuck by him, in one month's time (according to the contract) we would be paid.

A month after the exhibition closed, I happened to be in Vancouver with Stars on Ice. I had the afternoon free before an evening performance at the Coliseum. I tried never to mix my two careers. I did not want trouble in the painting department to upset my skating performance. Nevertheless I went to the Harrington Gallery and announced that I was there to pick up Paul's and my cheque (that had been due on the previous day).

Georgia waffled. Finally she simply said, "Look, I can write you a cheque for any amount you want. You can receive a cheque that bounces or no cheque at all. Which do you want?"

"You can't do this to us," I protested. "You have to pay us something."

She became vitriolic. Suddenly, she was the harridan Paul Douglas had described. I was upset, but I did not raise my voice. I simply said as calmly as I could, "Either you will pay me, or you will have a surprise that you will not like at all. I can step to the media and essentially destroy your gallery."

She replied, in essence, "Go ahead. I couldn't care less."

I skated that night, and I did worry a bit. Then I went back to Toronto, because the Stars on Ice tour had ended, and told Paul LaPointe, "Look, this is real trouble."

Paul has a much softer touch than I. He had accepted two post-dated cheques. Then Murphy's Law kicked in. The bank holding the two cheques tried to cash the one with the later date – at which point the Tremaines put a stop on both.

With Paul LaPointe, a good friend and personal art dealer.
Photo by Andrew M. Tourigny

Paul and I contacted a high-priced lawyer in Vancouver, who
phoned me several times in Mexico. The lawyer appeared to be far
more interested in learning about the joys of San Miguel de Allende
than in my lawsuit. He kept asking how the weather was, and was it
truly as beautiful there as everyone said it was?

I telephoned Paul LaPointe and told him, "Get that idiot in the
gallery. While it is still afloat, while there is still a chance, we might
be paid at least part of what we are owed." Paul backed down, the
lawyer impounded an empty bank account, and within several
weeks the gallery had closed its doors.

Paul and I were able to retrieve my unsold paintings at our
own expense – severely damaged. The Tremaines had not used a
professional packer. With regard to the many paintings that were
sold during the show (embarrassingly, many to friends of mine in

Vancouver), I never saw them again, and I didn't earn a penny from their sale.

Aries's Revenge

However, in true Aries style, I did what I had threatened to do. I turned a negative into a positive. I phoned every newspaper in Vancouver, every television station, and told the reporters exactly what had happened. That made big news.

As a result of my interviews, many artists came out of the woodwork with similar stories. The Tremaines owed some $500,000 to various artists. One of them, John Sund, phoned me. We engaged in an impassioned discussion. The Tremaines had pocketed the entire $15,000 proceeds from the sale of one of his bronze sculptures to a collector in Toronto whom the Tremaines had refused to identify.

The point of this story is not so much "Poor little me!" Rather it is the plight of the artist in the age in which we live, and the danger of exhibiting out of town or out of province. When stories like this come to light – and they are all too prevalent – they frighten artists and prevent them from taking chances. In a way, that influences the entire national art scene. It restricts artists to exhibiting in their own areas, and that produces a domino effect. Artists run scared and gallery owners get nervous, which is deleterious to the morale and emotional stability of any artist in the country.

Ultimately, though, ignorance is worse. If artists share and publicize their negative experiences, the artistic landscape will become safer for everyone.

31

The Double-Edged Sword

Between 1991 (when I was fired by the CBC, driven to a nervous breakdown by Christopher Bowman, and led by weakness and despair into cocaine abuse) and early 1994 (when I won my lawsuit against the CBC and got my life back in order), I lived in a condition akin to suspended animation. At times I was able to rally and take on skating jobs. At other times I foundered in a dank, dark hole. It was extremely important to me during that low period to honour my obligations and avoid disappointing people – especially myself.

In the early 1990s, I received a call from Thom Hayim, asking me to participate in an AIDS benefit that was to take place at the Maurice Richard Arena in Montreal. I agreed.

Meanwhile, IMG wanted to book me for a tree-lighting ceremony and ice show in Nathan Phillips Square at Toronto's City Hall. I agreed to do that as well. Only days before the two events, with advertising complete for both, it dawned upon me that they were scheduled for the same evening.

I phoned Thom in a panic and explained my dilemma, suggesting that the Montreal benefit go on without me.

"You can't do this to me," Thom protested, "especially with Cornelia Molson as the chair of the organizing committee."

I tried a similar approach with the Toronto organizers, but I could not wiggle out of either obligation.

Mrs. Molson made extraordinary arrangements to accommodate me. I would skate three outdoor shows in Nathan Phillips Square, scurry away before the last finale, jump into a limousine, and fly to Montreal in a private plane. Everything was timed to the second.

After my third Toronto performance, I ran off the ice in a white spandex costume, neckline cut to the navel, rhinestones and stars reflecting the moonlight from my chest and backside. I bolted through the crowd of spectators, grabbed my coat and the skate bag that contained a change of clothes, and ran – in skates and guards – to the waiting car. Kurt Browning, Barbara Underhill, and Paul Martini stood with their mouths agape as I dashed away.

Shoeless in Toronto

In the car en route to the Toronto Island Airport, I realized that I didn't have my shoes. They were still in the warm-up trailer at Nathan Phillips Square, and it was too late to retrieve them. I boarded the ferry for the Toronto Island Airport in my skates, spandex costume, and full make-up while a chauffeur walked beside me with my skate bag.

A car met me on the opposite shore and whooshed me to a tiny private jet. By then, my frozen feet had fallen asleep. As I flew from Toronto to Montreal, the seconds ticked away. I looked at my watch and realized that the AIDS benefit had already begun.

The plane landed at a private airport in greater Montreal. I ran through the terminal in full regalia like a demented superhero. I threw myself into a waiting limousine, my legs now asleep from the ankles to the knees. The chauffeur swerved dramatically into traffic and careened down the highway.

I ran panting into the Maurice Richard Arena just in time to see the end of the show's finale. As the crowd drained away, I demanded my music and skated a feeble performance for anyone who would stop and turn around in the aisle to watch me.

When I finally arrived backstage, I remember staring into the bewildered eyes of Isabelle Brasseur and Lloyd Eisler. I removed my make-up and costume, put on my street clothes, and quietly vanished wearing borrowed shoes.

When I reached my hotel, I made some furtive phone calls. Then I overdosed on cocaine as never before. My feet didn't touch the ice again for six months.

32

The Ice Princess

In December 1994, I broke my leg before a skating performance in Vail, Colorado. A difficult period ensued. I was off the ice show circuit and out of the loop. I had, at least for the moment, outlived my usefulness. I was prepared, with IMG's encouragement, to call it a day and launch the next (non-skating) chapter of my life. However, as vulnerable and unsure of myself as I felt, I was not at all certain that those who proffered advice were correct in their opinions, or even that they had my best interests at heart.

The Jolly Green Giant Goes to Germany

During the rehabilitation period, I admit, I did absolutely nothing to improve my situation. I let my leg heal in its own good time. I recognized that the injury was serious and that the chance of regaining my position in skating was remote. Still, throughout my career, everything had gone counter to the norm. When IMG asked me to accept a non-skating role in Katarina Witt's television movie *The Ice Princess*, being filmed in Berlin, I said yes without first

Katarina Witt. Photo courtesy of IMG

wondering whether I would be able to do what was expected of me.

Real movie stars might have said, "Send the script over. I will see if I'm interested." That is what a professional would do.

Amateurs agree to anything on the spot. I signed the contract. Then I read the script and got cold feet.

When I realized that the scenario was inane, my ardour for becoming a movie star chilled dramatically. The story line was an adaptation of the plot of *Cinderella*. Katarina was cast in the lead role, Ella. Rosalynn Sumners,[*] a U.S. and world champion with whom I had performed in Stars on Ice, played Katja, a plotter in the enemy camp and Katarina's romantic rival for the prince's affections. As Kraftstein, the evil head of police, I had two lines. One of them was particularly brilliant: "Good idea, Katja." That was how I was going to launch myself to stardom.

On the day I left Toronto for Berlin, I may have overdressed. I wore a pair of shimmering, silky forest-green pants, a Paddy-green Armani blazer, an emerald-green silk shirt from my Hong Kong days, and an acid-green satin tie. Although I do not believe that my underwear was green, the Jolly Green Giant could not have competed with me with respect to verdure.

A young German driver picked me up at the Berlin airport. He later drove me to and from the set on a regular basis, and we became friends. Rosalynn christened him Eyelashes, though his real name was Holgar. On that first day he drove me straight through the gates of Studio Babelsburg, where Marlene Dietrich had filmed *The Blue Angel* and so many other famous movies.

The Marlene Dietrich Stage was in a wooded area some twenty-five minutes outside Berlin in a prisonlike, communist-grey compound of sound studios, each with myriad dressing rooms and labyrinthine passages. The *Ice Princess* set itself was splendid: an outdoor pond surrounded by a forest. The Germans were so precise in their detail that they had individually wired dried leaves onto artificial tree branches. At the far end of the woodland pond was a

---

* Rosalynn Sumners was the U.S. ladies' champion in 1982, 1983, and 1984. She won the world title in 1983 and finished second behind Katarina Witt at the 1984 Olympics in Sarajevo, Yugoslavia.

wonderful rendering of the façade of a castle, with windows that lit up to reveal the outlines of antique furniture.

When I arrived, Katarina Witt was filming a woodland dance with the local peasants. I felt ridiculous in my Jolly Green Giant finery. Grunge was obviously the order of the day.

The director, Danny Huston, son of John Huston and half-brother of Anjelica, walked to where I was standing and shook my hand. He flashed a boyish smile and exhibited a brand of charm that devastated women. I do not think that it is too indiscreet to mention that Katarina was having a torrid affair with him. Flirtations habitually arise on film sets simply because those are closed, controlled societies. The rest of the world seems to fade into obscurity.

I thanked Katarina for inviting me to participate in *The Ice Princess*. She and she alone had chosen me for the role and had given me the opportunity to resume my career. She was gracious throughout the three weeks of filming on the rare occasions when I saw her, but each of us adhered to an independent schedule.

Action?

My foray into the film world began in the way I had most feared: *So glad to have you here. We'll give you your first call in three days.* That feast-or-famine style of scheduling, so typical of the film universe, drove Rosalynn and me completely insane. We valued the free time available to us in the summer, and we didn't like to be unproductive for days on end.

Rosalynn and I were bored after a day and one-half spent strolling the Kurfürstendamm looking at the shops. We did discover one little hot spot of activity: an encampment of hunger-striking Turkish dissidents. Rosalynn didn't understand why I was drawn to the scene time after time. What she did not know was that the entire Turkish encampment was rife with drugs. Although I remained aloof from the entrepreneurial action, making no purchases, I was hypnotized watching the behind-the-scenes machinations.

When I wasn't busy on the set, I spun out my time in tourist activities. I visited the famous Egyptian Museum, the city museum, the zoo, and the aquarium, all within walking distance. Rosalynn accompanied me to the aquarium, a visit that ultimately affected my painting. I was intrigued by the strange, amoebalike creatures, the miniature lace sea anemones, that danced around in their glass tanks like characters in *Fantasia*.

My favourite spot in Berlin was Schloß Charlottenburg, the residence of King Frederick the Great of Prussia. I wandered through the castle and stumbled into the ballroom. That genuine *Cinderella* interior dazzled me with its walls of pistachio-green damask. Each baroque panel was trimmed in gold. The domed ceiling (with three enormous chandeliers) glowed in strawberry pink. I do not believe that I had ever before seen a grand interior in exactly that colour scheme. How audacious the room must have seemed at the time it was decorated.

On days when we were called to the set, we ate breakfast at the hotel, arrived at the studio at 7:00 A.M., and went straight to the wardrobe department. The costumes had been borrowed from a German television movie about Catherine the Great, filmed at nearby Sans Souci, Frederick the Great's summer palace. Those incredible clothes were worth millions of dollars. My costume consisted of a tremendous hat with a huge feather, a fabulous black velvet cloak with a silver lining, and velvet pants. I was stuck in that outfit for ten or twelve hours a day.

Great and famous actors had been flown to Berlin, one from Gibraltar, where he had been making a fabulously expensive film with Geena Davis. A fine classical actor, George Murcell, dressed in bishop's drag to deliver a single line. Vernon Dobtcheff as the chancellor, a Shakespearean actor and Harvard graduate, had a grand total of three lines. That was my indoctrination into the absurdities of the film world.

In Katarina's woodland scene, the woodcutter's tame falcon was supposed to fly above a certain hut on command. When it came time for the falcon to perform, it did a 180° flip on its perch and hung upside down, ripped out of its mind on some sort of sedative.

Rosalynn had been cast as a giddy, brainless young woman whose manipulative sister tried to persuade her to marry the prince so that Ella from the forest would be left out in the cold. Every time the camera stopped rolling, the make-up crew further dishevelled Rosalynn's wig until the hair eventually unravelled.

I was on the bad-guy side as well. The first thing that I was called upon to do was to emerge from the bushes where I was spying on the prince and Ella and produce a grimace that could turn them both to ice. When my big moment arrived, my heart thumped. I skulked out of the bushes, delivered the grimace, turned with a flick of my cape, and walked away. There was a great round of applause and cries of "That was perfect! Wonderful! Great!"

Perhaps such a flattering reaction would have inflated an actor's ego, but for a skater it was all rather ridiculous. Please applaud if I give birth to a quad, not if I produce a mean look, turn on my heel, and leave the scene. I assured everyone, "I have been practising that look for the last forty-eight years. It really came quite naturally to me."

It was vital to be on friendly terms with the director and the cameramen. With three hundred people in the crowd scenes, getting a close-up shot was like winning the lottery. I became an intimate friend of the head cameraman, a charming Briton. I wanted very much to be discovered, so I tried hard to do everything well. In the end, I managed to be featured in several close-ups.

Back in Skates

I had not been expected to skate in the movie, but the ice was inviting, and the sound system and a stack of tapes were available during lunch hours. I slithered out of my crowd-scene costume and worked out every day. The skates felt good. My broken leg had healed. On that woodland pond, I recaptured my love of skating.

Michael Seibert and Danny Huston decided, "It is a bit ridiculous having Toller here if he is not going to skate in the film." They created a role for me, which made me very happy.

After two weeks of daily practice, the day on which I was to skate for taping dawned. I climbed into my velvet clothes and donned my plumed hat. For ten hours, I stood around and posed while crowd scenes were filmed. Finally someone said, "All right, put your skates on."

That moment was so important to me that I arrived on the scene like a volley of grapeshot. The entire cast of villagers, instead of leaving the set, stayed in full costume to watch me skate. I had decided that rather than go through the entire routine in one take, it had to be done in increments of tremendous velocity and fury. After waiting nearly a year since breaking my leg to perform once again, I jumped into my skin and caught fire, passionately executing every move in my repertoire.

Danny Huston announced, "You know, that was great. If you could just do it one more time so we can shoot it a different angle . . ."

I said, "Danny, I would love to, but I have nothing left."

It's a Wrap

One day the national press arrived to meet the cast. Because I had been well known in Germany as a skater, I thought that I would be asked a few questions. After a day of crowd scenes, I had my make-up retouched. Rosalynn, the world champion, expectantly put on her Catherine the Great wig and an elaborate costume. Along with the principal actors, we trundled off through the forest to the next sound stage in the kind of sartorial splendour that would propel us onto the covers of major German magazines. Sad to say, the reporters were interested only in Katarina. The star was everything.

That was a little sprinkle of reality for the rest of us, who were all dressed up with nowhere to go.

Seven months later, while staying in Germany with Norbert Schramm, I finally saw a telecast of *The Ice Princess*. The editors had used most of my work, but I realized that I came across as a caricature. My entire skating education had been about high theatre. For that particular role as Kraftstein, the exaggeration was fine, but I could never hope to perform naturally in front of a camera.

As Norbert and I watched intently, the *coup de grâce* was delivered. When it was time for my pathetically sparse spoken lines, I realized that a guttural German voice had been dubbed over my mellifluous Canadian tones.

III

Coming to Terms with Life, Death, and Retirement

Previous page: On Queen Street West, Toronto, 1996.

33

IMG and Me

Without rehashing the tales of woe told in *Zero Tollerance*, suffice it to say that I went through the wars in terms of early professional career management. Once my own theatrical ice show had collapsed, and with it my relationship with my manager, Elva Oglanby, I decided to look for more conventional representation.

During my German experience with Holiday on Ice at the end of 1978, I was living in a double apartment with a friend and admirer, the "Baroness" von Wolf, in the suburbs of Munich. She lived upstairs and I lived downstairs.

However, I had developed a crush on someone, which was highly unusual for me. I have been an emotional iceberg for my entire life, but one little spot of ice melted while I was in Munich, and I enjoyed a short flirtation with a German-Swiss actor. The situation was tricky. I didn't want the actor to know about the Baroness von Wolf, nor did I want the Baroness von Wolf to find out about the actor (although somehow she did).

So I skated all day and well into the night, returned to the baroness for a cosy little session of chit-chat over a very late supper, then went to bed. When I was sure that the baroness wouldn't notice, I sneaked out into the night in pursuit of a taxi that would

Performing "Les Bayadères" at Stars on Ice – still in shape.

take me to a rendezvous with my paramour in downtown Munich. It was the first time in a long time that I had *felt* anything for anybody, so I followed my impulse.

The actor had access to a huge alpine mansion in Mondsee, a small town close to Salzburg, Austria. (Mondsee is home to the church where Julie Andrews, as Maria, was married in *The Sound of Music*.) He asked me if I wanted to spend a week there after I had fulfilled all my Holiday on Ice commitments. Following the painful demise of my show, I had embraced the enormous Holiday on Ice workload, and I was thoroughly burned out from thirteen shows a week. I said yes.

Out of the Tub and into the Fire

I was driven in a Mercedes to a huge farmhouse in the middle of the picturesque Austrian countryside and spent several days resting, eating, and enjoying civilized conversation. One evening early in the week, I was immersed in a peaceful candlelit bath. At the height of that steamy bliss, the telephone rang and shattered my tranquillity. Nobody knew that the actor and I were there, we thought, so we both ignored the phone, even when it rang twenty times. Five minutes later, it rang another twenty times. On the third series of rings, my friend answered.

"It's for you," he said.

It was the baroness. She informed me that I had to phone my elderly socialite friend, Ruth Dubonnet, in New York City. I did so. Ruth, who knew that I had been looking for an agent, told me urgently that people at International Management Group, IMG, a highly reputable and well-known sports management agency, wanted to meet with me. Ruth, in her usual peremptory manner, insisted that I get on a plane immediately.

My once-in-a-lifetime idyll was destroyed.

The next morning I was driven from Salzburg to Munich, where I got on a plane and flew to New York. Ruth met me in a limousine at Kennedy Airport. She then informed me that she had set up the meeting for the following week.

I was highly irate. Instead of lazily indulging myself in the Austrian farmhouse, I had to spend an entire week as a captive in Ruth's huge brownstone at 43 West Sixty-third Street, functioning as her confidant and companion, while I waited for Friday to roll around. Then I would meet with IMG, the great wizards in the sky, who would propel me into the upper stratosphere of fame, wealth, and opportunity.

Signing on the Dotted Line

On the morning of my meeting with IMG, I went to a fortuneteller. She was a rather young, bland, barefoot-in-the-kitchen sort of woman, yet I sensed that she was the real thing: that is to say, reliably connected to the other world. She told me that I was approaching an extremely positive time in my life. All the planets were aligned. For the next six months, anything on which I placed my signature would pay out in gold.

My business meeting took place at the Box Tree Grill on East Forty-ninth Street. It was all very chi-chi and chic. I am not sure how closely I listened to Michael Halstead, the IMG representative. All I was interested in, above and beyond the excellent food, was signing the paper that would start my millions rolling in.

A printed contract arrived at Ruth's brownstone a day or two thereafter. I did not read it. My eyes beamed in on the signature line. The gist of the document, as it was explained to me, was that the agents at IMG were to aggressively pursue professional opportunities for me. Their services would cost me 25 per cent of my salary. In light of my earlier unfortunate experience with Toller Cranston's The Ice Show, I didn't mind paying a lot as long as I could trust the people in charge.

The Horses Are on the Track

Michael Halstead, an IMG vice-president, was Ivy League good-looking, intelligent, ambitious, and compassionate. He was a cut above the typical businessman. Moreover he was the perfect prototype, as I deduced some years later, for what IMG sought in upper management. IMG liked its top brass to be products from the right schools. Its ideal executives offered all-American good looks and sports backgrounds. I had the sense that I was entering a very high-priced milieu.

Mark McCormack had founded the agency with one client, Arnold Palmer, and was very successful with golfers and tennis players. In terms of skaters, the agency had managed one of the best, Janet Lynn, during the 1970s. The first thing that my new representatives did was negotiate a deal for me to skate for three months in Paris. I made $5,000 a week. That $5,000 had to cover apartment rental, food, transportation, and everything else, but I was perfectly happy.

I lived on the Left Bank. It was thick with *antiquaires*, so I was forever phoning IMG to ask for money with which to acquire more antique *objets d'art*. With my lavish lifestyle in the Seventh Arrondissement in a swanky apartment staffed by a full-time maid, and with a $6,000 dental bill due during the last week of my Parisian experience, I doubt that I left the City of Light with any money at all in my account.

There were only about four major stars of the ice at the time: Peggy Fleming, John Curry, Dorothy Hamill, and me, with Robin Cousins waiting in the wings. What I lacked in golden Olympic credentials, I made up for with my international reputation. JoJo Starbuck and Ken Shelley, lesser gods, were not quite of the same calibre or credentials but were well known in the United States.

I was among IMG's first skating clients, but subsequently a number of other stallions joined the stable. At the time of the 1984 Olympics, I had a call from Mr. Carruthers, father of American champions and Sarajevo competitors Peter and Kitty. Mr. Carruthers told me that IMG had been courting his son and daughter. How did I feel about the agency? I remember thinking that I didn't really want any other horses in the barn. Regrettably I was quite curt with Mr. Carruthers, and later somewhat flabbergasted at Peter and Kitty's silver-medal success. They had caught the momentum, thanks in part to the many Americans in the crowd.

Americans, I must say, support their own, giving their athletes the lift they need. The Carruthers' second place was virtually unprecedented in a division of the sport that was thoroughly dominated by Soviet skaters.

Nonetheless, the pairs favourites at those Olympics were Canadians Barbara Underhill and Paul Martini, whom I didn't fully appreciate until much later. They made a disastrous showing in

Sarajevo, but David Dore, now director general of the Canadian Figure Skating Association, held up a 5.8 and put them second in the short program. I was commentating at the time. So often I have been asked to go on national television to rant, rave, chastise, and spew at international judges. If the Russians are historically guilty of national bias, Canadian judges are no less so. Dore's days of judging ended that day. As for Underhill and Martini, they went on to win decisively the pairs world championship a month later in Ottawa.

Some people within the employ of IMG began to recognize that figure skating had the potential to make money. More and more skaters became clients. Within that group, I was the trusty work-horse who ran around and around the track.

I was working a lot at the time. I did anything available, including both Holiday on Ice and Ice Capades. I think that I was the first to perform on two continents virtually simultaneously, although Robin Cousins and the dance team of Torvill and Dean later followed in my footsteps. There was such a small group of big-name skaters, connected either through IMG or through agent Michael Rosenberg, president of Marco Entertainment, that we got just about every gig that came along, whether it was the World Professional Championships in Landover or a documentary filmed in China. If you weren't in one of those two stables, there was no significant work for you outside the traditional ice shows. Over the years, I had some wonderful experiences that were directly attributable to being an IMG client.

Just Show Me the Money

I read perhaps one in ten letters that arrived from IMG. The others I threw in the garbage. I simply didn't want to know about finances. Meanwhile, I overwhelmed IMG with my demands for money, so I was able to live with impunity well beyond my means.

Robert Foster, a multimillionaire whom I knew at the time, sometimes came to my black-tie dinner parties for ninety people.

"You know, Toller," he said to me once, "if somebody didn't know better, he would think that you were very rich." That, of course, fed my ego. I wasn't very rich. I just had a heavy cash flow. Whatever flowed in flowed out just as precipitously.

Meanwhile Mike Halstead left IMG to start his own agency. Jay Ogden, who had been working with Michael, became my primary manager. Today Jay Ogden is a major player in the skating world.

Shuffling towards the Exit

Every time a new champion turned professional, the old champions dropped a rung on the ladder or moved out horizontally. As the IMG fold increased with new horseflesh, the older horses, whatever their breeding, decreased in importance. I began to get the jobs that the new A group found too bothersome. I eventually moved laterally to assignments such as Winterlude. My reputation and status within the skating world were completely incidental. *This is the gig. Do you want it?* A Kristi Yamaguchi would not have dreamed of skating seven shows a day at Winterlude. By then, I had to. There was no option.

A turning point in my relationship with IMG occurred in Vail, Colorado, where I trained with the cast of Symphony on Ice before we went on to open in San Diego, California. It was the summer after the 1988 Calgary Olympics. All of a sudden, considerations such as billing and position in the program assumed new importance. It dawned upon me that I had to fight for my status. Being a performer, being a "star," moving with the A group, involved certain harsh realities. Even though no one discussed the fact, such people were perennially unsure of their relative positions. We all wanted to hold on to what we had. I may have appeared strong, aggressive, forthright, and a whole lot of other things, but I was deeply insecure about my skating ability and about performing with skaters twenty years younger than I.

Although I could not understand why, IMG had slotted Tracy Wilson and Robert McCall, brand-new Olympic bronze medallists in ice dance, above me. I flew into a rage, had a screeching fight with Jay Ogden over the questions of billing and skating order, threatened to pull out of the agency, and then ceased to speak further to Jay. I didn't feel that I could expect to compete with 1984 and 1988 Olympic silver medallist Brian Orser, another free skater and many-time Canadian champion, but I saw no comparison between my credentials and those of Wilson and McCall.

Jay arrived in San Diego, where I subjected him to extreme *froideur*. Because we skaters had all been training hard at high altitude, we performed very well – and especially me. I proved myself.

As an aside, I almost missed one of my San Diego performances. It was difficult for me to push open the curtain when I really wanted to stay backstage to watch the Olympic race televised from Seoul, Korea, between Ben Johnson and Carl Lewis. I thought about letting the audience wait the ten seconds until the race ended. Symphony on Ice just won out by a nose, but it took all the determination that I possessed.

Jay kindly began to humour me. "I will come to Dallas for the next Symphony show," he said, "and we will go out for lunch and discuss the situation." I was mollified.

Stars on Ice

A year and one-half after Scott Hamilton's 1984 Olympic win, IMG started up its own little ice show tour, originally called Scott Hamilton's America Tour and soon thereafter renamed Stars on Ice. Scott had not instantly emerged from Sarajevo as a megastar. He had won by the skin of his teeth in the face of a better free-skating performance by Brian Orser. It was only as a professional that he later developed a fabulous career, made his name, acquired numbers of fans the likes of which few people have ever enjoyed, and became the darling of America. Just after Sarajevo, however, Scott was not commercially appealing. He wasn't asked to do endorsements for toothpaste and Gatorade. The creation of the America

Tour was all about giving him a vehicle when he left Ice Capades. Within the new show's cast, Scott was on the highest rung of the ladder, but it wasn't his show.

I was on the ground floor too, along with Rosalynn Sumners, who'd switched management from Lee Mimms to IMG. She had hated her two seasons with Disney on Ice and was sliding downhill. Then she completely changed her work ethic and became one of IMG's longest-lasting and most professional skaters. The original Scott Hamilton's America Tour cast also included American ice dancers Judy Blumberg and Michael Seibert, pair Lisa Carey and Chris Harrison, ladies' singles skater Sandy Lenz, and my good Canadian friend, fellow men's singles skater Brian Pockar. Not long afterwards, the American pair of Lea Ann Miller and Bill Fauver joined the cast. Subsequently there were many additions and subtractions.

The early shows went to third-rate venues with a few second-rate cities sprinkled in. We played Burlington, Vermont, Durham, New Hampshire, and Syracuse, New York. I think that we made something in the neighborhood of $2,000 per performance, but even though I wouldn't have admitted it, the tour was the only gig in town for me, the only thing that I could do. The motel accommodations and tour buses in those early days were primitive. There was no per diem for expenses. There was no glamour. We were performing in a show that was losing money, but maybe it had a future.

For the handful of years during which I performed with Stars on Ice, I was an IMG standard. I was never in peril – at least that is what I thought – of losing my position. Inevitably, though, I reached the end of the road.

After the final performance one night in some southern U.S. state, we all went to a restaurant where IMG paid for our dinners. Hooray! In the middle of the meal, Jay Ogden stood up and gave a speech about how great I was and what a pleasure it was to have me along on the tour. He singled me out over all the other skaters.

The significance of Jay's testimonial did not dawn upon me until I received a birthday card from Lynn Plage, the Stars on Ice publicist. She congratulated me on my retirement and said that she was sorry that I would no longer be with Stars on Ice. I had really added something to the show.

After I left Stars on Ice, IMG continued to arrange work for me. In the book that chronicled my relationship with the agency, several chapters remained to be written.

34

The Varsity Drag

In 1997, the writing appeared in faint outline on the wall, indicating that my skating career was nearing its natural end. I had skated since the age of seven and had performed professionally for more than two decades. I wanted to quit before I became a parody of myself. My body was still strong, but my spirit wasn't always willing. I planned to concentrate on my painting career and spend more time in San Miguel de Allende.

IMG kindly suggested a special evening, a tribute show. Due to my own profligacy, there was not a single penny in my account, and I needed help to launch myself into the next phase of my life. In essence, I needed a retirement plan.

In August, Jay Ogden informed me that the agency was planning a televised tribute show to take place at Varsity Arena on

December 8 at 7:30 P.M. If there were net proceeds from ticket sales and television rights, I would receive a cash gift.

With the launching of *Zero Tollerance*, a work that addressed the foibles and triumphs of a life, planned for October of that year, it made sense to mark the end of something and the beginning of something else. I would have the chance to break free of the molasses of my life – professional, emotional, and drug-related – and commence the next chapter with a nest egg that would buy some paints and pay off a few bills.

In September, when I spoke to Jay on the phone, problems had arisen. "The date has been cancelled," he told me. "We really don't think that we can get the skaters, and the CBC isn't going for the concept."

I watched the bombshell as it whistled towards my doorstep, then voiced my profound disappointment.

The next time the telephone rang, it was Jay telling me, "I don't know *how* we are going to do it, but we have decided that we *will* do it."

Wendy Kane of the IMG Toronto office was chosen to mastermind the event. I submitted an outline of the premise of the show. I had discovered a young skater in Moncton whose name was Shawn Sawyer.* The story line was not about my own glorification. It was a skating lesson for the boy who reminded me so much of myself when I was very young. Throughout the evening, the skaters would perform for Shawn, then talk to him as he sat on a chair at the edge of the ice. They would proffer advice that they had gleaned over the course of their careers, in order to help him become a skater like me – or like them. He would ultimately learn that there is no one magical route to becoming a champion. Each skater finds his own way, by hook or by crook.

---

* Shawn Sawyer, a promising New Brunswick novice, placed tenth at the 1999 Canadian national championships, then won the novice title in 2000.

Just Don't Make Me Ask

IMG had a stable of international skaters who were major draws: Kurt Browning, Brian Orser, Rosalynn Sumners, Caryn Kadavy, Ekaterina Gordeeva, Isabelle Brasseur, Lloyd Eisler, and Scott Hamilton, to name a representative sample. The key to the success of the event was in assembling an appropriate cast of skaters, but there was a major problem in that regard. Many of the skaters, and maybe rightly so, wanted me to phone and invite them personally and individually: in essence, to beg them to come and skate for me. But that would have amounted to asking them to do me a favour, asking them to give me their performances free of charge so that I could receive the profits. I just couldn't make the phone calls. The skaters were baffled, and I truly could not explain to them why I behaved as I did.

Kurt Browning was particularly baffled and disturbed by the fact that I did not phone and personally invite him to perform. I understood his feelings, but I couldn't ask him. I just hoped that he would come because he wanted to.

During the weeks before the event, I had several phone calls from the agency suggesting that I should be out doing publicity. I replied, "Look, if the show were a benefit for a charitable cause, I could do that. If it were Kurt Browning's show, I could do that. But how can I, in good conscience, go on television, speak on the radio, give quotes to the newspapers, and tell everyone that they have to come to my tribute – and, by the way, I'm getting the gate as a going-away present?"

I felt somehow like a person who was paralysed, looking at his reflection in a three-way mirror with a front and a rear view, the future and the past. I couldn't take a step forward. I couldn't take a step backwards. Whatever was going to happen to me would depend on the actions of the people around me. I was so insecure that I was powerless. I didn't feel good enough about myself to take the bull by the horns and become aggressive.

As the show approached, ticket sales were so poor that the projected house had dwindled to practically nothing. IMG would have to dig into its own pockets to present me with a retirement gift.[*]

On the personal front, things turned ugly. For two weeks I could not practise. And instead of practising, I overdosed on drugs. I was just too traumatized to cope.

Getting On with It

What sometimes happens, though, is that in spite of the scum and algae on top of a pond, the water underneath runs very deep. The pure, clean water below consists of one's life experiences. I decided to drink of that water and go forward with the show.

On the day before the tribute, all the wonders of true professionalism went on display. Thanks to the lighting people, the sound people, IMG and the skaters themselves, within hours a dingy arena became the setting for a first-class Broadway show. It looked magical, incredible, and as professional as possibly could be.

I had invited two skaters who weren't big Olympic stars. (Both of them appear in *Zero Tollerance* as Great Unknowns.) First was Katherine Healy, one of the most uniquely stunning performers in the world in any medium. Second was an excellent and interesting artistic skater, Chris Nolan. They were special guests and special friends of mine.

Scott Hamilton had just gone through a bout with cancer. He must have felt quite vulnerable at the time. He looked thin and hadn't returned to his old self yet. But if there is anybody who came through in spades, it was Scott. Showing both loyalty and generosity, he came – without a phone call from me.

Jozef Sabovcik, a Czechoslovakian and European champion, an Olympic bronze medallist, and an old and good friend, came to watch the show and offer encouragement. Alas, he was ill and

---

* According to Jay Ogden, IMG in fact lost $200,000 on the show and generously dug into its corporate pockets to present a cheque to Toller for $25,000.

With Shawn Sawyer. *With Liz Manley.*

Backstage with Liz Manley and Brian Orser. Photos by Martha L. Kimball

Barbara Underhill

With Scott Hamilton

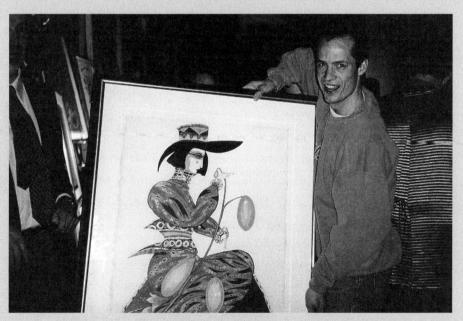

Kurt Browning displays his thank–you gift. Photos by Martha L. Kimball

couldn't skate. That put a hole in the running order, but Caryn Kadavy, a world bronze medallist and an attractive artistic skater, arrived to fill the void. Josée Chouinard, Gary Beacom, Rosalynn Sumners, Brian Orser, Kurt Browning, Elizabeth Manley, Barbara Underhill and Paul Martini arrived as well. Tracy Wilson kindly served as emcee. That wasn't a huge cast, but it was well rounded, heavyweight, and fabulously professional.

It's Showtime

On the day of the tribute, Rob Leon, a friend from Strateco Communications Group who had designed the souvenir program, drove me from my studio on Queen Street West to Varsity Arena to be sure that I actually got there in one piece. My frame of mind for several days had been such that my arrival was by no means assured.

I had brought my collaborator, Martha Kimball, into the project to help me with scripting and with the general story line of the show. I proclaimed to Rob and Martha that I really had only three requirements, and then I would be perfectly fine: a haircut, a massage, and a jockstrap. Rob arranged on the spot for a very competent hairstylist to meet me later in my room at the Inter-Continental Hotel across the street from Varsity Arena. IMG provided me with a backstage masseur. Martha, who was rather stunned by the development, did some hasty research and then made her first shopping trip for a gentleman's dance belt, size medium. Let the show begin!

Shawn Sawyer, the young boy, was exceptionally good, both in skating and in acting his part. He truly reminded me of myself, and I felt that the old Pied Piper was passing the baton to his successor, someone on the brink of a figure skating odyssey that would involve both learning and experimentation.

The most remarkable thing about the show was that, without exception, when the skaters revealed their truest characters and personalities by proffering advice to Shawn, they exactly mirrored their various skating styles. If it was Gary Beacom and his droll way of talking, of course! That is how he skates. If it was Caryn Kadavy talking like the girl next door, the girl every mother wants her son to marry, that is also how she performed. Whether the words and movement were strong, strange, or sweet, the fibre of championship stock was conspicuous in each performer.

Paul Martini and Barbara Underhill closed the show with an element of perfection that is rarely seen on the ice. During my life I have witnessed few performances more memorable than theirs.

The Final Performance?

For my final evening of skating, I had chosen to dress in three simple costumes, all in primary colours: cherry red, vicious-lemon yellow, and electric-cobalt blue. I would never have considered scripting what I was going to say to the audience before I skated the last performance of my life. I have traditionally been glib and smooth with a microphone in my hand. But when the moment came, I was vulnerable and very human.

The only words that I remember saying are these: "For your whole life as a skater, you wonder when the last performance will be and what it will be like. Well, here it is now. It is before me." Like pulling the plug in the bathtub, I lost my composure. For all my blasé, I-don't-really-give-a-damn, I'm-sick-of-skating attitudes and poses, the feelings came to me in such a rush that I was overwhelmed.

Oscar Wilde once said and this did enter my head at that moment – that we always kill the thing that we love most.[*] I had been trying for a long time, through lack of practice, lack of communication, drugs, and furious painting, to kill the very thing that I loved most of all. Suddenly that fact was crystal clear to me. And there it was now: the last time that I would perform as a skater. It is probably sad and not especially poetic that my skating wasn't

[*] "Yet each man kills the thing he loves, /By each let this be heard, /Some do it with a bitter look, /Some with a flattering word. /The coward does it with a kiss, /The brave man with a sword!" – Oscar Wilde, "Sonnet to Liberty."

remarkable that night. As fate would have it, though, it was not to be my last performance after all.

During the rehearsal, I had enjoyed the chance to chat with every single skater in the show. I talked to them in a way in which I would talk to very few people. The conversation that I particularly remember was one with Gary Beacom.[*] Gary was being prosecuted in the United States for tax evasion. I told him, "Look, you are in trouble. You haven't paid your taxes. You are a Canadian. You are in Canada. Please don't go back to the United States. Fight this from Canadian soil. You can save yourself."

Gary did go back to America, however, and four weeks later he was in jail serving a twenty-one-month sentence.

After my chat with Gary, a shard of irony pierced me. I thought, "Isn't it funny? Everyone believes that this is *my* last performance. Maybe it isn't. Maybe it is Gary Beacom's." That turned out to be true.

The house on the evening of the show was papered to the max, yet the people who were there truly enjoyed it. Rosalynn Sumners and Caryn Kadavy said that it was among the top three skating experiences of their lives.

The Aftermath

When I finished the show, I remember milling around backstage. There should have been an aura of humour, charm, and warmth. However, I realized that the evening, as great as it had been, ultimately had failed, because the production had lost money, and it was my fault. So I wasn't euphoric. I felt more as though I had just attended a special, unique, sensitive, and very sad play.

After the skating, there was an enormous reception and exhibition of my paintings at the Art Gallery of Ontario. I was galvanized

* Gary Beacom, a Canadian skater who evolved a highly original vocabulary of movement, spent the significant years of his amateur career in Brian Orser's shadow. He hit his heights as a professional show skater based in Sun Valley, Idaho.

to a certain height, but it was like buzzing Valium. I wasn't genuinely flying. I didn't even change my clothes for the reception or bother to make an entrance. I wore the same casual outfit that I had worn backstage at the rink. I was too tired and too disinterested to expend any further effort.

The evening ended in a large, rectangular gallery with a microphone that didn't work particularly well. I had offered as an incentive to give each participant a substantial oil painting from my gallery: thirty-five or forty thousand dollars' worth of paintings. I tried to get the skaters to draw numbers out of a hat. Those numbers would correspond with the paintings the various performers received. However, many of the skaters were intent upon going home with specific paintings, so I rigged the draw to a certain extent to accommodate them.

Rosalynn Sumners made a most extraordinary request with respect to the painting that she had received, a large portrait of a woman with closed eyes and flowers on her head. Rosalynn wondered if I could just take back the painting and open the woman's eyes. I told her that I really couldn't do that. Only Rosalynn would fully understand this: with respect to her personal life, her eyes had been closed for a very long time. The one person who could open them was Rosalynn herself. I found it quite poetic that she had received that particular painting.

Somehow the evening ended. I went back to the Inter-Continental and had a drink with my good friends Carol Ann Letheren and Michael Murnaghan. Then I sank into my rented bed with an aching body, thinking of cocaine but too tired to go out and look for some. Everyone believed that I flew to Mexico the next day. In truth, I stayed in Toronto, went through some unsavoury experiences, and eventually arrived in San Miguel two days late.

"Toller Cranston: A Tribute" was produced by IMG, Trans World International, and Insight Productions. It was some time before I saw a recording of the show that aired nationally three months after its taping. The production had been far greater live, as is often true of figure skating. Nonetheless, in a pleasant twist of fate, the television program was nominated for an ACTRA Award as the best drama or documentary of the year.

35

Midlife in Moscow

One March day in 1998, the telephone rang in my minuscule temporary atelier overlooking the red tile rooftops of San Miguel de Allende. It was Jay Ogden. Would I like to skate in Barry Mendelson's production of the Nutcracker on Ice in Moscow? And, by the way, could I leave tomorrow?

It is not as though I had been certain that the Varsity Arena tribute would be my swan song. I had always felt ambivalent about saying goodbye to skating, a creative outlet that was part of my very muscles, bones, and soul. In the show's narrative, as I faded into obscurity, I suggested to Shawn Sawyer that we might meet again as competitors at the 2006 Olympics. I enjoyed the ambiguity of that little plot twist. One can rarely predict what lurks around the corner.

Without missing a brush stroke, without showing the slightest evidence of the shock I felt – Why would Barry Mendelson want me? Didn't he know that I hadn't skated in three months and that I wasn't exactly the latest news? – I inquired coolly, "How much is he going to pay me?"

"Twenty-five thousand dollars U.S. plus first-class travel and hotel accommodations."

My brush continued to stroke the canvas as I reviewed the situation. The offer struck me as too good to pass up. Nearly a decade earlier, producer Dick Button had asked me to compete against Scott Hamilton, Brian Orser, Brian Boitano, and Gary Beacom at the 1989 NutraSweet Challenge of Champions at the Luzhniki Stadium in Moscow. However, with Dick's power to maim a skater's dignity by withholding an opportunity, he declined to invite me to its sister event, the more prestigious World Professional Championships in Landover. When it came time to board the plane for the Soviet Union, my ego was sufficiently bruised that I thought somewhat irrationally, "If I am not good enough to skate at Landover, then I am not good enough for Moscow." I did not go.

It had not yet occurred to me that I had been demoted in the hierarchy of skating in order to make way for the newer Olympic graduates, so I felt that the omission was unjust. If I had thought about life then as I do now, I would have jumped at the opportunity. Later I learned that the citizens of Moscow had eagerly awaited my arrival, but I had disappointed them and dashed their expectations. Now I was being offered a second chance, and so were they. I liked the symmetry of the arrangement.

Painting meticulously and summoning all my sangfroid, I said, "Yes, I will do it. I'll go in a flash. I was thinking about what $25,000 could do for my Mexican property.

"We will get back to you with the details," I was told.

I experienced, one could say, an intellectual frisson but not an emotional one. I felt no palpitations of the heart, no "Oh, my god, I can't believe that this is happening to me again, the Magic of Life." Still, an interesting thing happens to jaded old professionals like me. We automatically shift into performing mode, like aging firedogs instinctively answering the alarm. Preparation for skating starts as soon as the seed of opportunity is planted in our heads. Therefore I ate nothing for dinner. Instead I drank great quantities of water, determined to shed the ten pounds I needed to drop within a week in order to fit into my costumes.

The next day, when I was due to board a plane for Toronto to pick up my skates, then do an about-face and hop onto another plane bound for Los Angeles to commence practising in the depths of the night, the telephone failed to jingle with confirmation. I waited for most of the following day as well. At about five o'clock in the afternoon, a call came from the Toronto office of IMG. Wendy Kane said, "You are booked on a plane out of Leon, Guanajuato, at nine o'clock tomorrow morning. Don't miss it."

The Phoenix Rises

I woke up at 4:30 A.M. I had arranged for a taxi to pick me up at my lower gate, opposite the town park, for the hour-and-one-quarter trip to the airport. In the silence of the deserted streets, I could almost hear my brain speaking aloud. Who would believe that the solitary figure waiting on sixteenth-century cobblestones was en route to perform in a 20,000-seat Moscow arena? I doubted that anyone in that remote Mexican town had ever embarked on such an odyssey, especially so early in the morning. As the orange sun peeked over the horizon, I flew on an American Airlines jet towards Toronto.

With one day to spend in Canada, I grabbed my skate bag at my Queen Street West studio and took a half-hour taxi ride to the Cricket Club to see how much damage three months off the ice had done. I had recently returned from Puerto Escondito, one of the few non-working holidays of my life. I was as brown as a nut, and the salt and sun had bleached my hair to platinum blond. My appearance was incongruous in the Cricket Club's frosty milieu, and my warm-up clothes exposed a protruding stomach that owed its girth to too much tasty food and too little exercise.

I brushed with a brilliant new Russian pair team as well as with two members of the old guard who happened to be at the Cricket Club that day: Grzegorz Filipowski, a former Polish skating champion and world medallist, and Tracy Wainman, a long-ago Canadian Wunderkind. They were surprised to see me. I announced that, although I hadn't skated since December 8 at Varsity Arena, I was about to headline a show in downtown Moscow. Grzegorz and Tracy seemed more depressed than impressed by my skating demonstration, and I felt rather ashamed of the way in which I had allowed myself to fall apart. I didn't bother to reassure them, "Don't doubt this old dog. I know how to get it together." I just wanted to quietly set my feet on the ice to see how bad bad truly was. Bad was awful.

Where's Barry?

I flew to Los Angeles in economy class, something that I do not enjoy, particularly on Air Canada, where strangers often recognize me and make me feel self-conscious. Sandwiched at the back of the jumbo jet in the fourth seat of the middle section, I told myself, "No matter what unpleasantness or difficulty I experience, no matter how embarrassed I am about my lack of performing ability and my irregular appearance, I will do this for the money."

Income from painting is hit or miss, and I was remembering the planned addition to my house in Mexico. My two modest rooms (a small studio that I no longer used regularly and a bedroom that I shared with my elderly black-and-white English setter, Flora, sadly since deceased) were about to explode in size and ambition. The new incarnation was slated to include a living room, a kitchen, a much larger bedroom, an expanded studio, a roof garden, and an airy art gallery with twelve-foot ceilings and clerestory windows. Therefore I would skate, and if people whispered that Toller Cranston had disgraced himself in Moscow, I would deny every-thing. That was my strategy. It worked for Bill Clinton.

Barry Mendelson was to meet me at the Los Angeles International Airport and drive me to my hotel. I waited for half an hour. There was no Barry Mendelson. I treated myself to a chocolate-and-vanilla ice-cream cone.

Then I asked a security guard what I should do with my baggage while I made some phone calls. LAX is a scary airport. If a hapless traveller momentarily abandons his luggage, he will never see it again, at least in this lifetime. It will be seized by a bomb demolition squad and exploded on the spot. I dragged my suitcases, heavy leather skate bag, and garment bags full of costumes to a secure storage area.

Then I phoned Jay Ogden.

"Look, Mendelson is not here. What do I do? Where do I go?"

I was annoyed but not in a tizzy.

Mother

Three hours later, after my third or fourth ice-cream cone (my get-thin régime had broken down by then and the adrenalin flow had dried up), a man named John-something appeared at the ground transportation pick-up area. Calling me Mr. Cranston in a deferential tone, he behaved in a polite, apologetic, and professional manner. For my part, I was courteous but just a bit chilly (as I am when I feel justifiably miffed).

John was charged with overseeing the Nutcracker on Ice cast in Russia and skating the Drosselmeyer role, as I later learned. Because he immediately let me know that everyone called him Mother, his real name did not sink into my head. Mother looked less like an ice skater and more like a badger with dark hair and owlish glasses, and there was no doubt in my mind that as long he lived he would never marry and father children. He drove me to a considerably understated Holiday Inn in the middle of nowhere, settled me into my room, and asked me to wait.

You Are the Magic

Then I received a telephone call from Lisa Ware, a young woman whom I had met in the past in connection with some long-forgotten skating project. She was the choreographer who optimistically planned to whip the production into shape. She suggested that I join her for a drink at the bar.

Lisa was a little nervous, which I could understand. The show virtually did not exist at that point. Her scanty resources included someone who remembered choreography from a distant production of the Nutcracker on Ice plus a whole new cast that had to learn the show in three days, fly to Moscow on the fourth day, and perform it in public on the fifth.

Our full complement included Karen Armstrong, Lisa Auwenger, Carla Ericson, Rio Foster-Ross, Linda Fratianne, Heather Gruner, Fred Haug, Natasha Ivanova, Jeff LaBrake, John Niles Merrill, Chris Miller, Jennifer Nestelberger, Adrian Robertson, Grant Rorvick, Cheri Rae Russell, Mark Schmitke, Nicole Sciarrotta, Patrick Seeley, Joshua Starbuck, Lonni Suttenberg, Marina Utechina, and Kristy Vanesky.

"What are you going to be in the Nutcracker on Ice?" Lisa asked me. To my way of thinking, the obvious character was Herr Drosselmeyer, and I said so.

Lisa replied vaguely, "The role of Drosselmeyer is so enormous. . . ."

I assured her, "Whatever you want I will do. Don't worry."

"Well, why don't we just create a role for you? You become the magic element in the show. You are the magic!"

I wanted to agree with her, but I had absolutely no idea what the hell she meant. *You are the magic?*

I arrived at the rink that night, a double rink not too far from the Holiday Inn, looking like an aging surfer boy. There I made the acquaintance of a textured, variously experienced and inexperienced cast of show skaters. There is an onus on any principal skater to stir the pot and excite the cast, but my skating abilities were so infe-rior that I could not stir very briskly. Lisa gave me two pieces from Tchaikovsky's *Nutcracker Suite*, with which I was quite familiar, and said, in essence, "Go out there and be the magic."

Karen Armstrong, an Ohio girl, the lead who played Clara, was normally an adagio pairs skater in ice shows. She had come virtually cold turkey to our production and was required to learn the entire role in three days. My assignment amounted to just two minutes and thirty seconds in each half of the show.

When the music played on a crackly little tape recorder, all I needed to know was what general role I was interpreting (magic), how I entered the ice, and how I exited. I stumbled and bumbled around on a much-reduced ice surface, which meant not having to worry about my lack of conditioning. What I did was little more than a tragic attempt at marking direction, with nary a spin nor a jump. I played the music once, twice, three times. I assured Lisa, who wanted to believe me but couldn't quite summon sufficient faith, "Don't worry. I've got it. I know exactly how this is going to work."

Cheri Rae Russell

Other skaters came to me over a period of time to introduce them-selves (a ritual I enjoy). That is how I began the traditional process of establishing individual relationships. I bonded with each skater. The cast members and I were going to share a significant experience, so I wanted to know what form of skating they regularly did for a living, where they came from, who their teachers had been, and what events and achievements made up their personal skating histories.

If the Nutcracker on Ice heading off to Moscow was a junk car out of control, at the wobbly wheel was a phenomenal creature named Cheri Rae Russell. Cheri Rae was a Los Angeles-area skater who hadn't made her mark in the amateur ranks, but her personal-ity and her multifaceted talent (manifested by her acting in such leg-endary movies as *Motorcycle Mama*) made her a driving force. She

Cheri Rae Russell.

displayed a voracious enthusiasm for quality skating and for skaters whom she had admired over the years. When she met me, she prostrated herself on the ice *à la* Friday and Robinson Crusoe and made the cast aware that God had arrived. Her conspicuous adoration instantly opened a channel of communication between us that the others could not access.

Cheri Rae possessed a personality so electric that she short-circuited everyone around her, exhausting them and leaving them dying by the roadside. But we needed an electric personality if we were ever to make a miracle happen in Moscow. Cheri Rae was a crucial ingredient in our mix.

A Second-Rate Production

If I had been Lisa Ware, I would have folded my wings and announced, "Look, this cannot be done." However, those remarkable and disciplined choreographers such as Lisa attack their projects like pit bulls. They are relentless. Lisa drove the skaters until six o'clock in the morning, picking through the creative rubble to find some sense of numbers with which they could work.

The next day, my entire body ached. I lay in bed watching CNN throughout the afternoon, becoming progressively more nervous. There were only two days left for the impossible to occur. On the first night, I had been able to do an Axel: in literary terms, A in the alphabet. On the second night, I had no stamina and failed to skate any better. Staying in bed all day ordering room service hadn't helped my cause.

The valiant cast worked again until six o'clock in the morning. Linda Fratianne, a former world champion and Olympic silver medallist, had arrived by then to skate the role of the Sugarplum Fairy. Meeting Linda was like making the acquaintance of a distant relative, a legitimate member of the royal family of skating. She held global credentials. Successor to Dorothy Hamill, Linda had reigned as U.S. ladies' champion from 1977 through 1980. She had won world titles in 1977 and 1979 and had placed second – although I thought that she should have won – behind Anett Pötzsch at the 1980 Olympics in Lake Placid.

I hadn't been friendly with Linda on an intimate level during the days when we both competed for Dick Button at Landover, but she was young then and wet behind the ears. The Nutcracker on Ice gave me a chance to get to know her better. The naïve star of Disney on Ice, in becoming a married woman with a child, had developed some depth and maturity. Suddenly we could chat on an even footing. Her skating was not quite as I remembered it from her amateur days, but she was not the least bit perturbed by that as I was perturbed by my own shortcomings.

I went to a hair salon at the local mall to reacquaint myself with my former image. That meant getting a haircut, having my hair dyed dark brown, and stocking up on various hair products and make-up. When I arrived at the rink later as a brunet, I felt more like my old self.

That night, the third and last, there was some sort of vague run-through. My skating ability was starting to kick in, which armed me with a smidgen more confidence. I didn't stick around for the end of the run-through. As far as I could see, we were mounting a second- or third-rate show. I reminded myself that, if word got out, I would simply deny everything. Then I dreamed contentedly about my Mexican construction project.

On a Wing and a Prayer

Experienced performers know that they can be ill prepared right up to the brink of crisis, but even in the moment, magic can happen. They can pull it off. If young skaters could remember that, it would alleviate much of their anxiety. When something goes wrong at home before a big event, there is really no need to worry. It is impossible to predict what will happen in the space of three or four days. The competitive climate can change one's destiny.

Christopher Bowman, a talented American ex-champion whom I coached between August 1990 and November 1991, was a master of that philosophy. He could leave for an event without so much as a three-jump in his arsenal, then skate brilliant triple Axels in the heat of competition. Sometimes he even improvised during his routines, an inclination that properly horrified his long-time coach, Frank Carroll.

The chorus skaters finished their final rehearsal, returned briefly to the Holiday Inn to pick up their bags, and then flew straight to Moscow. Those old show gypsies were genuinely excited – with the particular reinforcement of Cheri Rae Russell's energy and antics. Linda and I enjoyed the luxury of leaving on a later flight at two-thirty in the afternoon.

The First and Second Natashas

Barry Mendelson's attractive Los Angeles connection, a promoter named Natasha, was to meet Linda and me at the airport with our tickets and visas, then fly with us to Russia. Natasha was a Radcliffe kind of girl: well educated and chic. She and her mother did not show up until half an hour before departure time, so there was a certain amount of angst in the boarding lounge, most of it mine. I was not as upset as I otherwise might have been, however, since I had already been paid.

Linda and I sat together on the plane and reminisced about many things, including common skating experiences that we had shared independently from different viewpoints. We changed planes in Frankfurt, Germany, and headed to Moscow.

There was one coincidental juxtaposition that struck me as pleasantly ironic. I was airborne, devouring Lufthansa's first-class shrimp en route to my comeback skating performance, on the very same day that my valedictory show, taped before a live audience at Varsity Arena three months earlier, aired nationwide on CBC. My bittersweet departure from figure skating had lasted just hours through the magic of videotape. I came to think fondly of the phenomenon as my seven-hour retirement.

A welcoming committee that included print journalists and even television crews met Linda and me at the airport. A splendid woman, a second Natasha, greeted us and held out a sparse bunch of spring flowers just as I realized that I had left my passport on the plane.

Linda and I never did go through customs, already an indication of our position (or the Russians' perception of our position). We were stars. That was the sort of treatment about which I had almost forgotten. We were ushered into a holding tank: a VIP bar, discotheque, and restaurant. Natasha II and another official took our visas and passports through customs for us while we gave some brief interviews and quaffed champagne. After twenty minutes, we were slipped out the exit to a waiting car.

I had visited Moscow eleven times during the 1970s, making tremendous waves with my exhibitions. One memorable night after a competition, I had performed eleven encores that were later featured on Russian television as part of the introduction to every hockey game of the decade. That pleasant memory was well buried in the past, I thought. Part of my growing sense of security was rooted in the belief that no one would recognize me this time. If I failed, I would do so anonymously.

Moscow had grown and grown since I last saw it. During the ride from the distant airport to our hotel thirty minutes outside downtown Moscow, I dozed intermittently and watched out of the corner of my eye as the outskirts of the city passed in review. The Moscow that I knew in the 1970s was dark, gloomy, and dingy. Already this new Moscow seemed more impressive. The historically and architecturally important buildings, especially the Russian Orthodox churches, were illuminated like nocturnal Disneylands.

Whether or not Moscow is one of the most beautiful cities in the world has everything to do with whether one sees it in the daylight or at night. After dark, Moscow has no equal. The Moscow that I saw on that fourteen-day trip was a magical cloisonné fairyland at night with hundreds of onion domes in enamel green, sapphire blue, turquoise, and ruby red, all glittering grandly like Fabergé eggs, a real-live, audaciously mad *Nutcracker Suite*.

The Cosmos Hotel at 150 Mir Prospekt, built by the French in 1980 to house their competitors at the Moscow Olympics, was splendid in its own way, officially rated first-class, but no more than a two- or three-star hotel by North American standards. It was an enormous relic of the Soviet Empire, a vertical Grand Central Station teeming with conventioneers, businesspeople, and tourists. Built on an arc, it contained twenty floors and 1,777 rooms. Mine offered tremendous vistas of contemporary Moscow.

On our first night in Russia I fell asleep early, relieved to have arrived but knowing that a major effort would be required to complete the next leg of the journey, the show itself. Although Cheri Rae had liberally imbibed on the plane, revving up all her fellow passengers, on that same night, as I slid into the arms of Morpheus, she dragged along two friends and went running off to a performance of the Bolshoi Ballet. Her companions fell asleep during the performance, but Cheri Rae, with bright eyes and bushy tail, stormed the stage and threw flowers to an aging diva.

Lions and Tigers and Bears

A day of publicity dawned, a young spring day full of promise. I knew that the hours ahead would be long, arduous, and draining both emotionally and physically, so I fortified myself for what was to come. I joined the line for an elaborate, diverse breakfast buffet in one of the hotel dining rooms. The myriad offerings were a marked contrast to the sparse fare of twenty years earlier: typically then an egg, a slice of bread, and perhaps a piece of cheese.

The rink complex was even bigger than the Cosmos Hotel and more centrally located. The building had been designed to gild the Soviet Union's lily during the 1980 Olympics, but its full impact was minimized when much of the West boycotted those summer Games.

The rink itself could not have been more my cup of tea. I cannot think of any rink that I have come across during my performing career, including Paris's wonderful Palais des Sports, that I would have preferred. The ice size had been cut down to approximately eighty feet by sixty feet, making the work easier for someone without stamina. Most of the seating in that enormous arena was far away from the performing surface, welcome news for a forty-eight-year-old skater. I was sensitive about the ravages of aging, so those many feet of separation filled me with a certain restored confidence.

The lighting was dim that first day, and the ice was as good as could possibly be: tank ice of a splendid quality and moistness, with inky blue-grey striations. Colour grounds a performance. When a skater jumps on a pure white surface, he can't be quite sure where the floor is.

One question nagged at the back of my mind. If I had been asked to perform in Moscow with less than a week's notice, what kind of publicity could have been done in that short time? Barry Mendelson had sold the show and had transferred all responsibilities to the Moscow promoters. Would anyone come to see the production? Right or wrong, every principal skater feels that a lack of spectators in the seats is his responsibility or his failing.

Although it was never an issue with me, never more than a tiny cloud on the horizon, inexplicably it was Brian Orser's photograph, not mine, that graced the posters in Red Square.

Somewhere in the complex that contained our rink, there was a world-renowned centre for the training of wild animals. Every night as we showered, dressed, and prepared to return to the Cosmos Hotel, a parade of trainers passed by the snack bar with leashed baby animals. Some of the skaters obtained permission to pet the animals, but I chose not to. With my history of debilitating animal encounters, I simply enjoyed the colour that the nightly animal promenade lent to our evenings.

The Metropole

Linda and I made a brief sortie to the Metropole Hotel where we had stayed in 1971 with the rest of the cast of the ISU tour after the Lyon world championships. The Metropole, under the Soviet régime, was a grand-turned-seedy, prisonlike seat of rumoured espionage, a fact that we skaters enjoyed and milked for humour. I habitually entered my room and announced myself to the bugs I presumed were planted under each faded lampshade: "Hello. This is Toller Cranston. I am a skater. I will be staying here for a few days."

Millions of dollars had subsequently been poured into the Metropole. By 1998, it was no less opulent than the Ritz in Paris. Not the tiniest shard of familiar décor remained. Gilt, marble, chandeliers, and oriental rugs had replaced the shabby appointments Linda and I remembered so well. We left without treating ourselves to tea.

A Glittering Success

By opening night, I felt strong. My legs had stopped shaking. Having adhered to a precise dietary regimen and forgone further ice-cream lapses, I was beginning to feel conditioned for the first time in a long while.

A small audience saw the opening show: perhaps two thousand people in a forty-thousand-seat building, but I have seen worse. It was just this side of respectable.

I wore the costumes that Angela Arana of the Canadian National Ballet had made for my tribute show: the three simple bodysuits with different necklines and sleeve styles, one in red, one in yellow, and one in blue. Not a single sequin glittered under the spotlights.

As a professional, when I was at my best, I could execute up to two triples in a show as well as many, many double Axels. But when a skater's technical repertoire slips away, he ends up with only a name and a dusty medal. That is the last chapter. Then he vanishes. Performing the double Axel had become a major psychological hurdle for me. I had not bothered, or attempted, to practise the two-and-one-half-revolution jump in recent years, and as a result I had become double Axel shy. For some reason, things were different in Moscow.

There is a certain galvanizing effect that occurs backstage. When the music plays, the adrenalin kicks in. On the first night, I performed two double Axels. That armed me with the knowledge that I could continue to do them at subsequent performances. If, on opening night, a skater lies on his back on the ice, he may tell himself, "I don't think that I should lie on my back tomorrow night, so I'll take that particular jump out of my program." Luckily I was spared the decision.

There was a gasp of recognition that I did not expect when I skated out to centre ice. Something else happened that was almost as scary. Thanks to Lisa Ware and the energy of the various cast members, the show received tremendous reviews. That exerted a positive effect on attendance. The audiences grew.

My ego steamed into fast forward, and I became the star that I had been in an earlier era, an era that I had thought was long gone. I started to take my role as the co-captain of the Nutcracker on Ice extremely seriously. The chorus played a part in helping me to regain my long-lost confidence. Mark Schmitke, a Canadian professional who lives in Massachusetts, an excellent skater in his own right, made a point of coming out from backstage every night to watch my performances, along with various members of the supporting cast. That helped a lot.

There was one little puzzle that I did not solve until the run of the show was over. Although I consistently performed my brains out, at the end of my numbers there was little if any applause. I later realized that the Russian audiences received the show as they would a ballet or a symphonic performance and saved their enthusiastic applause until the finale.

When I arrived at the curtain for my entrance each night, I reached into a jar of golden glitter that I kept backstage. I took two large handfuls before skating onto the ice. On the opening notes of the music, I threw the glitter into the air, first with my right hand, then with my left, and let it rain down on me, because I was the magic – in case someone hadn't figured that out yet. From all reports, the glitter was effective. During my final bow, I took two more handfuls, ran through the line of skaters to the front, and showered myself (and sometimes part of the audience) with golden sprinkles. It was a touch, however hokey, that seemed just right under the circumstances. Miraculously the glitter held out as long as I did. The jar hit empty at the last performance.

The production took on a life of its own. Wonder of all wonders, it began to make a fortune. Thirteen, fourteen, or fifteen thousand spectators attended each performance. The dressing rooms were miles from the ice along a circuitous obstacle course behind the seats. Before each show I peeked out at the audience with trepidation. *Is anybody out there? It happened last night, but will it happen again tonight?* The attendance continued to increase.

The promoters kindly attributed the success of the show to me. I was the forerunner of *Perestroika*, the free creative spirit who had returned after two decades, like the prodigal son, to receive the kudos of the citizens who had – as a direct result of my inspiration – freed themselves. That was a far-fetched theory, but I believed it because I wished to. As the magic of the show, I announced each night to the audience (at least in my own imagination), "You see, I knew that you would all be free one day, and here I am to congratulate you."

Only one person was not aboard that magical mystery tour. The young wardrobe woman took her own wild ride. She was far more interested in sharing vodka with her boyfriend on the lighting crew than in ensuring our costumes were cleaned, pressed, and mended. After my third or fourth plaintive "Could you help?" and her customary "I really don't feel well, but maybe if I have time," I knew that the job was not going to get done.

Midnight in Moscow

The Moscow subways are the deepest in the world – several times deeper than New York's – and architecturally glamorous with their marble floors, chandeliers, and bronze torchères. I watched the towering escalators flow quickly up and down, up and down, conveying a roiling sea of humanity. The entrances and exits in particular were hives of activity. People sold whatever they could: second-hand clothes, a few scrawny flowers, and homemade cookies. The ruble was in a perilous state, soon to further decline. Certain kiosks offered gorgeous roses, but who could afford to buy them? During my stay in Russia, I saw a vast divide between the haves and the have-nots. There was virtually no evidence of a conventional middle class.

The cast had been sternly warned, "Do not go out at night. In fact, do not go anywhere at any time without a companion." The pervasive sense of danger in the streets was unlike any that I had experienced in East Los Angeles, Harlem, Mexico City, or even the menacing São Paulo, Brazil.

The point was moot for me, because I was too tired to go out after the show. For others, ignorance was bliss – at least temporarily. Many in our group were eventually accosted by thugs or by the police (two events that were equally unappealing). Mother was robbed of three hundred dollars, and Mark Schmitke was attacked and roughed up on the street.

The most overwhelming and sad feature of the new Moscow was the multitude of prostitutes who worked at the Cosmos Hotel. They roamed the lobby, always opulently dressed. After observing them night after night, I realized that each owned only one set of working clothes. Fourteen, fifteen, or sixteen appeared to be the median age. The prostitutes didn't frequent the hotel's bars and restaurants, probably because they couldn't afford the prices. Instead they prowled like solitary animals: up the staircase, down the staircase, posed in a state of ennui against a railing.

Many of the Nutcracker on Ice cast members, including me, received phone calls from Russian girls who had managed to obtain our room numbers. Speaking poor English, they proffered their sexual services. I don't believe that they generated any interest among us, but we felt genuinely distressed at their plight.

The Glories of the Kremlin

One day when Linda and I had some free time, we visited the Kremlin. Our arrival at the correct location had far more to do with luck than intelligence. President Boris Yeltsin had fired the prime

Queen of the Dawn, *inspired by the Moscow experience.*

minister and his entire cabinet only the night before, so there was virtually no government in evidence. Entering the Kremlin compound, I sensed a strange anxiety – or perhaps not so strange, since the guards were all armed with machine guns.

A refined middle-aged woman, Natasha III, a freelancer whom we encountered in the courtyard, offered us her services as a certified guide. She was a veritable oil well, a gusher of information.

Little did she know that she had fallen upon someone whose interest in Romanov history was no less than her own.

The first stop on our tour was a collection of ecclesiastical vestments of the twelfth and thirteenth centuries. Those clothes were covered from top to bottom with hundreds and thousands of pearls and precious stones, almost without any real sense of design. The wealth was beyond imagining. There were cases and cases of those vestments, all exhibiting a mystical element unlike anything I had seen before. One particular priest had died owning one hundred and eighty such garments.

Similar pearls and precious stones solidly encrusted the footmen's livery and the harnesses of the Imperial Guards' horses. The individual coaches of the czarinas and czars struck me as fantastic and self-indulgent. Those golden carriages with translucent windows had diamonds embedded in their wheel spokes.

The wedding dress worn by teenaged Catherine the Great for her marriage to the son of Elizabeth I, Grand Duke Peter of Holstein, was made of spun silver – and had a ten-inch waist.

One of the thrones on display struck me as quintessentially Russian. It was a double seat designed for the crowning of Peter the Great and his older half-brother, Ivan V. I recognized the extent to which the Russian empresses and czars had taken on mystical images in the minds of their subjects. The accoutrements of their coronations and other rituals had fanned the fires of their myths and had cemented their autocracy.

Since my Russian adventure, I have painted an extensive series of imperial Russian portraits that I believe are among the best work I have ever done – a direct result of my inspiration on the day I spent with Linda Fratianne at the Kremlin.

The Last Lambada

There was much talk about the same cast taking the show on to St. Petersburg, but the Russian economy was by then in shreds. There was such economic turmoil that few citizens could imagine paying to see an ice show. As is often true of magical experiences, our Russian fantasy ended prematurely.

The Moscow promoters, however, their coffers nicely overflowing, wanted to entertain us in some way. After the final performance, they told us to dress up in evening clothes. Then they took us to a discotheque in downtown Moscow, the hottest and the newest. There was a whiff of dirty money in the air. It was as glamorous a nightspot as any that exist in Tehran, Paris, or London, yet its security guards carried rifles.

A sumptuous display of food was laid out before our entourage, and we took advantage of one last chance to fraternize and chat. The same thing happens at the end of any important skating event – it could be the Olympics, the world championships, or something more modest. There is one final glut of energy that must be expended before the event is truly over. I was coaxed onto the dance floor by numbers of hot young chicks from California.

We felt no inhibition. It is one thing to act uncool in New York where people know who you are. It is quite another to behave that way among Russian mobsters and prostitutes whom you will never meet again. Because we didn't care what anyone thought, a number of us, including me, but spectacularly eclipsed by Cheri Rae Russell, performed such indecent, lewd, and suggestive dance interpretations that Moscow had not seen their like. Several times we all crashed to the floor, bodies sandwiched on top of bodies.

Natalia the interpreter became so vodka-saturated that she made up her mind to seduce any cast member she could persuade. She began her quest with me but soon moved on and on down the line. Natalia was truly barking up the wrong trees.

Cheri Rae had brought along her American boyfriend to share the Moscow experience with her and celebrate the two-year anniversary of their liaison. He was utterly overwhelmed, both by the experience and by Cheri Rae. I later heard that the moment their plane touched down in the United States, as Cheri Rae sashayed down the concourse, he ran as fast as he could in the opposite direction.

The dutiful interpreters were to take us to the airport, but our scheduled van did not arrive. There we all were at the Cosmos Hotel with heaps of skate bags, garment bags, and suitcases. Where could we find a taxi at 4:00 A.M. in the depths of Moscow? Somehow we did. Natasha II, probably the premier interpreter in the city (she had previously interpreted for the Béjart Company and the Royal Ballet), was clearly nervous. It did not register on me exactly why, but now I realize that leaving Moscow through miles of red tape is not easy to do. Many unwary travellers have gotten stuck there. Natasha walked us right through the security checkpoint and into the departure lounge to make sure that we arrived safely with the proper clearance.

Cast members told each other goodbye, hoping that we would perform as a group again. Linda and I left on the same flight, but someone had taken a little jab at me. My first-class ticket had been cancelled and reissued for economy. Meanwhile Linda enjoyed business class. When I arrived in Frankfurt, Lufthansa kindly upgraded me for my continuing flight to Mexico City.

The Turn of the Screw

Back in San Miguel de Allende, I went to El Buen Cafe near my studio one day for a cup of coffee. An acquaintance handed me a clipping that a friend in Cairo, Egypt, had mailed to her. According to the World Press, a remarkable production of the Nutcracker on Ice had sold out in Moscow thanks to the legendary Canadian skater Toller Cranston. I have never received a greater compliment in my life. Nothing has touched me more. That clipping is a bit thin and worn, because I have shown it to so many friends, casual acquaintances, and virtual strangers.

I can look back now on that wonderful adventure in Russia, something that perhaps I did not deserve, as one of the magical opportunities of my life. Everything worked just right. With my poor luck and lack of preparation, it shouldn't have, but it did.

In late 1998, my studio addition was completed, a permanent monument to the glittering memories of Moscow.

36

Dylan's Lesson in Living

It is a privilege to be appointed godfather, especially if one's godson is Dylan Caldwell. Dylan is less a student than a teacher. He is living proof that God tests most harshly those best able to rise to the challenge.

Clive Caldwell and his wife, Marianne (who died in February 1999), were special friends and long-time surrogate members of my family. Prominent entrepreneurial success stories, together they owned and ran the Cambridge and Adelaide athletic clubs. Dylan was their first-born.

For reasons that no one was able to determine, Dylan arrived in the world twenty years ago with enormous physical handicaps. His lower body is severely truncated. His hands and fingers are mis-shapen. Beyond those undeniable facts, Dylan is a perfect human being. No young man in Canada is more handsome.

Dylan has always had his work cut out for him. In addition to his physical challenges, he has been forced to hold his own against a father who was once a professional squash player: tall, strong, athletic, and handsome. Marianne, too, was both physically and

Dylan Caldwell. Photo by Thom Hayim

socially adept. Children of high achievers often feel disadvantaged by comparison.

One tragic day, Dylan's younger sister, Ashley, a perfectly normal and beautiful three-and-one-half-year-old, fell out of bed and suffered a spinal stroke that severely impeded her ability to walk. Marianne and Clive then adopted their third child, Devon, who grew into a handsome young man of six-foot-three. Devon's attributes compounded Dylan's daily torment.

However, Dylan, like my friend Sherika, was cut from exceptional cloth. God has a way of simultaneously taking and giving. Whatever he took from Dylan in the physical realm, he made up for one hundredfold through gifts of personality and charm based on ingenuousness, honesty, and enthusiasm. Dylan rarely alludes to his handicaps. He does not display self-pity.

From the earliest days of our association, Dylan and I have treated each other as equals. All he has ever asked from me is love. That is an easy requirement to fulfill.

Dylan has come three times to visit me in Mexico. Not five minutes after he and I walked into a crowded restaurant in San Miguel de Allende, a group of interested strangers had gathered around our table to talk to Dylan. Later he approached the Spanish-speaking musicians during their break. Without knowing their language, he engaged them in conversation and behaved in such a natural, unselfconscious way that I marvelled at his courage, spirit, and character.

The next afternoon, as I walked through my gate, I saw three policemen on the grounds. Fearing the worst, I quickly learned that Dylan had met them in the park and had invited them to see our gardens.

There is one particular action that Dylan performs so nobly that it commands enormous respect. Whenever he meets someone new, he extends his deformed hand for a firm handshake.

Occasionally Dylan and I paint together. Although painting is not an activity that particularly interests him, it means doing something together, godfather and godson. The hours that we have spent working together in Mexico, chatting, helping each other, and bestowing mutual compliments, rank among the most cherished of my life.

Someone else with physical impediments might have thrown in the towel when it came to sports, but Dylan developed himself into a fine athlete. He can knock anyone's socks off on the tennis court. With his custom-made clubs, he has beaten his father in golf. He drives an adapted car and rides a specially constructed bicycle. Competitive almost to a fault, Dylan takes what he has and makes the best of it. That is the ultimate secret of life.

While I taught a young Swiss skater, Lucinda Ruh, Dylan developed a crush on her. On Saturdays he often came to the Cricket

The fabulous second-storey studio in San Miguel.

Club, put on his skates, and joined us on the ice. Once, in a sensitive moment, he remarked, "You know, if my body were right, I would have been a great skater." There is no doubt in my mind that he could and would have been.

Marianne Caldwell developed ovarian cancer. As Dylan watched his mother die and his family fall apart under the strain of grief, he confided to me, man to man, in a sincere and intense way, "I know that my mother is dying, but I can survive it. I'll be all right. I'm more worried for my brother and sister." Such was and is his strength of character.

37

Wendy's Lesson in Dying

Until recently there was a close-knit group of four women in San Miguel de Allende who had eaten lunch together every Thursday afternoon for five years. Three of them were my friends too, so I learned about the fourth, Wendy, from their conversations.

Wendy developed terminal cancer that spread throughout her body. A month before I met her, she was airlifted (to the tune of $16,000) from San Miguel to Palm Beach, Florida, where her sister, Linda, lived. Her condition was so extreme that she simultaneously vomited and excreted green bile.

Refusing to Die

There were many tears. *Wendy is going to die.* To everyone's surprise, however, Wendy returned to San Miguel. One day I went to her rather artistic, eclectic colonial house to meet her and say hello. With her two boxer dogs and her three closest friends, she was holding court on the patio. She looked like the Ghost of Christmas Past as she sat cross-legged in a nightgown, smoking a cigarette. Her long, attractive legs had withered to the bone. Just a few thin hairs remained on her head, and her cheeks were as sunken as a concentration camp victim's, yet her lips were meticulously made up, and she sported a touch of eye shadow.

A certain type of person with a fatal disease, if she has the confidence, the arrogance, and the sense of humour, persistently asks her friends what they want from her house when she dies. That is what Wendy was doing that afternoon. She plainly enjoyed the emotional torment she wreaked on her guests and beneficiaries. That can be rather funny if one can glimpse the humour beyond the pathos. Wendy demanded like a perfect martinet that so-and-so's name be affixed to the back of this painting or that piece of bric-a-brac. I later learned that half of her substantial trust fund was bequeathed to her dogs' veterinarian (with whom she was in love).

Upon my introduction to Wendy, I presented her with two dozen tangerine-coloured roses. I continued to see her often after our initial visit. I habitually first went around the corner to a vendor who sold roses in the most extraordinary colours for fifteen pesos a dozen. I bought at least sixty stems at a time. Wendy was irritated by what she viewed as my extravagance, but I revelled in the sort of floral bargain that is entirely unknown in Canada and the United States.

Wendy generally held court in her grand rococo-barocquo living room. She took great pains to dress up every day in Guatemalan vests and multicoloured skirts. Wearing full make-up but never a wig, she paraded around like an exotic, bald water bird. Her conversation was feisty, salty, arrogant, honest, intimate, and infuriating. As demeaning as the effects of the disease had been to her body, her ethereal beauty hypnotized me.

Wendy carried her head and bones with confidence, even though her flesh had been ravaged. The result was masklike, theatrical, and surreal. She was always onstage. I never saw a single crack in her armour, even when her pain was extreme. The administration of morphine was not legal in Mexico. Fortunately Wendy was eventually able to obtain a supply through nontraditional channels.

One day Wendy dined at La Lola, a restaurant where I had hung a large painting depicting a red rose and a beautiful white dress on a hanger. She summoned me and said that she could not afford the full price of the painting, but she wanted to buy it anyhow. How would it be if she gave me a substantial down payment? Then I could reclaim the painting when she died. I agreed on the spot. That painting assumed a place of prominence in her living room.

What other woman who expected to be dead in several months would buy an expensive painting? Others might have said, "Why bother? I won't be here to enjoy it," but that purchase was Wendy's weapon against dying. She shopped for new clothes, pretending that life was normal. Her bravado reinforced her spirit.

Wendy received word from her doctors in Palm Beach that the chemotherapy she received in San Miguel was becoming ineffective, and they were afraid to increase her dosage lest she go into cardiac arrest. Before returning to Florida, she threw what we all believed would be the Last Supper (except that it turned out to be the Last Luncheon).

Wendy's friends converged on the scene. We felt that it was the final time we would speak to her, and we wanted her to know how she had inspired us, helped us, and given us strength in our own lives. There was a tearful farewell, and off Wendy went the next day to Palm Beach to die.

At least *we* all presumed she was going to die, but she told us, "I'm taking ten suitcases with me because of all the parties I'll be attending in Palm Beach. Then I will continue on to Boston, and I plan to go to New York to see some shows."

Meanwhile the rest of us thought, "Keep on dreaming."

Wendy went to Palm Beach to stay with her sister. True to her promise, she visited New York, although she didn't quite make it as far as Boston. Then she returned to San Miguel. Every time she had left, we had buried her, but she kept coming back.

I do not know whether, before Wendy became ill, her friends had perceived her as a great human. She was a product of her society, a wealthy woman who led a pleasant existence. At the end of her life, however, she was selected to play a great role, one that she may not have been conscious of playing. Her performance, enhanced by natural feistiness and greediness for life, was inspired.

Wendy taught her friends some of the supreme lessons of life: how one can survive at all costs; how physical unattractiveness need not prevent one from becoming more beautiful each day; how the human spirit has the ability to call the shots over one's impermanence. She made dying more understandable, more of a living process for us all. She gave us a fuller appreciation of life. Wendy and I talked about how she could make the experience of her death positive for her friends. She was magnificent in the face of that challenge.

While she lived on borrowed time, Wendy declared (without really fooling herself), "You never know. There could be a miracle cure."

I told her, "Wendy, you *are* a miracle. You are a living miracle right now."

Towards the end, I saw Wendy only sporadically – because of a lack of character on my part or because I recognized that, at a certain point, the act of dying from a debilitating disease becomes private. My temporary studio was across the street from her house (I was waiting for my own studio addition to be completed), so I observed the comings and goings without joining in.

Wendy developed a brain tumour that changed her personality. She became aggressive, dictatorial, and sometimes almost violent, according to reports from her intimate friends. She was hospitalized in San Miguel, but I chose not to visit her in that state.

One day Patricia, Wendy's long-time companion, broke the news to her: "Look, Wendy. Cards on the table. You have maybe a week to live." Wendy insisted on returning home from the hospital.

Just days before she died, she announced with perfect clarity, "Tell Toller to come and get his painting. I don't want any problems with the estate taxes."

The Final Act

The death scene, I heard, was remarkable. Wendy's closest confidants, male and female, the ones who had supported her throughout her months of torment, were all at her bedside. Wendy wore the red lacquer nail polish she had demanded two days earlier.

Finally she asked her friend Rodolfo Maldonado, a wealthy banker, "I'm dying, am I not?"

"Yes, you are."

"I'm afraid. I don't want to go alone."

"We will close our eyes and go with you," he offered. "Close your eyes, Wendy. Can you see the angels?"

Wendy closed her eyes and said yes, but still she was fearful. Then Rodolfo struck a deal with her.

"We need you on the other side to help us. Will you be our ambassador?"

Wendy agreed. Then she asked her friends to leave her alone with her nurse. She explained that she could not die with so much energy surrounding her. The group of friends left for a short time and went to lunch. When they returned, Wendy's life had ebbed quietly away.

On that particular day, unaware of what was happening just blocks away, I dressed in electric-royal-blue pants and a silk shirt and headed towards a downtown art shop. For some reason, as I passed Wendy's street, I turned into it and rang her doorbell. The usual friends were on the patio, arranged in a circle.

"So how is she?" I asked.

"She died fifteen minutes ago."

In a way, I was not surprised. As happened just before the death of skater Rob McCall, an internal clock had urgently told me, "Go right now. This is the time." I was the last member of the group to arrive on location. I asked for champagne.

A golden rose hung in its basket from the top of the loggia, spotlighted by the last orange rays of the setting sun. The luminous beam seemed to point towards God. I said, "Look. That's Wendy's soul going to heaven." We lifted our eyes and our glasses to toast that glowing orange-yellow rose.

What happened next was out of *Edie: American Girl*, the life story of Andy Warhol groupie Edie Sedgwick. The subject herself was not interviewed for that book. Rather, the spoken views of others created Edie's patchwork biography. Similarly I began to learn about Wendy, much more than I had known while she was alive. She had been a social renegade in the golden circles of New York, an iconoclast in a staid environment, rejected by her wealthy father and raised from early adolescence by her grandmother.

Ashes to Ashes

It was Wendy's final wish that her best friends travel to New York, ride in a limousine to a pet cemetery, and sprinkle her ashes over the graves of her best-loved pets. I do not know whether one is allowed to do such a thing, but that was her plan. The limousine would then convey the group to a fabulous restaurant, Wendy's favourite.

Linda, Wendy's sister, arrived from Palm Beach to oversee the arrangements and execute the will. She was an utterly glamorous woman of indeterminate age, redheaded and magnificently made-up. When I took her to lunch, she confided to me that she was having difficulty obtaining the correct paperwork that would allow her to transport Wendy's ashes to Palm Beach. She informed me with a perfectly straight face that drug smugglers lately had been using human ashes to camouflage their contraband. Narcotics police tested suspicious undocumented substances in any manner that they found convenient.

"Can you imagine?" Linda exclaimed "If I don't get the proper papers, Wendy's ashes could be snorted by border guards!"

I agreed that such an event would be monstrous. My interior voices, however, told me otherwise. If there is anything that would have amused Wendy Johnson's immortal soul, it was the thought of being snorted by attractive young Mexican customs officials as she made her way to her final resting place.

38

How to Guarantee Skating Immortality

As we begin a new millennium, why has skating, blessed as it is with an unprecedented abundance of popularity and innovation, become boring and silly? Why have the great personalities of the sport all but vanished, leaving behind few or none capable of filling their shoes?

In the 1990s, television, newspapers, and newsmagazines were inundated as never before with skaters' performances, information about skating, and skating gossip, yet a certain segment of the public grew cold and disinterested. How can that be? When figure skating starts to bore the bank tellers and the shopkeepers, our sport is in trouble.

Quality vs. Quantity

During the 1970s, the epoch in which I performed as an amateur skater, a champion did what everyone else did, but he did it the best. If he could win Canadians with a triple Salchow and a triple loop, why on earth would he want to try his luck with a triple Lutz and a triple flip? He pushed himself to the potential of the era, but not to the ultimate human potential available to him by virtue of his athletic abilities. As a result, the jump repertoire became static within certain periods of skating history.

Janet Lynn, for example, could and did win the world free-skating title with two double Axels. Of course, Janet could have

As Tybalt in "Romeo and Juliet."

learned to do triple jumps, but that was never the point. She was doing what everyone else did better than anyone else did it.

If you do a quadruple-revolution jump today, someone else will do two (or four) quads tomorrow, so you'd better learn how to do more quads. Athletes such as Elvis Stojko, some of the Russian men, and even American Todd Eldredge[*] may think that the way to improve as skaters is to add an additional rotation to a jump. If so, they could not be more mistaken.

As a result, they ensure themselves a less significant role in skating history than they would occupy through developing other strengths. As soon as someone new comes along and adds yet another rotation, their accomplishments will fade. However, when the accomplishments are artistic and innovative, when a skater changes the medium of skating and moulds it to his personality as Gary Beacom and the quirky, humorous French skater Laurent Tobel have done, he guarantees himself skating immortality.

At the 1998 Olympics in Nagano, Tara Lipinski's win in the ladies' division was justified by the "experts" on the grounds that she had executed one more jump than Michelle Kwan, the beacon of light, the ultimate contemporary skater, and perhaps one of the ultimate skaters of all time. Such a rationale in itself is a crime. That should not be the reason why a skater wins an Olympic gold medal.

Although there have been much more egregious examples, that sort of thinking tells the skating audience at large that the quality of skating, the quality of jumping, choreography, musicality, and beauty mean absolutely nothing. The only important criterion is the number of jumps executed successfully – in direct contrast to the way skating was judged in the 1970s and 1980s, when figure skating built to the crescendo of popularity that it now threatens to fritter profligately away.

---

* Todd Eldredge, five-time U.S. men's champion and 1996 world gold medallist, maintains his Olympic eligibility.

The Danger of Playing It Safe

As I had always suspected, and as I learned once and for all from the public reaction to my exhibition program *Pagliacci*, to succeed artistically one must go the extra mile. Playing it safe creatively and choreographically is the kiss of death. Both as a skater and as an artist, I have rarely played it safe. I have habitually put my neck on the chopping block. That was my natural inclination. Sometimes it got me into trouble, but often it led to triumph and intense satisfaction.

The annals of figure skating are littered with the remains of safe choices that led to disappointment. Isabelle and Paul Duchesnay played it safe with their free dance at the 1992 Olympics in Albertville, France. Until that point, they had engaged in a thrilling and triumphant game of Russian roulette with both their judges and their audiences. Instead of continuing in the same vein as their electrifying and controversial programs *Jungle* and *Missing*, they settled for *West Side Story*, which made them look sadly mediocre when they were anything but.

Jayne Torvill and Christopher Dean committed the same error after securing reinstatement as Olympic-eligible skaters in order to make a comeback at Lillehammer in 1994. They had built their reputations on a series of groundbreaking free dances, notably *Mack and Mabel*, *Barnum*, and *Bolero*. For the 1994 season, they were intimidated by the powers that be into contriving an amalgam of their greatest hits. That was the wrong creative decision, and it blew up in their faces (insofar as a bronze medal can be viewed as a disaster – they certainly felt that way, as I did in 1976 and as Debi Thomas did in 1988).

The great moments in figure skating occur when a performer is true to his own nature and puts his heart and soul on the line with no holds barred.

The Acid Test

What can happen to a skater – and perhaps it happened to me – is that he may start to spin his wheels, become limited and one-dimensional. It is time for Elvis Stojko, for example, to try something choreographically different and challenging. He needs to look out into the world for inspiration and further his education in the sport. He would become better rounded.

Elvis views criticism as bad energy, but that view is counterproductive. It is only through analysis and constructive criticism that one grows creatively. A *Toronto Star* reporter phoned me in Mexico and asked me to respond to something Elvis had told a German newspaper. Elvis had directly attributed the negative perception of his artistry to me. I had jaundiced the world against him, he thought, and that was an albatross he still carried around his neck.

I was deeply flattered that he attributed that much power and influence to me, and I will not deny it, but the criticism I proffered related to a program he had skated at the Junior Worlds in Oberstdorf, West Germany, more than ten years earlier. My question to Elvis was the great acid test of skating: Have you ever received higher artistic marks than technical?

I do not ignore for a moment Elvis's incredible credentials and competitive record, but anyone who cannot earn higher artistic marks than technical will not become one of the skating world's historical elite. Only those who score the highest second marks become immortal: Torvill and Dean, the Duchesnays, Robin Cousins, John Curry, and I ever so humbly add myself to the list.

Brian Boitano and Todd Eldredge, U.S. and world champions, are like high-quality machines. They are not artists, but they are so finely tuned that their artistry is in their refined technique. Scott Hamilton is short and slight, yet he has pleasing lines. On the other hand, I do not think there is anything beautiful about Elvis Stojko's jumps. He doesn't stretch his leg or point his toe. He is not flexible. His form is not aerodynamic. Rather, it is the combination of the confidence and the strength with which he jumps that commands profound respect. The effect has absolutely nothing to do with aesthetics.

Four Decades of Memorable Skaters

Throughout skating history, great skaters have been remembered for two things: first, for their unique conceptual approaches to the sport. Their vocabularies of movement were original. We were fascinated, because we had never seen anything similar. Second, they have been remembered for their individual stamps on the sport that reflected their personalities and temperaments.

In the 1950s, Tenley Albright was a shining example of harmonious movement, but her contribution went far beyond skating. It was as great off the ice as on. She was a humanitarian and an icon to the young.

Others who followed in her footsteps were Maribel Vinson Owen's American stable, including her daughter Laurence. To see those skaters perform was to remember them always.

Canadian Donald Jackson's victory at the Worlds in Prague in 1962 accosted our senses in every way. He fascinated us. If his was not an artistic contribution, the first triple Lutz was a major athletic achievement. More important, his personality took control of the arena and captured the imagination of the world. Each person who indelibly imprinted himself in the collective skating memory did so on an emotional level, never on purely technical grounds.

The 1970s were the golden age of innovation in skating, the most creative and diverse decade in the century. I think that I can fairly say that I was a major contributor in terms of personality and a unique conceptual approach, but I was far from alone. All around me were skaters who captured the public's imagination and provoked equal disdain. Often that combination is propitious.

Briton John Curry, the 1976 Olympic champion, transported classical ballet to the ice. That in itself was not unique, but he did it better than anyone else before or since. He and his many followers understood aesthetics. They knew that figure skating could be the perfect mixture of sport and art in equal increments.

American champion Janet Lynn enthralled the skating world during the same decade. The ability to create magic on the ice is rare. Janet combined lyricism, beauty, charm, and a spark of enchantment.

At Ljubljana in 1970, ice dancers Ludmila Pakhomova and Alexandr Gorshkov, the most important contributors to their branch of the sport, changed everything when they debuted a new and artful approach that carried them to six world titles (1970–73, 1974, and 1976) and the first-ever Olympic gold medal in ice dancing (Innsbruck, 1976). Ludmila, who has since died of leukemia, was able to combine dance, ice dance, and theatre in one program. Although she had a fine body, feature for feature her face was unattractive. Nonetheless, she had the ability that only the great magicians of the art of skating have: by stepping onto the ice, she became a mystifyingly beautiful swan through the way in which she expressed her feelings.

Other fabulous Soviet ice-dance teams followed: notably Irina Moiseeva and Andrei Minenkov, who won world championships in 1975 and 1977. They were so artistic they became one-sided and essentially self-destructed. Sublimely emotional, they allowed the balance between art and sport to go out of kilter.

The ideal Olympic champion, though he did not quite deserve the title on the night, was Great Britain's Robin Cousins, who won the men's gold medal at Lake Placid in 1980. He went on to become one of the greatest entertainers in the skating world: majestic, noble, artful, athletic, exciting – the perfect combination. There are few skaters in all the sport's history to whom one can point and say, "Oh yes. He was superior to Robin Cousins." Some have been as good, but few have been better. His skating is the supreme hybrid of beauty, sport, musicality, temperament, and personality. When added together, those ingredients create a magical, memorable experience for the audience.

In the early 1980s, Robin's fellow Britons Jayne Torvill and Christopher Dean brought a cool novelty to ice dancing. They were not passionate. Their great appeal was that they presented a welcome alternative to the over-the-top, dramatic Soviet style, invented by Ludmila Pakhomova, that had run its course. Torvill and Dean took centre stage and fascinated the world with their cleaner, more natural approach to ice dancing. Their English style perfectly countered the excessive drama of Natalia Bestemianova and Andrei Bukin, who regurgitated every excessive aspect of Russian creativity.

The last ice dancers to galvanize the global public were Isabelle and Paul Duchesnay, perhaps in part thanks to Christopher Dean's choreography. As brother and sister, they could not play romantic roles. Instead they relied upon a passion that sprang from aggressiveness. Theirs was a raw, visceral, and entirely novel approach. Their skating was kinetic modern art.

Midori Ito, who became the first Japanese world champion with her soaring triple Axel, was so astoundingly athletic that she arrested our senses.

The last major showdown, the last big blast of the volcano, was the memorable competition between Brian Boitano and Brian Orser at the 1988 Olympics in Calgary. It had little to do with art and everything to do with their shared voracious desire to win at any cost through their technical abilities. The struggle itself, like the match between Mike Tyson and Evander Holyfield, became a work of art. It will never be forgotten.

What Went Wrong?

There have been many other fine skaters since the 1980s, but the great public fascination with skating that those earlier contributors built up over the decades began to turn sour during the early 1990s.

The perception that jumps were the only legitimate way to improve one's technical mark became the misguided rule of the day, reinforced by judges who counted jumps because that was easier (or at least more quantifiable) than evaluating the mechanics of a spin or footwork. How many jumps can you do in four and one-half minutes? How many times can you rotate in the air before landing? The image of ideal skating slipped out of focus.

To a large extent, I blame the current trainers. Maribel Vinson Owen, Ellen Burka, and numbers of Russian teachers of earlier eras took an intellectual approach to the sport. In coaching, they conveyed their broad understanding of art, dance, and music. A one-dimensional teacher cannot create a perfectly balanced skater, but enlightened coaches have become rare.

In Canada, we have a system that has contributed, in my opinion, to the decline in the overall level of competency among skating coaches. Ironically, it was designed to do just the opposite. Coaches must go through a series of National Coaching Certification Program (NCCP) training sessions and examinations from Level One through Level Five, each with three components: theory, technical, and practical. Skating-ignorant secretaries and plumbers can learn to pass the exams, but numbers of skating geniuses have slipped through the cracks. It is time-consuming and expensive to adhere to the prescribed ritual.

The legendary Russian ice dancers Marina Klimova and Sergei Ponomarenko coached Shae-Lynn Bourne and Victor Kraatz at the Ice Castle in Lake Arrowhead, California. However, when Shae-Lynn and Victor arrived at the Canadian championships in Halifax, Nova Scotia, their distinguished teachers were not allowed to coach them. Marina and Sergei, who had won a world gold medal at that very venue, had not passed their Level Three exams.

I received my credentials through Level Two before I abandoned the effort. Level One alone required fourteen hours of theory classes and thirty-two hours of technical instruction, so it is a miracle of the highest order that I persevered for as long as I did. Suffering through structured programs is hardly my forte.

People with some of the most inferior skating minds in Canada can lay claim to Level Four or Five, yet they have not produced a single champion in their lives; whereas, with my lowly Level Two status, I have contributed to the development of numerous national and world champions, whether through coaching, choreography, or costume design.

Going for the Cheap Vote

During the 1970s and 1980s, skating appealed to many intelligent people who were not necessarily dyed-in-the-wool skating fans but who were captivated by the magic, the sincerity, and the beauty. That audience was all but lost in the 1990s.

Beginning with Christopher Bowman, skating began to zero in on the Spice Girls market: teenyboppers and younger. Tapping into that audience set the tone for other skaters to follow: Victor Petrenko as a professional, Philippe Candeloro, and Elvis Stojko. Those Bowman successors wanted the audience reaction that Christopher elicited, but they sought it at the expense of a complete, mature understanding of the sport. As a result, skating started to slip away from its broader audience.

Philippe Candeloro was easily the most culpable of the three. At formal ISU exhibitions, he removed his shirt and sometimes his pants to get a rise out of the audience. ISU officials were completely baffled. They didn't know what to do. Candeloro was popular and brought in the fans, yet his behaviour was the antithesis of the image they wanted the sport to project. As a result of their dilemma, they did nothing. Granted, Philippe is an entertainer, but his frighteningly bad taste has nothing to do with the art of figure skating and would be better suited to a Chippendale dancer on skates, a job description to which he has been known to aspire.

How to Ruin Ice Dance

As a result of Isabelle and Paul Duchesnay's wildly popular programs, the old guard, the sticks-in-the-mud, chief among them the head of the ISU dance committee, Hans Kutschera, an Austrian who knows as much about dance as my dog did (I'll grant you that Flora was musical), started to pull strings and change the rules of competitive ice dance. Maybe they knew how to count a foxtrot beat, but that wasn't really what audiences craved. Audiences didn't want to revert to the 1950s with *Seven Brides for Seven Brothers*. They wanted to surge into the future with the kind of material that the Duchesnays offered.

The ISU, by maintaining tight control of the ice-dance world, clipped the creative wings of the dancers and teachers. Instead of fostering the tremendous explosion of creativity that was evident all over the world, they squeezed everyone into the ballroom-dancing format and ended up with a glut of ice dancers who all looked the same: in a word, ridiculous. The wound was self-inflicted.

We the public were not interested in watching ice dancers who were clones of one another. We were not interested in watching ice dancers who had been forced into a narrow creative vortex. We especially were not interested in seeing judges slot skaters into boxes numbered from one to twenty, uniformly across the board, with no movement from one event to another. That outcome is simply impossible in a fairly judged creative sport.

I saw identical events occur at two consecutive world championships: in 1996 at Edmonton, Alberta, and in 1997 at Lausanne, Switzerland. At the end of Oksana Grishuk and Evgeny Platov's winning performances, they skated off the ice in stony silence. After the dance team bowed at centre ice and started towards the exit, both audiences stopped clapping. The couple then received some 6.0s. That mark should be used to indicate the creation of a sublime emotional experience, something that surpasses excellence. My question was "How can a judge award 6.0 to a performance for which the audience abruptly stops clapping?"

That sort of error in judgment contributes to the spiralling down of the sport's popularity. It insults the intelligence of the viewers who don't understand the marking system and feel frustrated by the complete dichotomy between their visceral reactions and the judges' marks.

At the Nagano Olympics in 1998, the greatest applause was for Canadian dance couple Shae-Lynn Bourne and Victor Kraatz, who placed a commanding fourth. That sort of travesty influences how fans feel about the sport. It chips away at their interest in skating.

In the 1980s, the popularity of ice dancing hit its height. For a number of years, ice dance was the premier event at skating competitions, the number-one ticket, the only sold-out event. With the disintegration of the Soviet Union, all the top trainers brought their teams to North America and set up shop. Then North American couples, including Americans Elizabeth Punsalan and Jerod Swallow and Canadians Bourne and Kraatz, began taking lessons from Russian coaches. North American and Russian styles then dissolved into a homogeneous pile of mush.

There are too many chefs in the kitchen. Nobody knows what the rules should be. The regulations seem to change every month. First try this, and then try that. You can't do this, and then you can't do that. Truly nobody knows. It is like changing a country's constitution every year. After the fiasco at Nagano, the head of the Canadian Olympic Association, my good friend Carol Ann Letheren, along with other ISU members, seriously considered voting to oust ice dance as an Olympic sport because it made no sense in that context.

My own solution to the ice-dance dilemma is to watch it supine in a fine hotel, propped up by fluffy pillows, ordering room service.

The Russian Nationals

With the breakup of the Soviet Union, a terrible thing happened to the sport of figure skating. Skaters who had once been under the Soviet Union's umbrella ran like animals in a forest fire to affix themselves to any former Soviet republic or foreign country that would accept them. Instead of going through the natural selection process that the Soviet nationals would have ensured, the erstwhile Soviets of varying abilities became champions of Armenia, Belarus, Estonia, Georgia, Kazakhstan, Latvia, Lithuania, Russia, Ukraine, and Uzbekistan. Ex-Soviets also volunteered to represent other countries, especially in ice dance. For example, former Soviet citizen Marina Anissina became the French champion with Gwendal Peizerat.

As a result, the Germans, to cite another case, were not as excited about their German champion as they might have been in other circumstances. Instead of being a home-grown native son, Anrejs Vlascenko was simply a Russian skating for Germany so that he could qualify for the Worlds. There were seventy-six Russians at one recent European competition. It was essentially the Russian nationals with a few invited guests. Worse, the Russians all had a similar approach to skating. They cancelled each other out. One Russian male skater was the same as another.

In the professional world, everyone left the sinking Soviet ship and moved to America. An Olympic champion such as Oksana Baiul is virtually unknown today in her home country. When almost every serious skater defected to America, so did the coaches. Some brought with them twisted and perverse notions of North American culture and tried to be more American than the Americans. Those coaches harboured misconceptions about style, fashion, costumes, and music, aping the glamour of the 1940s and the 1950s. That approach does not fly in the modern age.

In the clothes department, a monstrous parade of cartoon characters competed at international events. A prime example would be Ilia Kulik winning the Nagano Olympics dressed like a reticulated giraffe. The costumes that Alexei Urmanov chose to wear at Albertville (white gloves, lace, and a brocade vest) would have been more suited to Little Lord Fauntleroy.

The ultimate purveyors of the grotesque were ice dancers Oksana (Pasha) Grishuk and Evgeny Platov, who won two Olympic titles yet remained the least-known skaters in America. Their signals got crossed. Their motivation became twisted. They forgot about the art of skating and went for cheap publicity and sexually explicit routines. At the 1998 Olympics, their free-dance performance was completely eclipsed by Oksana/Pasha's absurd imitation of Marilyn Monroe. If she thought that she belonged in Hollywood, she should not have been in Nagano. Such silliness, artificiality, superficial spice, and complete lack of sincerity became entirely distasteful to audiences all across America and Canada.

Homogenization

Another mark of the latter part of the twentieth century was a lack of variety in musical choice. Soundtracks of violent movies – *Rambo*, *Rocky*, and *The Terminator* – became *de rigueur* as skating accompaniment. I watched Skate Canada one recent year, and the horror of the men's programs as a whole was the mind-numbing sameness of style and music. Certainly the audience applauded, but was that homogeneity what people truly wanted?

American male skaters are the most guilty of unoriginal musical taste. At the U.S. nationals, the sound system could blast out the same piece of music for most of the top-ten skaters without altering their routines. At first I tried to believe that the phenomenon was simply the flavour of the times, but now I fear that the deplorable trend is here to stay.

The men are choreographic clones, striving for the same jumps. That leaves little room for individuality. More frightening, the emergent generic style is little more than virtuoso cheap skating.

Of course there have been exceptions. Gary Beacom, before he went to prison for tax evasion, was consistently an exception. Paul Wylie, before he retired to attend graduate school, was a huge exception. So is Scott Hamilton. Kurt Browning today is perhaps the number-one exception, but those skaters can be counted on one hand. Hundreds and hundreds of skaters seem to be spiralling down into the vortex of the same generic whirlpool.

The legendary skaters of the past cultivated sensitivity, body lines, and aerodynamic shapes. Sensitivity has all but been thrown into the gutter. Elvis Stojko made national news by asserting, "Real men don't point their toes." The tragedy of that remark is that a large number of male competitors believe it. However, the perfect form of a body, the perfect harmony of music, and the perfect attention to detail in a painting have nothing to do with masculine or feminine traits. They are universal.

I have always been passionate about skating and interested in skating history. During February 1998, I was at home in Mexico. There was a television playing the Olympic Games across the garden path from my studio, yet I didn't bother to stop by to watch. I didn't need to see the performances. All I had to know were the numerical results. Those told me who had landed which jumps.

There was little to arrest our emotions, our senses, our sense of aesthetics, or our memories. I hoped at one time that the great family tree of skating would bear fruit of the highest quality as we entered the twenty-first century, but it is fair to say that the growth has been stunted. That wasn't due to any single factor. A trend that was built on the interaction of many variables took on a certain momentum of its own.

What Happened to Longevity?

At one point fans were exposed to certain skaters over time and learned about their personalities, the highs and lows of their careers, and the excellence of their skating, thereby developing long-term interest in those fixtures of the sport. Brian Orser won eight Canadian championships and twin silver medals over two Olympiads. Scott Hamilton won four world championships and an Olympic title. Michelle Kwan has remained in the eligible world to give pleasure to her admirers. By way of contrast, Tara Lipinski won the big prize in Nagano, then vanished from the scene, just as Oksana Baiul won the Olympics in Lillehammer, then virtually retired in the night. Many other skaters have done the same.

That sends an unfortunate message: we are here to compete for our own personal glory, not for the glory of skating, and not to give anything back to our fans. Such a message has a deleterious effect on the skating world at large. In 1998, Minneapolis hosted one of the most forgettable world championships on record. Many competitors participated in the Olympics, then lost interest in continuing to train for just one more month. That is the point at which agents, contracts, and greed can creep into the sport and contaminate it. Agents, rather than coaches, then begin to call the shots in skaters' careers.

No Comment

There was a time when audiences relied on commentators for information above and beyond what they could see for themselves. I tried to be one of those informative commentators, but I was not alone. There were others with skating credentials who talked intelligently about the medium. Most of today's television personalities are out of the loop. The prattling is so disturbing that the viewer often turns down the volume when the commentator isn't telling him anything that he doesn't already know.

Non-skaters proffering their personal opinions regarding artists and sportspeople about whom they know virtually nothing is insulting to viewers and turns viewers off. Nonetheless, virtually every intelligent, sincere, and passionate commentator in the history of the sport has been fired: Judy Blumberg, John Curry, Brian Pockar, Toller Cranston, and others. We stirred the pot. Skating audiences are too well informed and too intelligent to suffer through the superficial prattle to which they are often exposed as the new century begins.

An Embarrassment of Riches

Confusion is another element that has caused the skating ship to sink at its moorings. At one time everyone understood that the premier competitions were the national championships of various countries, the world championships, and the Olympics. Now the mixture of amateurism and professionalism confuses skating fans: some events are all amateur (or "eligible"); some are all professional; some are a bit of both. Some professional skaters asked to be reinstated for the 1994 Olympics while others did not. Then reinstatement was banned.

Now there is a Champions Series instead of the individual, autonomous fall internationals. There are so many competitions, both major and minor, that the impact of each has been watered down. That has especially undercut the ultimate competitions: world championships and the Olympics.

The ISU has pulled the rug out from under its own feet. At one time the organization controlled all amateur competitions. Now, in order to get in on the financial action, the ISU has teamed up with companies such as IMG and Candid Productions. The competitive scene has been muddied by widespread confusion. What do the competitions mean? Why are only certain people invited, yet the promoters can call an event the world professional championships?

Familiarity Breeds Contempt

I think that it is fair to say that in professional competitions, the practice of inviting the same skaters over and over again was a mistake. Greedy promoters, inventing more and more events, repeatedly aired the same routines at different venues. That bored the public. There are many creative professional skaters waiting to be discovered: witness the relatively recent successes of Jozef Sabovcik, Scott Williams, or Anita Hartshorn and Frank Sweiding.

You Be the Judge

I once saw a skater place second yet rank third in the short program because of a strange twist in the ordinals. Such outcomes confuse and disturb the viewing audience, not to mention the competitors. If I finished second in the short program and received the second-highest marks, why have I just ended up in third place going into the long program? Such outcomes are baffling.

One action that I advocate, because skating is big business now, is the hiring of a corps of paid professional judges who are experts in the sport. The figure skating hierarchy clings to the feeble theory that if you do all your homework and you hang in long enough, you can become a competent international judge. With today's network interest and high financial stakes, how can the sport afford an Olympic judge who hasn't been an international skater?

Moreover, every judge should be able to defend his position. An extreme mark is not necessarily the wrong mark. Staying strictly in line is the sign of a weak judge, yet the system today rewards those who do so. Professional judges should not be loved. They should be paid. Then, if they develop reputations for partisanship, they should be fired.

The thing that ultimately pushed me off the deep end in amateur skating was the question, How can my destiny and my career be determined by people with one-twentieth of my knowledge? That was what bothered me the most.

Once, I watched a judge officiate at the Lalique competition in Paris. An excellent Russian pair, Elena Betchke and Denis Petrov, skated right off the top. The judge gave them a technical merit mark of 4.7 while each of his colleagues had them a full point higher. What was the judge's defence? "I didn't know who they were." That was his defence! Judges must have worn skates on their feet. Only former skaters have the necessary experience.

Loyalty to One's Coach

I was intensely loyal to my coach, Ellen Burka, both as an amateur and as a professional. I was offered an opportunity at one time to switch to Carlo Fassi, but I did not seriously consider it. Ellen and I were a team.

Katarina Witt, during her amateur days, listened to and obeyed her coach as few have ever done, with staggering results. She was loyal to Jutta Müller, and loyalty breeds the kind of confidence with which a long-time teacher can infuse a student. The loyal athlete is the dog with a loving home rather than the dog that must roam the streets.

Brian Boitano maintains a similar relationship with Linda Leaver; likewise Todd Eldredge and Richard Callaghan. Michelle Kwan stands virtually alone among women with her impeccable attitude and rapport with her coach. As rich and successful as she is, she still respects Frank Carroll and adheres to his advice.

Other skaters today are like water bugs zooming across a pond. Nicole Bobek all but ran out of pros in North America and went back for seconds.[*] What such skaters may not know is that when they change pros after reaching a high competitive level, it is like getting a divorce. There is a tremendous emotional cost to pay, even if there were legitimate reasons for the breakup. Such a skater becomes rudderless. He and his new coach don't share a history of competitive experiences on which to fall back. What a pro of long-standing knows about his skater's personality and reactions is worth its weight in gold in intense situations.

Only months before the Olympic Games in Sarajevo, Norbert Schramm switched to Carlo Fassi. It is true that Erich Zeller, his German teacher, was an old-fashioned stick-in-the-mud, but Zeller had taught Norbert since childhood. By going to an American teacher, Norbert lost the weight of Zeller's German influence, and he

---

[*] Nicole Bobek was trained by Richard Callaghan, Frank Carroll, Kathy Casey, Carlo Fassi, Evy Scotvold, and several other talented coaches before returning to Carlo Fassi until his death at the Lausanne world championships in 1997.

also lost the common experience and the bond of trust he had shared with his coach. The second German, Rudy Cerne, stepped into Norbert's place, and Norbert ended his career in a bed of ashes.

Swiss skater Lucinda Ruh worked with coaches (including me) from Japan to Canada to California. She even ran to the Great Wall of China, hoping that she would find a triple Lutz there. Such an effort is tremendously expensive and, more often than not, entirely futile. No coach can automatically elicit a consistent triple Lutz. It is more effective to adhere to discipline and remain loyal to a familiar teacher. That said, I must note that Lucinda had some beautiful moments at the 1999 world championships in Helsinki, Finland, and finished thirteenth in the ladies' division. I was very happy for her.

A skater makes a naïve mistake in thinking that a coach can push a magic button to allow him to accomplish the thing that gives him the most difficulty. At a high level of skating, the coach is little more than a caretaker and organizer. One learns through repetition, through watching others perform, and through experimentation. A skater can find a close-to-perfect coaching relationship virtually at home, because the onus is on him to push his own buttons through effort and discipline.

With the advent of money in amateur competitions, the balance of power has shifted. Now students control the teachers. In earlier eras, teachers controlled the skaters. Ilia Kulik, reigning Olympic champion, dismissed his teachers. He coached himself, choreographed himself, designed his own costumes, and subsequently did poorly in most of his competitions. He would not listen to advice. For such skaters, money has completely clouded all rationality. They are superficially independent; they are independent financially; but they are completely vulnerable emotionally and professionally.

Success and Failure

Such exceptional skaters as Brian Orser, Kurt Browning, and Brian Boitano have found their satisfaction in winning. After Brian Boitano

won the 1988 Olympics, he realized that money, fame, and professional projects paled in the light of his moment on the victory stand
in Calgary, so he reinstated as an amateur and tried again to capture
that feeling, though with less success. (In his 1994 Lillehammer
comeback, Brian placed eighth in the technical program and sixth
in the free skate for a sixth-place overall finish.)

I, on the other hand, generally revelled in tragedy and felt
ambivalent about success. Success never made me happy. I was
uncomfortable with it. The successes of my life left me feeling
empty. Yes, they caused a superficial kick, but that was just a condition of the moment. My finest achievements, either in painting or in
skating, always contained an element of tragedy or failure. They
were soothing to my character, because I suspect that I lusted after
the role of artistic martyr.

That paradox played out in spades during my skating career.
Perhaps it helps to explain why I never won a world championship.
I subconsciously passed on the win. I was uncomfortable thinking
that I could achieve it. Others – perhaps Paul Wylie at one time –
have done the same.

Tonya, Nancy, and the Decline of American Culture

The Tonya Harding–Nancy Kerrigan phenomenon was in many
ways similar in its effect on American culture to such *causes célèbres*
as the Lyle and Erik Menendez and O. J. Simpson trials: warm-up
acts for the ultimate cultural fiasco, the Bill Clinton impeachment.

Tonya Harding's indirect attack, through her cohorts, on Nancy
Kerrigan was about avarice, power, ambition, and lack of character.
Fantastic and incredible as it was, the situation was not contained,
as it should have been, as it *would* have been in any other country.
One does not earn a place on the Olympic team simply through
one's placement at the national championships. A committee of
figure skating association members who wield discretionary power
chooses the Olympic team.

In the past, both in Canada and America, junior champions and others have been chosen in lieu of legitimate third- or second-place finishers. That has happened because the committees have deemed it more sage to send someone new in order to give him or her the experience; or because they have sent someone more seasoned who was forced to sit out the national championships due to injury. Had Tonya and Nancy been Canadian, the situation might have ended in lawsuits but never in an Olympic showdown at Lillehammer. Such a confrontation would have been equally unimaginable in such serious skating countries as France, Russia, Germany, and Japan.

The Perversion of the Olympic Ideal

How can it be that competitive figure skating has devolved to such an extent that a primitive mind can contemplate such extreme measures? The prize at the end of Tonya's rainbow was a pot of gold. It had nothing to do with technical excellence and everything to do with greed and jealousy.

Nancy Kerrigan, whacked on the knee by a crowbar, could have become a cripple for life. The fact that she actually competed at the Olympics was miraculous. More miraculous still, in light of her past inconsistency, was her excellent performance in both the short and long program. However, there was a faction in America that turned against Kerrigan and rooted for Harding, the indirect perpetrator of the crime. The perverse glorification of Tonya Harding as a celebrity reached its nadir when Connie Chung's network paid for Tonya's first-class travel in exchange for interviews along the route to Lillehammer. *How are you doing, Tonya? What are you thinking? How much pressure are you under?*

Who cared?

Americans cared. In my opinion, there was only one reason why Tonya Harding was permitted to compete, regardless of what the pundits said about potential lawsuits or her entitlement to do so in the absence of a guilty verdict. That reason was commercial. The networks and sponsors hoped for the ratings that her confrontation with Nancy ultimately generated; but by so profiting, they glorified her complicity in the crime. I found that odious and completely contrary to every tenet of the Olympic ideal.

Meanwhile, the influence that Tonya exerted on the sport, on the American team, and on all the Olympic skating competitors was unsavoury, to say the least. Katarina Witt, two-time Olympic champion, who made a comeback and finished a respectable seventh, was virtually overlooked because of the Harding–Kerrigan sideshow. Canadian champion Josée Chouinard's moment in the spotlight was all but obliterated by Tonya's antics just before Josée's performance.

Many people, including me, became fascinated by the situation and watched the Olympics for all the wrong reasons. We were interested in skaters and skating for events that happened off the ice, not because of excellence on the ice (which distinguished the skaters of the past). That shift is detrimental to the sport. Civilized people have begun to lose interest.

Tonya Harding hovered for a time at the outer fringes of respectability. Her role in the attack on Nancy Kerrigan had not been precisely determined. Producer Dick Button floated a trial balloon among the Landover World Professional Figure Skating Championships judges. (I was one of them until I was executed for giving an honest mark, but that is another story.) He asked, "Wouldn't it be great if Tonya Harding competed?" The answer was a resounding no.

Tonya had no right to compete with any respectable skater, and I doubt that any respectable skater would have competed against Tonya at that point. I know that Katarina Witt would not have. However, consideration was given to including Harding not because of her skating skills but because of the publicity and viewing audiences that she would have attracted. Again, all the wrong reasons.

Now Tonya has a legitimate agent, Michael Rosenberg, and the spectre has raised its head once again. At her first competitive outing, the 1999 Pro Skating Championships at Huntington, West Virginia, Tonya won a sympathetic crowd reaction.

The Boomerang Effect

Tonya Harding contributed to a huge increase in the popularity of figure skating. Salaries doubled, tripled, and quadrupled simply because skating became hot. Ultimately that was more negative than positive. If one takes the progression a step further, it is precisely the indecent amounts of money that attract avaricious agents and promoters who will destroy skating. The potential of earning vast sums has already altered the career courses of skaters such as Oksana Baiul, Ilia Kulik, and possibly even Tara Lipinski, largely because of the rockslide begun by Tonya Harding.

Tonya represents a genuine American cultural tragedy that transcends skating. History will cite individuals such as her in explaining how American morality declined. Tonya was not in the Peggy Fleming or Dorothy Hamill mould, but she was a fantastic skater, if infinitely more masculine than feminine. Her strength and virtuosity would have assured her a comfortable seat among the royal family of skating.

Nobody's soul is as black as cinder, and that includes O. J. Simpson, the Menendez brothers, and Tonya Harding. They got off on the wrong track and made terrible mistakes, some far more heinous than others. Tonya's ultimate fate is not dissimilar to Simpson's however. They are allowed to be free, yet the world is their jail. They are prisoners in their everyday environments.

A final common thread that I detect among fallen turn-of-the-century cultural icons is denial. There has never been an element of public emotion that would indicate that either Simpson or Harding feels the slightest remorse. Bill Clinton shares this trait with them.

Maybe they can justify their transgressions to themselves, but that is
even more terrifying.

The Disconnect of Canadians 2000

When certain skaters who have been around the track and over the
obstacle course end their careers, either voluntarily or involuntarily,
they are so bitter that they become estranged from skating. They
develop disdain for the very activity they loved so much, practised
throughout their lives, and viewed as the embodiment of their identities. Someone who comes to mind in that regard is Julie Lynn
Holmes, a world silver medallist in 1971 but never an American
champion. Because of the preferential treatment that ABC commentator Dick Button accorded Janet Lynn, Julie had to undergo counselling to exorcise her resentment.

There was a two- or three-year period after my retirement from
amateur skating when I could not view the sport on television. I found
it too painful. If I watched a world championship, for example, all my
shortcomings resurfaced and paraded through my conscious mind,
especially if I saw contemporary skaters suffering unfortunate situations similar to ones with which I was all too familiar.

In the year 2000, I experienced another wave of bitterness when
I watched the Canadian men's championship. I hadn't seen the event
in a long time. I had usually been in Mexico during January and
February. I decided to acquaint myself, in an open-minded way,
with the newest group of Canadian men. As I did so, I felt as though
I was witnessing a terrible crime with my mouth taped shut. I had
no way to report the crime I witnessed, and the television commentators seemed oblivious of it.

During the 1970s, thanks to many skaters in addition to
myself – John Curry, Robin Cousins, Sergei Chetverukhin, Yuri
Ovchinnikov, Igor Bobrin – the development of the mind and the
understanding of the sport of figure skating kept pace with

the development of the body and technical abilities. Among the elite of skating, there was a global understanding of the body as a kinetic work of art.

I hadn't watched Elvis Stojko perform for some time, and I was interested to see his development. He had left long-time coach Doug Leigh and had gone to Philadelphia to train with choreographer Uschi Keszler and coach Tim Wood, an Olympic silver medallist and two-time world champion, the immediate predecessor of Ondrej Nepela. One could only expect a new presentation, a new concept, a new *something*.

In deference to Elvis, what I saw on television that Saturday in February was a phenomenal competitor with a superhuman ability to concentrate and to zero in on particularly difficult jumps, invariably landing them on one foot. That was the positive element. What traumatized, disappointed, and saddened me was the fact that the new program wasn't new at all, and I was baffled by the total disconnect between the commentary that I heard and the visual images that passed before my eyes.

Elvis performed his program to the soundtrack from the movie *The Mummy*. I saw *The Mummy* on a flight between Texas and San Miguel. Had a parachute been available, I would have made use of it. That's how cheap, corny, and unbearable I found the film. I don't believe that I have ever seen a serious skater use more superficial music. The effect produced by the choreographic elements made me think of a hockey player – or, worse, a football player – masquerading on Halloween as an Egyptian pharaoh. Because Elvis was able to land his jumps very well, the commentators apparently could not discern the inferiority of the overall program.

Ideally, choreography is the use of the human body, from the top of the head to the tip of the toes, as an instrument to interpret a musical score. All that I saw was a caricature: arm gestures, with a couple of neck rolls thrown in, to signal the Egyptian theme.

The sport of skating, which once aspired to heights of refinement and sensitivity, had degenerated to the level of the cheapest talk show. It was a Jerry Springer approach to the ice.

Prior to Elvis's performance, Emanuel Sandhu[*] had skated. Emanuel, a tall, lean, serious skater with a background of dance at the Canadian National Ballet in Toronto, had turned in a clean short program the night before. That program had included a quad. The fact that he had done so and had finished a close second to Elvis (who had also executed a quadruple-revolution jump) was completely ignored on the night of the long program.

Emanuel happened to draw to skate first. His lace became undone. He probably felt a little nervous. However, although his performance was not the world's greatest, there was conspicuous evidence of very fine technical ability. That evidence included a triple Axel, a triple toe loop, and a quad that Emanuel rotated but missed. On the positive side of the ledger, however, were a superb program, a superb costume, superb music, superb interpretation, and perfectly respectable content. Emanuel's artistic impression was as superior to Elvis's as Elvis's ability to jump was superior to Emanuel's. Nonetheless, the commentators were unable to perceive, or unwilling to remark upon, Emanuel's maturity, sophistication, sensitivity, and uniquely different approach from Elvis's.

Quoted in the newspapers the next day, the CFSA, in the person of director general David Dore, basically decried the performance of Emanuel Sandhu by saying that he had blown too many chances and shouldn't be named to the Canadian world team. The CFSA could count on Stojko but not on Sandhu.

I am particularly sensitive to other skaters who have achieved greatness but not easily. One who comes to mind is Paul Wylie. For most of his life, Paul was unable to put together the perfect short

---

[*] Emanuel Sandhu, born on November 18, 1980, in Toronto, Ontario, won the Canadian junior title in 1997 and subsequently finished second to Elvis Stojko in three consecutive senior championships.

and long program. There was always a problem with one or the other. But America is much more generous than Canada, and America understood the unique sensitivity of Paul Wylie. Sooner or later, the odds were that Paul was going to achieve the double whammy. He did that in Albertville and probably should have won the Olympic gold medal.

Rather than publicly demeaning Sandhu, the CFSA should have recognized that unique and sensitive artists, finely tuned Stradivarius violins such as Paul Wylie and Emanuel Sandhu, need special handling if one is to get the best music from them. What the press did not report was Sandhu's increased sophistication and maturity. The press did not report that Sandhu had skated an internationally superior short program the night before, equal to Elvis's, with identical content. The press did not report that although Sandhu had made two mistakes in the long program, the overall quality and technical ability had been of international stature. And what the press really missed was that once again, as in the 1970s, there had been a window into something with great substance, sincerity, and beauty that was the absolute antithesis of the program that Elvis skated.

No one could report those events, because nobody saw them. Today the trained eye has been rendered blind. McDonald's hamburgers feed the proletariat.

I believe that the Canadian machine foolishly gave some misleading signals. When Elvis goes to Worlds in Nice, France, there will be a faction among the judges who will not buy into his routine.[*] If there is not such a faction, then all the work that the great skaters have done will be negated. The efforts and passion of Paul Wylie, John Curry, and Robin Cousins – not to mention my entire thirty-year career – will mean nothing. We will have had no lasting impact. It is very disturbing for a serious performer/artist to see how badly skating has slipped.

---

[*] In Nice, Elvis Stojko finished fifth in the short program, second overall, after a long program competition in which several of his competitors' programs were marred by technical errors.

My frustration raged as I watched Canadians. I saw exactly what had happened but stood alone. If there were other witnesses who understood, they were too afraid to report the crime.

The Search for Honesty

In any art form, the genuine artist searches for honesty and truth about who he is, what he does, and how he performs. In the skating world, avarice and the quest for power are supplanting the quest for honesty. Truth no longer seems important. The magic of Janet Lynn was the honesty of her emotions, the kind of emotion that one cannot find in the phoniness of a Philippe Candeloro. In every age, there are exceptions. Michelle Kwan is one superior example.

It would be nice to think that the recent negative trends in skating are temporary. Perhaps it won't be long until someone grabs that artistic torch and throws it into a small, dark spot that has never been illuminated before. That is all that we can hope for, but it is enough.

39

Send in the Clown

I hadn't set foot on a sheet of ice since an AIDS benefit in Sacramento, California, on August 1, 1998.

The old Maple Leaf Gardens arena in Toronto was scheduled to be supplanted by the new Air Canada Centre on Front Street. IMG hired the Canadian choreographer Sandra Bezic and her

American assistant, Michael Seibert, to produce and direct a historical extravaganza to celebrate the arena's first figure skating event. The March 2, 1999, show was to be called A Legendary Night of Figure Skating.

Nearly every living Canadian figure skating champion would somehow participate, either by skating, speaking, or walking out onto the ice on a carpet to accept the crowd's accolades: Barbara Ann Scott, Brian Orser, Karen Magnussen, Osborne Colson, Suzanne Morrow, Donald Jackson, Frances Dafoe, Maria Jelinek, Isabelle Brasseur, Lloyd Eisler, Michael Kirby, Josée Chouinard, Elizabeth Manley, Petra Burka, Elvis Stojko, Debbi Wilkes, Tracy Wilson, Barbara Underhill, Paul Martini, and the list went on and on. There would be memorabilia displays, historical video clips, and a review of Canadian figure skating during the late nineteenth century and throughout the twentieth. As a six-time Canadian champion, I was one of a relative handful of people who agreed to skate solo numbers.

The Hero and the Fool

I hauled myself out of mothballs about a month before the show, flew from Mexico to Toronto, jammed my feet into those painful skates again, and worked out at the Cricket Club. At first I was creaky. My muscles felt sore from disuse. The skates had not fit correctly since the day I bought them, and I had trouble forcing myself to take a taxi to the rink from my studio on Queen Street West more often than two or three times a week. As the event drew close, inspiration took over to some extent. I decided to revive "Vesti la giubba" from *Pagliacci*, the pivotal number that secured my career at Munich in 1974.

I had always found Leoncavallo's music more of a caricature than something to be taken seriously, but I felt that the role of hero and fool – that is how I see Pagliacci – would be the poetically correct role for me on the particular night in question. The heroism of Canio as the clown Pagliacci resides in his belief that nothing is impossible to a willing heart. The fool in his character continues to chase an impossible dream, a comet tail of hope that he can never catch. I would skate my final show (for that is what it would be) in the dual role of hero and fool. I simply had no choice. It was natural and correct in the context of my life.

March 2 arrived at last. I took a taxi from the Royal York Hotel, where the cast was lodged, to my Queen Street loft, where I usually slept. I ate a minimal breakfast, dashed out to buy stage make-up, then made a last-minute trip to René and Jake Brunott's skate shop in Thornhill to have my tired, dull blades sharpened to fine twin edges before the afternoon dress rehearsal. I had planned to get a haircut too, but ran out of time.

That evening, backstage at the shiny, impersonally new Air Canada Centre, I took out my skates (for the millionth time) in the cavernous men's communal dressing room. I was in the company of men who ran the chronological gamut: from Donald Jackson, who was still skating solo performances punctuated by double Lutzes after three and one-half decades, to Emanuel Sandhu, the wonderfully lyrical yet strong young skater. I had designed the costume in which Emanuel placed second to Elvis Stojko at the 1999 Canadian men's championship.

I was running a little late, seduced by the camaraderie in the air. It was exciting to talk with the many old friends and historical relics of my past who were in attendance. The numerous veterans of Toller Cranston's The Ice Show from my Broadway days proposed a class reunion (which hasn't quite happened yet).

There were just three numbers to go before my turn to skate *Pagliacci*, the penultimate performance of a lengthy and draining evening. On one end of the ice, Canadian and world champions sat expectantly on folding chairs three rows deep. I spent an inordinately long time getting into my costume and putting on my skates. I wanted everything to be just right. As I slipped my feet into my boots, perhaps for the very last time, I suddenly realized that I was up against the clock (or, more exactly, up against the new Wittnauer watches that all the participants had just been given by the sponsor), and the timepieces were winning. One of the greatest fears of any performer is that he will not be ready when his name is called.

Just then my right lace broke. That was a bad omen. I began to suspect that the elements were conspiring against me. I am not particularly well organized, as the reader will have gathered by now, so I had no extra laces in my skate bag. I dashed around backstage, trying to borrow one. There were no spare black laces to be found, so I tied together my damaged lace ends and rethreaded the eyes of my skates. It was a slow process. The worn, frayed lace tips didn't slide easily through the small punctures in the leather boot.

Time was running out. Now there were only two more numbers before mine. My old friend Karen Magnussen, currently a coach, was announcing a performance by one of her students, tiny Mira Leung, when my second lace broke. That double jeopardy had only happened to me once before. How could it be occurring again on such a significant night?

I recognized the opening notes of the program just before mine, Brasseur and Eisler's campy, reverse-gender "Patricia the Stripper" piece. What could be a more pointed contrast to *Pagliacci*? I had no time at all to warm up backstage. As I continued to bend over my recalcitrant left lace, my feet tingled with numbness. It was Bratislava all over again.

I was wearing a brand-new costume that had been made according to my design by Angela Arana of the Canadian National Ballet. It was royal blue with nude glissette inserts that swirled across each other's wakes in both the front and back, culminating in audacious twin curves across my derrière. The sheer fabric was peppered with enormous rhinestones that cast prismatic shards of refracted light. It was a great costume. I had called for it at the National Ballet just the night before and had tried it on only once, during the dress rehearsal. In my panic, alone now in the men's dressing room, I somehow couldn't fasten the unfamiliar hooks.

I frantically ran down the echoing concrete hall in my skate guards and asked someone to help me. I had hoped to find my old friend and hairstylist Sherika Bakova. Instead I ran straight into Hillary Clinton. The American first lady had been invited to deliver a special speech about the evolution of North American figure skating.

"Please," I begged, "can you help me fasten the snaps on the back of my costume?"

Her response was not encouraging.

"I'm not some pathetic little cookie-baking woman standing by her man, you know. Anyhow, I can't find the hooks. I detect a vast right-wing conspiracy."

As the public address system broadcast my pretaped narration of the video clip that introduced my performance, the situation seemed surreal. My own voice boomed from the nearby arena as the sharp red nails on the tips of Hillary's icy fingers dug at my back.

"Forget it," I told her in irritation. "I'll skate with the costume unfastened. Maybe the bits of Velcro will hold it together."

At the rehearsal I had been bathed in a warm pink glow, but now the glare of the television lighting blinded me. I couldn't see two feet in front of my face. I felt disoriented as I stood at last at centre ice, motionless, waiting for my music to begin. My greatest fear was that when I jumped – if I had the nerve to jump – I would slam, unseeing, into the boards.

My music boomed, but it was soon apparent that the tape had been miscued. Leoncavallo's opening notes had passed me by, and the middle section of the piece was already racing. Since the Legendary Night of Figure Skating was being broadcast live, I could not decide in that split second whether to stop the music and ask that the tape be rewound. By default, I opted to pick up my program halfway to the end.

The intense heat of the television lights melted the ice in spots. I skated through huge puddles that grew deeper and deeper until my blades scraped along the cement below. At that point I metamorphosed into a synchronized swimmer in the water off Marshall's Bay near my family cottage. My costume turned into a peacock-coloured Esther Williams bathing suit, and I danced a water ballet with nine glaring judges. Then the bay became a huge vat of tomato soup with floating lemon wedges. Just as the lemons turned into toothy, twenty-five-foot sharks, I awoke.

Nightmares, Night and Day

The mind is fantastic. At one time I could mentally relive good skating performances in my dreams. I remember lying in bed, sailing effortlessly across the ice. Now, because of the passage of time and my lack of practice, when I skate in my dreams, my body doesn't work as it used to. I can no longer simulate that sublime, gliding feeling.

Real dreams no less extreme than the one described above, nurtured by a lifetime of skating anxieties, came to me nightly as I slept during the months before and after my valedictory tribute show at Varsity Arena. People who work in other professions have nightmares about their working lives as well. Teachers tell me that theirs are surreal and persistent: hearing the bell ring yet unable to find their classrooms; standing in front of their students in bathrobes or underwear.

The most difficult challenge for any skating performer is to stop doing the very thing that he has done for his entire life. His body hungers for skating – demands it like an addict's body – but his rational, conscious mind forbids it, so he lives in perpetual torment. Slipping into retirement has been anything but peaceful for me. It has been more torturous than continuing to skate. That is the cruellest irony of all.

I lived for some time in a Jekyll and Hyde world. By day, while I was busy painting, I no longer thought about skating, but throughout many nights my dream world was filled with skating nightmares. In my unconscious state, I ran out of time, failed to fulfill my obligations, and skated out every hang-up that I had ever experienced during my waking hours on the ice. I moved across a frozen pond of guilt. The only relief came with the dawn. If I was able to ignore or block out the signals of my id during the daylight hours, the next night's dreams were even more extreme.

It was precisely because of the deep-seated anxieties manifested in my dreams that I decided to skate at the opening of the new Air Canada Centre. I thought that perhaps my inner voice was telling me that the final paragraph had not yet been written in my skating book. Against my better judgment, I resumed practising, arranged for Angela Arana to make yet another splendid costume, and prepared to honour the obligation of performing at an historical event. Perhaps then I could make peace with the gods and allow the poison to seep away. Perhaps then I would no longer skate in my dreams.

Little did I know that the reality would be worse than the nightmare. Five days before the show, in a state of acute anxiety, I went on a drug binge that lasted forty-eight hours. Through the help of watchful friends, I was able to pull myself together. I spent the last two days before the event either cocooned in the safety of the Royal York Hotel or performing prosaic neighbourhood errands on Queen Street West. I avoided as much as possible the arena and the agitation that it provoked in me.

The Legendary Night of Figure Skating itself, as great as it was for Canadian skating, was something of a personal letdown. Somehow I had wanted to be frozen in time forever. In the back of the tunnel, before I skated out onto the ice, I had tried to make a deal with God. *Just let me be wonderful. Let those people like me.* I was able to skate well enough. Yet, as I performed under the lights in that blue velvet suit covered in pigeon-egg-sized rhinestones, the kick – the long-familiar thrill – did not come.

I watched Barbara Ann Scott, 1948 Olympic champion, stand up at the end of my performance. She glittered like a platinum-blonde diamond in a silver sequin dress, holding on to who and what she had been and remains to this day. I told myself, "That represents an option that you have. Or do you want to grow up?"

I decided then and there that the red shoes wouldn't be dancing any more. To pronounce those words out loud is so scary. When you say them, do you really mean them? The next day I fled to the safety of San Miguel de Allende and gripped my paintbrush as a drowning man grabs on to a life preserver.

40

Butterflies and Jacaranda Blossoms

In early April 1999, 250 people on the famous San Miguel House and Garden Tour poured across my Mexican property like extras in *The Ten Commandments*. My role was similar to the one I play at a painting exhibition. I stood at the front entrance, at the mouth of the tunnellike vine-covered arbour, to greet my guests individually, shake their hands, and direct them around the grounds. In essence, I sent them forth to scrutinize my life.

A decade ago, I acquired that property only with the greatest difficulty. It was as though I was jumping ahead of my destiny. The

In San Miguel. Photo by Thom Hayim

purchase of what were then four charming but derelict houses and vast, tangled, undisciplined gardens was accompanied by great nervous agitation. Since then, Arturo, my wonderful gardener, and his three helpers have honed the estate to perfection little by little. Marietta de Aubrey, who is no longer with me, stalwartly ploughed every penny I provided into the property.

To me, my San Miguel de Allende estate had always before been a foreign work-in-progress to which I fled whenever I was overwhelmed by my skating career or my Toronto life of drugs, anxiety, and perennial impecuniousness. I did not realize that it had become a finished product until I saw it through the eyes of others from all across the world. I suddenly knew that it mirrored in the material sense what my life could become – and perhaps already had become – emotionally.

April had been strategically chosen for the House and Garden Tour. That is the San Miguel flower month. In particular, April is the time of year when my colossal jacaranda tree rains great periwinkle-blue blossoms. As I stood greeting my guests, the blossoms fell in profusion on the paths and patios.

I thought about life cycles. I had eagerly awaited the jacaranda's bloom, knowing that an enchanted moment would arrive. All around me, periwinkle blue would dance across the sapphire sky. Now that all too ephemeral beauty fell around my feet like purple rain. Among the piles of blue petals, numbers of dead saffron-and-black monarch butterflies further reminded me of the immutable rules of nature.

All the secrets of life can be found in nature by those with the eyes to see them. In enjoying beauty and wonder yet gracefully accepting their demise, one can scale the ladder of maturity.

When I agreed to skate at the Air Canada Centre opening, I bucked one of nature's primary rules. Everyone – and this certainly applies to the hierarchy of figure skating – has a moment in which to bloom. There is also a time to drop lightly to the garden path like a drying petal or a moribund monarch butterfly.

For reasons of personal insecurity, vulnerability, and ignorance, I had been unable to read the signs that told me to hang up my skates. I had started to pay a terrible emotional price, simply because I had refused to heed nature's demand.

Happy Birthday

A week or so later, on April 20, I turned fifty in the company of Linda Cranston, my sister-in-law; Priscilla and Brian Caldwell, Toronto friends of thirty years; and Margaret Barnard and her son,

Adam, dear British friends. Seventy other people whom I had gotten to know in Mexico came to my birthday party.

Heretofore I had looked back at what I used to have, trying to fit the old square peg into the new round hole. I had always thought that skating, performing, and the friends with whom I had worked for so many years were the only true joys in my life apart from painting, so I looked back wistfully. Because of the intimacy skaters enjoy within their world, being on the out looking in is a painful experience. Yet that happens to everybody, skater or not, sooner or later in one way or another.

In *The Wizard of Oz*, Dorothy explained her newfound wisdom to Glinda the Good Witch. To find her heart's desire, she had only to look in her own backyard. In the month of my fiftieth birthday, I had finally done that, both literally and figuratively, and had seen it as though for the first time. If the past was clouded in shadow, the future was bright and new. Surrounded by the comforts of home and friends, I *got* it. My mind finally clicked. I shrugged off the mushrooming phantom that I had fought for a decade and recognized the glory of living for tomorrow.

Index